D0856564

302565

Date Due

W/D

THE LAST GREAT CAUSE

by Stanley Weintraub

AN UNFINISHED NOVEL BY BERNARD SHAW (*ed.*)

PRIVATE SHAW AND PUBLIC SHAW: A DUAL PORTRAIT OF LAWRENCE OF ARABIA AND G.B.S.

C. P. SNOW: A SPECTRUM (*ed.*)

THE YELLOW BOOK: QUINTESSENCE OF THE NINETIES (*ed.*)

THE WAR IN THE WARDS

THE ART OF WILLIAM GOLDING (*with Bernard S. Oldsey*)

REGGIE: A PORTRAIT OF REGINALD TURNER

THE SAVOY: NINETIES EXPERIMENT (*ed.*)

THE COURT THEATRE (*ed.*)

BEARDSLEY

BIOGRAPHY AND TRUTH (*ed.*)

EVOLUTION OF A REVOLT: EARLY POSTWAR WRITINGS OF T. E. LAWRENCE (*ed. with Rodelle Weintraub*)

THE LAST GREAT CAUSE: THE INTELLECTUALS AND THE SPANISH CIVIL WAR

THE LAST GREAT CAUSE

The Intellectuals and the Spanish Civil War

STANLEY WEINTRAUB

WEYBRIGHT AND TALLEY
New York

Published in the United States by
WEYBRIGHT AND TALLEY, INC.
3 East 54th Street,
New York, New York 10022.

Library of Congress Catalog Card No. 68-12866

PRINTED IN THE UNITED STATES OF AMERICA

In memory of William L. Werner
who taught one to honor good causes
and good books

Acknowledgements

I am indebted to the following authors and holders of copyrights for permission to reprint material in this book:

From Herbert Read, *Collected Poems*, reprinted by permission of the publishers, New Directions Publishing Corporation and Faber and Faber Ltd. From "Looking Back on the Spanish War" from *Such, Such Were the Joys* by George Orwell, copyright, 1945, 1952, 1953, by Sonia Brownell Orwell. Reprinted by permission of Harcourt, Brace and World, Inc., and Secker and Warburg, Ltd. From *Mediterranean*, copyright 1938, by Muriel Rukeyser. From *Short is the Time: Poems 1936–43*, by C. Day Lewis, copyright, 1940, 1943, Oxford University Press New York Inc. Reprinted by permission of the Harold Matson Company, Inc. From the poems of John Cornford, by permission of Christopher Cornford, Esq. From "Arms for Spain," by Rex Warner, by permission of Professor Rex Warner. From *Volunteer in Spain* by John Sommerfield, by permission of Paul R. Reynolds, Inc. From *Autumn Journal*, by Louis MacNeice, by permission of Faber and Faber Ltd. From the poems of Tom Wintringham, by permission of Mrs. Kitty Wintringham. From the poems of Edgell Rickword, by permission of Edgell Rickword, Esq. From "Spain 1937" by W. H. Auden, by permission of the author, Faber and Faber Ltd., and Random House, Inc. From the poems of Stephen Spender, by permission of the author, Faber and Faber Ltd., and Random House, Inc. From *Geneva*, by Bernard Shaw, by permission of the Public Trustee and the Society of Authors. From "The Old Man at the Bridge" and *For Whom the Bell Tolls*, by Ernest Hemingway, by special permission of Charles Scribner's Sons. From the NANA dispatches of Ernest Hemingway, by permission of the North American Newspaper Alliance. From the *Collected Poems of W. B. Yeats*, reprinted with permission of the Macmillan Company, and Mr. W. B. Yeats and Macmillan and Co. Ltd., from "The Great Day" and "Politics," copyright 1940 by Georgie Yeats.

From "Defense in University City," by Robert J. C. Lowry, by permission of the author and Doubleday and Co., Inc. From the *Collected Poems* of Roy Campbell, by permission of the Bodley Head, Ltd.

In some cases I have attempted without success to locate executors or estates of deceased writers, and must conclude with the general acknowledgement that I trust I have quoted these authors fairly and responsibly.

I am grateful, too, for the assistance of the Pennsylvania State University's Central Fund for Research, and the staff of the University's Pattee Library. Many individuals have also helped, among them Alvah Bessie, Malcolm Cowley, Moe Fishman, Hugh Ford, Richard Gidez, Gladys Greenfield, Allen Guttmann, August Jennings, Arthur Koestler, Dan H. Laurence, Arthur O. Lewis, Jr., Robert J. C. Lowry, Charles W. Mann, Jr., Ann and Bernard Oldsey, Prudencio de Pereda, S. Leonard Rubinstein, Allen Trachtenberg, Samuel S. Vaughan, Rex Warner, Marcia and George Wellwarth, Philip Young.

Lastly, my chief debt remains, as always, to my wife, Rodelle, for her intelligent editing and wretched typing.

Contents

. . . a devotion to Humanity . . . is too easily equated with devotion to a Cause; and Causes, as we know, are notoriously bloodthirsty.

James Baldwin
EVERYBODY'S PROTEST NOVEL

I suppose people of our generation aren't able to die for good causes any longer. We had all that done for us, in the thirties and the forties, when we were still kids. There aren't any good, brave causes left. . . .

Jimmy Porter in John Osborne's play
LOOK BACK IN ANGER

INTRODUCTION
The Last Great Cause

*Spain caused the last twitch of Europe's dying
conscience.*
   Arthur Koestler,
   THE INVISIBLE WRITING *(London, 1951)*

IN THE DAYS OF REVOLUTION and civil war in Spain, there was a
story often repeated:

> . . . of how, after the Creation, the nations of the world, counting up
> and comparing their various blessings, were envious of the dispro-
> portionately large share of the good things of this world that had
> been given to Spain. It had rich soil, a sun that always smiled but
> yet did not burn, wine, and the world's most beautiful women—a
> land of song and plenty.
>
> Accordingly, they formed a deputation to place their grievance
> before God himself. And God looked upon Spain, and saw that it
> was good, and too closely resembled that Eden of which the world
> had proved itself unworthy. And after he had weighed the matter, He
> spoke as follows, "What I have created I will not destroy, but to
> show you that I will not favor this country beyond any other I will
> grant the right in perpetuity to my Enemy the Devil that he may give
> to Spain her governments."
>
> And the representatives of all the other nations of the world
> pondered upon these words, and went away satisfied.[1]

If the Spanish Civil War and the cause of its ill-fated government do, like an amputated arm or leg, continue to produce an

occasional twinge in places where the English language is spoken and read, it is very likely because they exerted an emotional appeal upon English and American writers, artists and intellectuals, affecting not only what they wrote, but what they did. It was, on a larger scale, the equivalent of the Greek War of Independence which drew Byron to his death, or the Italian *Risorgimento* which magnetized writers more than a century ago. It was, too, the last great cause for many of them, those who never came back, and those whose lives and whose perspectives were forever changed by the experience of Spain. Never since has a cause so captured the moral and physical influence of so many makers and molders of the language, or created such relentless pressure upon so many members of the intellectual communities in the English-speaking world to take sides, to make a stand. No "Ban the Bomb" movement or crusade for Negro rights has been more than fractionally its equal in its impact upon writers and writing.

At perhaps no other time did the makers of art feel so strongly that art could be a weapon. Writers brandished their typewriters against the enemy, and many went even farther, putting down their overheated typewriters and picking up rifles they at first had no idea how to use. And if the Cause later betrayed them, or was itself betrayed, in a complex international ballet choreographed outside Spain, it remains suffused with a nostalgia beyond ideology and politics. "I suppose people of our generation aren't able to die for good causes any longer," playwright John Osborne had his heel-hero Jimmy Porter complain in 1956. "We had all that done for us, in the thirties and forties, when we were still kids. . . . There aren't any good, brave causes left." "For all its blood, cruelty, intrigue, and corruption," an historian writes, "there was something pure about the Spanish war. The enthusiasm it engendered was a springtime that briefly loosened the wintry grip of a world grown old and weary and cynical. As did no other event of our time, it caught the conscience of a generation."[2] Men of his generation, Albert Camus wrote, "have had Spain within their hearts . . . [and] carried it with them like an evil wound. It was in Spain that men learned that one can be right and yet be beaten, that force can vanquish spirit, that there are times when courage is not its own recompense. It is this, doubtless, which explains why so many men, the world over, feel the Spanish drama as a personal tragedy."[3]

Not all the writers who took up pen or machine gun for the cause agreed on what the cause was, and a handful of unreconstructed Rightists even took the cause to be that of the *other* side, the holy crusade of General Francisco Franco to restore the old order in Spain, and oust the atheists, murderers, and hooligans of the Left. One English author, in fact, could lay claim to having started the Civil War on its way. He was forty-three-year-old Douglas Jerrold, publisher, writer of books on history and politics, and, in the summer of 1936 in his seventh year as editor of the near-Fascist *English Review*. Early that July he received a phone call in his Fetter Lane office from Luis Bolín, London correspondent of the Spanish Monarchist daily *ABC*. Would Jerrold see a friend of his? He would, and the unnamed friend turned out to be a Rightist conspirator who wanted English help in procuring fifty Hotchkiss machine guns and a half a million rounds of ammunition for them. It was, he said, raising his voice slightly to be heard above the traffic outside, "a question of saving a nation's soul." For about ten minutes he offered Jerrold—who needed no rationalizations—some justificatory tales of "murder, outrage, and sacrilege."

The business details were ended quickly; Jerrold said his good-byes, and explored the possibilities of procurement. The next day, he informed Bolín that the matter which had been discussed could be arranged; but the offer was never taken up, the requisite weapons apparently having been acquired elsewhere. Before Jerrold had learned this, there was a second call from Bolín, barely a fortnight later. Would he have lunch? "I'm afraid it must be today. It's important." Assuming it was connected with the visit of the anonymous Spaniard, Jerrold agreed, and the pair (with a third party, monarchist and autogiro pioneer Juan de la Cierva) lunched at Simpson's with appropriate preliminary conspiratorial gestures, much whispering and shifting about to tables which afforded more privacy.

The matter was brought up by de la Cierva: "I want a man and three platinum blondes to fly to Africa tomorrow."

"Must there really be *three?*"

At that Bolín turned to de la Cierva triumphantly: "I told you he would manage it." And, after a pause, "Well, perhaps two would be enough. But of course the man must have had some experience; there might be trouble."

Anxiety registered on the Spaniards' faces as Jerrold sat saying nothing. When he noticed it, he assured them that he was troubled only by the rival qualifications of three men, all suited for the assignment, and by the probable expense of three platinum blondes. Money was no obstacle, they assured him.

From the restaurant Jerrold telephoned Hugh Pollard, a retired major, for "after all, the job was Pollard's by rights, for he had experience of Moroccan, Mexican and Irish revolutions— and, of course, this meant war. And he knew Spanish."

"Can you fly to Africa tomorrow with two girls?" Jerrold inquired, and heard the expected reply, "Depends upon the girls."

"You can choose," he told Pollard, and added that he would bring two Spanish friends to work out arrangements with him. "There's only one point I ought to mention," Jerrold concluded. "The aeroplane may be stolen when you get there. In that case, you come back by boat."

"First class?"

"Why not?"

"Can do. Good-bye."

When the conspirators reached Pollard's home in Sussex, Jerrold explained that the private plane, containing three English "tourists," would be appropriated by the military at the Canary Islands (where General Francisco Franco had been banished, for the Republic's safety, to be commander of the garrison), "if the anticipated crisis arose." It would take the General to Spanish Morocco, where he would seize command of the Army of Africa. Bolín had already chartered a *Dragon Rapide* at Croydon Airport and arranged for a pilot. An English plane, with English pilot and passengers (the idea of platinum blondes to give the air of a different sort of intrigue), the Spaniards assumed, would arouse little suspicion, while the government of the Republic, wary and worried over the possibilities of an imminent coup, might keep careful control over its own aircraft.

The ostensible route to Casablanca via Lisbon (where Bolín was to be deposited) was mapped, and money was arranged for. All that was needed—since Pollard's eighteen-year-old daughter was to be one of the party—was the second girl. After a frantic search down Sussex lanes, the four men located her (a fair-haired friend of Pollard's daughter) in a pub. Two days later, on Saturday, July 11, the party of "pleasure-seekers" took off from Croydon for Las Palmas, in the Canaries, without landing papers, planning on being able to talk—or to stall—their way out of that omission. During the confused week following, during which risings, and some counterrisings, occurred all over Spain and Morocco, the English airplane sat innocently in the Canaries.

For the Madrid government, it became obvious by the eighteenth that no compromise could be reached with the Rightist generals. "The Popular Front cannot keep order," General Mola told the Republican Minister of War (via telephone from Pamplona). "You have your followers and I have mine. If we were to seal a bargain we should be betraying our ideals and our men. We should both deserve to be lynched."[4] The remark would cost Spain hundreds of thousands of lives, including Mola's own.

Primarily an internal affair at the start, the rising of the generals against the Republic had little to do with European Fascism and international Communism. There had been some assurance of help from Mussolini as early as 1934, but the generals were interested neither in a religious *cruzada* nor in extending an ideology borrowed from Berlin or Rome, and assumed a quick Latin-style *coup d'état*, not a long war. At first, the Civil War was a military mutiny, backed by the Church and the aristocracy, intended not to impose Mussolini-style Fascism but to restore feudalism. The weak and indecisive Republican government Franco set out to overthrow, rather than being the tool of the Comintern, did not include even one Communist or Socialist, and only fifteen members of the four hundred and seventy in the Cortes were Communists. It took the outbreak of war to evoke the mood of *cruzada* on the Right, and inspire a nearly spontaneous social revolution on the Left. The longer the war went on, the more it was to become polarized at the extremes.

When the generals struck, the army-less government, to retain control of its own capital, fell back on its most drastic alternative. At dawn on Sunday, July 19, trucks from the Ministry of War began unloading arms at the headquarters of the Socialist trade unions, the UGT and CNT, the Madrid radio having announced the step as the Government's way of accepting "Fascism's declaration of war upon the Spanish people." The waiting masses received the weapons with enthusiastic shouts of *"No Pasarán!"* and *"Salud!"*

Prudently, General Franco bided his time until the last Republicans in Morocco had been overwhelmed. Then, flown in the English *Dragon Rapide*[5] on the same Sunday that the civil population of Madrid took to arms, the General, who had supposedly been relegated harmlessly to the Canaries, landed in Spanish Africa, at the San Ramiel airfield at Tetuán. There was no difficulty about landing papers.

Not all writers were committed to the cause of the Left or the Right in Spain, not even all English and American authors resident in Spain. The land had long been an Arcadia to foreign writers, and to an unmalleably obtuse few it remained so, even in the confusion, incendiarism, and carnage of the opening days of the rebellion in Barcelona. An English lady novelist who often wrote about, and from, Spain even dismissed church burning (with which she had no sympathy) as "the second national sport of Spain"—after bullfighting.

Of all the battles fought on the day Franco landed in the borrowed *Dragon Rapide*, the bloodiest had been in Barcelona, capital city of independence-minded Catalonia, dominated below its seething surface by respectable labor unions and illegal Anarchists. Before the day was over, the Atarazanas barracks had been stormed by militant Anarchists, and armed workers had advanced on rebel led troops with such disregard for personal safety that many of the panicky soldiers turned on their officers and surrendered. While shots ricocheted through Barcelona's streets, Cedric Salter (correspondent for a London paper) and a journalist friend had hurriedly paid an unexpected call, at six in the morning, on writer friends of Salter's companion. Uninvited, they were seeking safety—and a view of the fighting from the penthouse flat. The occupants of the penthouse were three young Englishmen "who lived together in complete harmony in a graceful world of their own," the peace of the establishment unmarred by female intrusion. They favored as working attire "Byronic shirts in the palest shades of silk, and corduroy riding breeches," and "the nearest thing to work permitted to approach their threshold was the rare issue of a book of belles lettres, by one of their number."

One of the trio, clad in lilac silk, opened the door, and the men, breathless from their bolt across the street and the climb to the top floor, were hospitably invited in. Their gasped explanations about revolution and civil war were swept aside:

> "You can hardly guess," one of our hosts assured us, "what a happy thing is your arrival. You are just in time to help us decide on the color scheme for our tiny roof garden," and we were piloted out of the bay window. At irregular intervals a bullet whined up from the street.
>
> "Did you know," chimed in he in palest blue, "that every year in Barcelona they hold a concourse of poets, and after they have heard them all the poem which is judged to be the third best is rewarded with a rose fashioned in silver, and the second best one made of gold.

That which is the very best is given a perfect natural bloom." My confession that I did not, together with an unworthy impulse to remark upon the fierce competition there must be in order to persuade the judges that the other fellow's poem was just a shade better than your own, was drowned by a thunderous hammering on the door. A second later, without a word, six Guardias de Asalto pushed their way into the flat, flung open the windows, and began firing rapidly into the street.

"And now," continued our host, utterly undisturbed, "what do you say to our scheme for a flood of something really bizarre, like bougainvillea along that wall. Alaric here wants petunias, but I think it is so drab and middle class of him—the dear boy."

Correspondent and friend, feeling "a little unequal to the situation," seized the first conversational opportunity they could find to take their leave "from this world where revolutions were clearly too uncouth to be allowed acknowledgement."[6]

There were ivory towers occupied in England and in America, as well as in the increasingly incongruous setting of Spain; but, for the most part, writers took sides. If there were far fewer on the Right than on the Left, they were no less passionate and no less committed. Rightists regularly used the term "crusade" in supporting Franco, while an English historian has called the Civil War in Spain "the first and last crusade of the British left-wing intellectual. Never again was such enthusiasm mobilized, nor did there exist such a firm conviction in the rightness of a cause."[7] The puzzle for thoughtful people since has been why events moved so many intellectuals outside Spain to offer *themselves* as well as their works for the cause Spain symbolized. In the writings of a distinguished French biologist, René Quinton, who volunteered at age forty-eight for active duty in the First World War, Rightist author Douglas Jerrold found an answer which satisfied him: "An idea for which a man is not prepared to die is not an idea sufficiently dynamic to stimulate the instinct to serve, and it is on the stimulation of this instinct, on its predominance over all else that, as a matter of mere biological necessity, the health of the race depends. For it is only in serving that the male can attain moral dignity, without which the race must deteriorate and ultimately decay."[8]

For writers on the Left, there were less subtle philosophical grounds for activism, although, like the Right, some saw the conflict in Spain simplistically as a conflict between good and evil. If there was more militancy from the English Left than from the American equivalent, it may have been because Englishmen in the mid-thirties saw cowardice elevated to national foreign policy. In the shadow of Neville Chamberlain's umbrella, pacifism, so fashionable since the Armistice—although it had been nurtured by the poetry of Wilfred Owen and Siegfried Sassoon, the *Death of a Hero* of Richard Aldington, the *Goodbye to All That* of Robert Graves, the stage pathos of *Journey's End* and the filmed horror of *All Quiet on the Western Front*—suddenly became intolerable. In the United States, pacifism had been underlined by isolationism, and sustained by the writers who created *A Farewell to Arms, Bury the Dead, Johnny Johnson, What Price Glory?*, and *Three Soldiers*. Suddenly Spain had made the pacifist stance seem obsolete. Writing and fighting had become, for many, inseparable. Regardless of how one did it, German emigré author Ludwig Renn told a meeting of writers, the contemporary writer's role was no longer to "make stories but to make history." Similarly, Upton Sinclair wrote of the international volunteers that they had formed "probably the most literary brigade in the history of warfare. Writers and would-be writers had come to live their books, journalists to make their news."

The making of that history was accomplished by men of whom only a small percentage were sufficiently articulate to write about it, or to hope to affect history by their writing. Those who fought the war included the confused and the misled, the unemployed and the unemployable, the misfits and the maladjusted; but they also included men from Brooklyn and San Francisco, from London and Liverpool and Glasgow, who risked everything they had to go to Spain to fight. They ranged, too, from the

peasants in remote Spanish provinces who walked all the way to
Madrid to help defend it, and then had no weapons, to the steel-
worker from Budapest[9] who traveled all night hanging on to the
undercarriage of the Orient Express in order to get to Paris, from
where he could be sent on to fight. As W. H. Auden described
the urgency of the appeal,

> *Many have heard it on remote peninsulas,*
> *On sleepy plains, in the aberrant fishermen's islands*
> *Or the corrupt heart of the city,*
> *Have heard and migrated like gulls or the seeds of a flower.*
>
> *They clung like burrs to the long expresses that lurch*
> *Through the unjust land, through the night, through the alpine tunnel;*
> *They floated over the oceans;*
> *They walked the passes: they came to present their lives.*[10]

However small the number of articulate combatants, possibly
never before had so large a proportion of a war's participants
been motivated to write about a war, from polemics to poetry.
Many were not—nor ever became—professional writers, but that
had nothing to do with the itch to set down what one saw or did.
Hemingway satirized the phenomenon in a short story, in a
dialogue between a mercenary American pilot and a volunteer
tanker:

> "Comrade," said Baldy. "I will describe the strange and beau-
> tiful scene. I'm a writer, you know, as well as a flyer."
> He nodded his head in confirmation of his own statement.
> "He writes for the Meridian, Mississippi *Argus*," said a flyer.
> "All the time. They can't stop him."
> "I have a talent as a writer," said Baldy. "I have a fresh and
> original talent for description. I have a newspaper clipping which I
> have lost which says so. Now I will launch myself on the description."
> "O.K. What did it look like?"
> "Comrades," said Baldy. "You can't describe it." He held out
> his glass. . . .[11]

For serious writers, particularly those who found morality
and art inextricably bound up with each other, there was an epic

quality to their activism. If the *Causa* seemed then like the last possible great cause, it was that, if it failed, the threatening darkness of Hitlerism would spread its stain across Europe, and even across the Atlantic. To Fascist poet Roy Campbell the Civil War was the beginning of the Ninth Crusade, and Stalin's use of the International Brigades had more in common with the Fourth Crusade* than the First; but it turned out to be, for writers, at least, a tragic epic without precedent, as so many who had lived by the pen suddenly found themselves living, as well as writing, their own epics. They came not only from countries where writers wrote in English: the cause of Spain was also the cause of André Malraux, Ludwig Renn, Paul Lukacz (Mata Zalka), Gustav Regler, Ernst Toller, Alfred Kantorowicz, and others; but this is the story of some of those whose impact then and since has been upon literature in English. It was a war conspicuous for the physical commitment of its intellectuals; and for the writers who lived to see their lives altered, or their later work shaped by the war, and most truly for the many who died in battle, it was the Last Great Cause.

* The Fourth Crusade (1202–1204) was shamelessly betrayed by Venice, which used the crusaders to further its political and commercial ends in the eastern Mediterranean.

1

A PLATOON OF POETS
The British Battalion

We cannot hide from life with thought,
And freedom must be won, not bought. . . .
John Cornford,
"AS OUR MIGHT LESSENS" *(1936)*

"THIS IS A FINE WAR," said John Cornford.

"Sure," John Sommerfield agreed. "It's a fine war."

A truck had just arrived with biscuits and buckets of hot coffee laced with brandy; and there was a frosty November tang in the air. Coming up from the slum district of Vallecas was the Thaelmann Brigade of German (and mostly Communist) refugees, on the way to the Madrid front. To the rhythm of their marching feet, their voices low and deep, they sang—most of them with the optimism of the unbaptized-in-battle—a Hanns Eisler marching song. At the head of the column was a red flag, and each company had its own red banner. For the two Englishmen, it was a glorious sight, obliterating momentarily the actualities of discomfort and frustration. They saluted the column with clenched fists as it went by and savored the vision of the determined faces and the song and the marching feet. It was why they were there.

Before the autumn of 1936 had ended, the first British volunteers had already made their way to Spain, most of them eventually to join the British Battalion of the Red-organized, yet not entirely Communist, International Brigades. Barely two dozen of the four hundred Englishmen claimed to be writers, half of that number poets; but they were articulate, militant, and unafraid. Intellectuals and mostly middle class, they were eager, whether they realized it or not, to find an association with the working class that their upbringing had made impossible, one which seemed guaranteed to inspiringly vindicate their liberal political ideals. Their declared motives had little to do with the comradeship of intellectual with miner, machinist, and longshoreman. As Cambridge-educated volunteer Miles Tomalin (who survived) believed:

He gives, but he has all to gain,
He watches not for Spain alone,
Behind him stand the homes of Spain
Behind him stands his own.

For some authors, writing was an insufficient commitment to the fight against Fascism: the final test was action—to expose the body to danger and discomfort and to offer it, if necessary, in sacrifice. Only then would the ideals about which one wrote be put to the ultimate test of sincerity. (And if one fought and lived? Certainly, then, the experience in the crucible could only sharpen and heighten one's powers.) Further, as writers such as W. H. Auden (who would be in Spain briefly in a noncombatant role) realized, the spread of Fascism over Europe—certain to continue if Spain were lost—"would create an atmosphere in which the creative artist and all who care for justice, liberty and culture would find it impossible to work or even exist."[1]

Perhaps never before had the intellectual felt his *raison d'être* so threatened, and the threat threw Communists and anti-Communists into each others' embrace in common cause. It was impossible "to remain an intellectual and admire Fascism," Cyril Connolly wrote, "for that is to admire the intellect's destruction, nor can one remain careless and indifferent. To ignore the present is to condone the future."[2] It was not a conviction lightly held or—by many—merely verbalized.

One of the first writers to turn up as a volunteer in Spain was twenty-year-old poet John Cornford, a professor's son. A brilliant student and a leader among young Communists at Cambridge, he chafed at home front pro-Loyalist activity, even while the first efforts at it were being organized, and on his own initiative left for Spain. Except for his having prudently obtained a *News Chronicle* press card identifying him as a free-lance journalist, Cornford's trip began as casually as a spur-of-the-moment holiday. He crossed France by train from Dieppe to Port Bou, and, on August 8, 1936—three weeks after the war had begun—was in revolutionary Barcelona. Impressed, he wrote home from there that he could "now understand physically what the dictatorship of the proletariat means. . . . Everywhere in the streets are armed workers and militiamen. . . . But there is nothing at all like tension or hysteria. . . . It is genuinely a dictatorship of the majority, supported by the overwhelming majority."[3] By his third day in Spain he had, in his enthusiasm, joined a column of POUM militia, the "uniformed" arm of the Party of Marxist Unification, an Anarchist-leaning, semi-Trotskyite party active in Catalonia. In its fashion, it was defending the Aragon front, where rebel armies had already penetrated to the east as far as Huesca, Saragossa, and Teruel. Afterwards, rationalizing his curious choice of troops with which to enlist (since he was a Communist), Cornford explained that when at Leciñena, in Aragon, he saw how useless he was as a correspondent, he decided to join the militia there, using "the strength of my party card" to prove his identity as an anti-Fascist.[4] The card had to be convincing: he spoke no Spanish.

What the POUM militia lacked in weapons (it did not even have enough ammunition for rifle practice) it made up in enthusiasm and spread its contagion through the villages it occupied. "One of the things I remember most vividly," Cornford observed later, "is how, when we marched into Tierz, three miles from Huesca, in spite of the fact that they had been deluged with stories of rape and atrocity by the retreating Fascists, the villagers

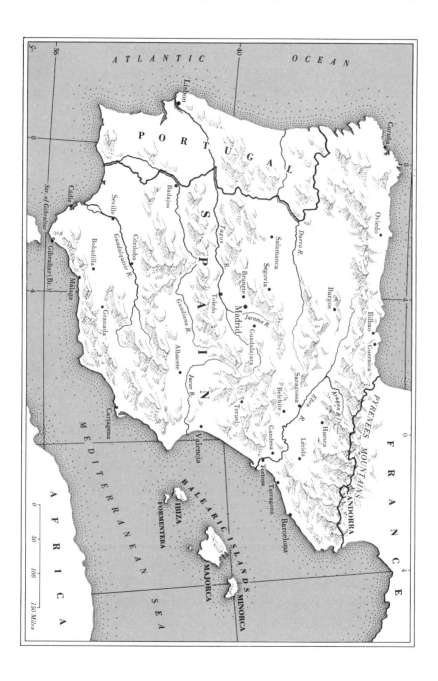

came out into the Market Square to welcome us, and took us off to their houses, where they had already prepared meals, and beds in the straw. In one village we passed through, the people's committee had taken a voluntary decision to continue paying their normal rents—to the militia."[5] A nonbeliever might have found the action almost incredible initiative on the villagers' part; but Cornford saw an ideologically loyal peasantry, not a group of apprehensive folk eager to appease the current occupying army.

He had joined impulsively, intending to stay only long enough to fire a few amateur shots at the enemy. But, with action dormant under the scorching August sun, Cornford felt idle after a few days and considered using his press card again, this time to extricate himself. Nothing seemed to be happening:

> At the moment I am on top of a hill. . . . A complete circle of rocky mountains, covered with green scrub, very barren. . . . Two kilometres away a village held by the enemy. A grey stone affair with a big church. The enemy are quite invisible. An occasional rifle shot. One burst of machine-gun fire. One or two aeroplanes. The sound of our guns sometimes a long way off. And nothing else but a sun so hot that I am almost ill, can eat very little, and scarcely work at all. . . . We lie around all day. At night two hours on the watch—last night very fine with the lightning flickering behind Saragossa, miles away. Sleeping in the open with a single blanket on the stones. . . ."[6]

His pride kept him with the column—"provisionally until the fall of Saragossa," he wrote. Each offensive against the city petered out into a false alarm before it began, but he determined that he was there "in earnest," however lacking in earnestness he appeared in his nondescript uniform—"a pair of heavy, black, corduroy trousers (expropriated from the bourgeoisie), a blue sports shirt, . . . alpaca coat, rope-soled sandals, and an infinitely battered old sombrero. Luggage, a blanket, a cartridge case (held together with a string) in which there is room for a spare shirt, a knife, toothbrush, bit of soap and comb. Also a big tin mug stuck in my belt." If action were limited, the unpredictabilities of Anarchist disorganization alleviated monotony at least some of the time, and Cornford had, for the first time in his life he thought, "unlimited opportunity to write. And I have plenty of things which for years I've wanted to write. But I can't get them together in my head, things aren't straight enough: all I can put down are my immediate subjective impressions. . . . I'll learn: I am learning. But it's going to be something of a testing-time."[7]

Their first real attack, in the direction of Perdiguera, turned into a floundering fiasco, although when Cornford read accounts of it afterwards in Catalan newspapers he discovered that the POUM press had played it up as a successful punitive expedition, not as one directed at recapturing territory. It gave him some additional reason, as a Communist, to believe Communist Party claims that POUMist activities were, at best, inept, at worst, suspect; yet he stayed and enjoyed political discussions with five German "comrades" in the column, four of them ex-members of the Party. After twelve days, the detachment was shifted to the Huesca front, where the incident at Tierz he described took place. The attack on Tierz was also the occasion for a long poem, parts of it sensitively phrased, parts of it jarringly political. In one stanza he worried about how he would react under fire, for the irrespressible physical fears demanded a kind of dedication he never needed to know as an intellectual activist:

> Then let my private battle with my nerves,
> The fear of pain whose pain survives,
> The love that tears me by the roots,
> The loneliness that claws my guts,
> Fuse in the welded front our fight preserves.[8]

In the unpretentious free verse of "A Letter from Aragon," he may have been more successful. Emotionally understated, it begins with a line which became an ironic refrain to four wartime vignettes: "This is a quiet sector of a quiet front." The best of the four was the most poignant and precise:

> We buried Ruiz in a new pine coffin,
> But the shroud was too small and his washed feet stuck out.
> The stink of his corpse came through the clean pine boards

> *And some of the bearers wrapped handkerchiefs round their faces.*
> *Death was not dignified.*
> *We hacked a ragged grave in the unfriendly earth*
> *And fired a ragged volley over the grave.*[9]

By September 13—only his thirty-seventh day in Spain—
Cornford was out of action. Ill and exhausted from what was
probably dysentery, he was being sent home. The idea of in-
validing himself all the way to England was his own. He had not
soured on the botched and divisive defense effort (one political
group seldom cooperated militarily with another); rather, he was
thinking in terms of organizing a group of Englishmen who could
serve as an example of discipline to the Spanish irregulars. Optimistic and enthusiastic during his three weeks in England, he
visited old friends, formally resigned his college scholarships,
enlisted volunteers, and returned to Spain, carrying with him a
symbolic but practical parting gift, the revolver his father had
carried in World War I.

Unknown to Cornford, his idea was already being carried
out on a more ambitious scale through the concept of the International Brigades; and, although he asked for and received financial support to transport his group of five Britons and a German;
from Communist Party Secretary Harry Pollitt, he learned nothing
in London about the polyglot Brigades, just then in their formative
stages in France and in Spain. The hastily organized Internationals
had resulted from suggestions by both Communists and non-
Communists among European radicals. But Communist organizing
efficiency made the difference, and the International Brigades
quickly came under Communist operational and logistic control,
funneling most of their recruits into Spain by sea via Alicante,
or overland through (or around) the French border town of
Perpignan, where a crack Yugoslav Communist named Shapayev
handled arrangements. A half-dozen years later he emerged in
another war as *Tito.*

In the little hotel in the Belleville district of Paris to which

Cornford and his group were directed by the *Comité d'Entr'aide au Peuple Espagnol*, they discovered the Internationals in organization;* and when they arrived in Spain, in a ship alarmingly—for most of the volunteers—flying the Anarchist ensign, they were reassured by the sight of the flags of the Spanish Republic and the Communist Party alongside the Anarchist flag above the customs house at the port of Alicante. Transportation was waiting, and late that night they arrived at Albacete. South of the main Madrid-Valencia road in the province of La Mancha, it was the city where, a few days before, the first contingent of Internationals —French, Poles, and Germans—had begun training. Whether or not Cornford had wanted to rejoin the POUM militia in Aragon, he and his group were clearly headed from there to the Madrid front. Because they were so few, the Englishmen were difficult to assimilate into an organization dividing itself by national origin into battalions; and they were grateful to have the problems of foreign cooking and foreign languages, haphazard uniforms and hazardously old and multivarious weapons, superseded by urgent orders to Madrid. The capital was in immediate danger of falling, and it would have done little good to have had men training to fight a battle while that battle was being lost 150 miles away.

With Cornford on the troop train was the young English writer he had described to the Spanish Peoples' Front Information Bureau in London—when he expected to be returning to the Aragon—as "the good shot John Sommerfield." Sommerfield, who had just published a "working class" novel titled *May Day*, had begun to keep notes for a book. His *Volunteer in Spain* (the result of his notes) would present a vivid picture of the early months in the field and the first desperate fighting around Madrid, from the time training was suspended until his last look at the front.

Sommerfield and Cornford made the final stage of their journey to the Madrid front in the last vehicle of a convoy of open,

* Until then Cornford had expected to return to his POUM unit.

dark green trucks, through the cold of the highland nights into the raw chill of the dawn. In sultry days, Cornford had been laughed at for trailing about with a monstrous old overcoat, mossy with age and so large that it flapped around his heels. "With that," Sommerfield wrote, "an ammunition belt strapped around him, rifle slung on one shoulder and blanket across the other, his high cheekbones, and sculptured almost Mongol face, he looked like something in a bad picture of the retreat from Moscow." But along the switchbacked roads which wound around icy summits at grades which forced the trucks' straining motors to a boil, Cornford had the last laugh. No one else had a coat.

Under rebel pressure, Cornford and Sommerfield backtracked their way into the Madrid suburbs, fighting alongside Polish and German refugee volunteers. University City was already partly in enemy hands. The great blocks of red-brick buildings with white stone facings, the immense clinical hospital, laboratories, lecture halls, and libraries which stood in broad landscaped islands, had to be fought for one by one. The immediate Republican objective was the retaking of the Philosophy Building, accomplished in darkness relieved only by flames reflected in the structure's remaining unbroken windows. It ended in a new kind of stalemated fighting, far different from what Cornford had known in the Aragon, and in the country around Madrid. At first they had lived in the open, in a way Sommerfield described in mannered passages which strove for prose-poetic effects while communicating something of the least romantic side of war:

> We grew filthy and hairy, slept with weapons in our hands, huddled together for warmth like cattle in the snow; our rifles became part of us, so that to be without them even for a moment gave us a sense of loss; we ate quickly, on the alert, like hunted animals, crouching close to the ground and slicing with jack-knives at hunks of tinned meat held in muddy fingers; our hair grew matted, our unwashed bodies took on the smooth, coppery patina of gypsies' flesh; we blew our noses with our fingers, and used our handkerchiefs for cleaning guns. We forgot that once we had lived in rooms and slept between sheets, had sat down to eat at leisure and vanquished the darkness

with electricity. We went back to the days of prehistoric man, to the days before fire was known. We were always cold, often hungry, wary for danger, and accustomed to sudden death. It made no difference that the perils that beset us were the product of a scientific age, that men had learned to fly so that our enemy could kill us from a thousand feet above our heads, that the poetry of mathematics had made it possible for him to direct death at us invisibly from behind the flanks of hills five miles away, that instead of teeth and hands and clubs with which to attack us the sublimities of chemistry had given him power to pierce the bodies of five men with a single leaden fragment darted across the valley faster than the sound of its own passage, so that men died before they heard the shot that killed them. In defending the advance of mankind we lived like men of the Stone Age, and learned these things. . . .[10]

What they also learned, according to Sommerfield's slim book, written like so many of the firsthand accounts of the war while memories were still vivid, were "the different music of bullets," the "hawk-shadows" of aircraft across the fields, the "white, hoary bloom of the cold" on the clothes they slept in, the "new depths of exhaustion" that made them forget at times to care about danger or death, the "various ways of broken flesh," the "curious attitudes" of the dead, the cacophony of the screaming shells:

Now we learned to know the shells, all the different sounds of their flight and explosion; we learned a new instinct that could trace their course in the air and tell us where they would fall, a new reflex that jerked us forward on our faces at a certain note. We learned strange singings overhead, strange rushings and commotions, ghostly aerial concerts, shrieks and howls sounding from clear skies. And sometimes, while we stayed in a valley, the big guns boomed overhead as loud in the air as the great trains roaring through the night. And we learned how they fell right among us, the whirling scythe-like splinters of hot metal, razor-sharp, able to slice a man in two, the hurtling jagged lumps that blotted head and limbs into scarlet shapelessness, the fountaining earth, the flying stones, the broken boughs of trees tossed upwards with twisted rifles and bits of men, and then the scorched hole in the earth, rimmed with burnt grass and baked, steaming clay. . . .[11]

Among the once elegant edifices of that pride of Madrid,
University City, the survivors

> learned a new kind of fighting, the shooting amongst buildings, the
> machine-gun duels between men behind barricaded windows two hun-
> dred yards apart. Then we slept in rooms, out of the rain; our lives
> had a different routine: there was much sniping for us to do; we
> built barricades with sand-bags, with furniture, with books; we found
> sofas to sleep on: in the night we dug communication trenches be-
> tween buildings, and made tunnels under the roads: we watched aero-
> planes circling above that could not bomb us because they did not
> know which buildings were in their hands and which ours: we saw
> the buildings burning in the night, we watched blank windows all
> day for a single movement: we lay down on velvet cushions beside
> our guns: we sniped from arm-chairs: and at night there were bomb-
> ing parties.[12]

The rebel half of University City, on the Madrid side of the
river Manzanares, opposite the Casa de Campo—the former royal
grounds—was sparsely wooded park land, studded with the once-
showpiece University of Madrid structures. While the Medical
School building was Republican, the nearly gutted Hospital
Clinico housed the spearhead of the rebel forces. It was a vast
building of brick and reinforced concrete which once had towered
magnificently over the park, but the tides of fighting had cost it
whole sections, and twisted girders and broken bricks littered the
ground. Nearby were the Institute of Hygiene, and, Fascist-held,
but half-collapsed, the Institute of Agronomy.

In Philosophy and Letters, across no man's land, Cornford,
Sommerfield, and others used lulls in the fighting to build interior
barricades with thick, bulletproof volumes of early nineteenth-
century German philosophy and Indian metaphysics. The contrast
to their experience in the countryside was polar: there were
carpets on some of the floors, clocks and barometers in working
order on the walls, and a "Come to Sunny Spain" poster acquired
somewhere and tacked on a wall. Between attacks, life was
orderly. On clear mornings, they were regularly bombed at eleven
o'clock, and, during each hiatus in attacks, they engaged in sniping

and patrolling, and in shouting jeers at the enemy Spaniards, Moroccans, Italians, and Germans holed up in the adjacent buildings.

In the building's reading room, antitank guns faced out of the windows. The valuable books and manuscripts had been removed from the library for safekeeping, but there remained a shelf of Everyman classics, in English. It was cold, and Sommerfield rolled himself up in a carpet one morning to read, from that shelf, De Quincey's reminiscences of the Lake Poets, leaving his rug and his book twice to help shell the buildings opposite. Through the afternoon he read, and was near the end when there was a crash, and the room filled with dust and smoke. A hole appeared where the "Sunny Spain" poster had been, and figures moved confusedly in the haze. Among the wounded was Cornford, the shrapnel felling him and two others in the room later identified ruefully as having come from a spent Loyalist antiaircraft shell. In two days, he was back from the *Secours Rouge* Hospital, his head bandaged and his pockets full of oranges. It was still, sometimes a good war.*

At sixteen, Cornford had written to his mother (poetess Frances Cornford), "Are the poems that you write really your most important experiences? . . . It always seems to me that you have a great deal that needs to be said more urgently but can't be, because of the limitations of your view of poetry . . . because I should guess that until recently you would have denied that every subject is equally poetical. . . ."[13] But, at Trinity College, his own creativity had taken the form of intense political activity, and he had found it difficult to transmute the experience into verse. In three years at Cambridge he wrote a mere nine poems. Only in Spain had he begun to write poetry again.

Cornford's few poems—although often cluttered with political messages—made clear that he was satisfied that in going to Spain he had done the right thing. He had released himself, at

---

* But he had left the hospital too soon; after two days spent digging trenches in the frozen clay, he was hospitalized again.

least temporarily, from academic and personal commitments, and found a kind of new freedom in the discipline of the ranks and the sense of physical danger. "Not by any introspection / Can we regain the name of action," he wrote, and, in a merging of motives, observed that

> *We cannot hide from life with thought,*
> *And freedom must be won, not bought.*

One of his Spanish poems—fruit of his Aragon experience—had been a lyric pure in its freedom from ideology:

> *Heart of the heartless world,*
> *Dear heart, the thought of you*
> *Is the pain at my side,*
> *The shadow that chills my view.*
>
> *The wind rises in the evening,*
> *Reminds that autumn is near.*
> *I am afraid to lose you,*
> *I am afraid of my fear.*
>
> *On the last mile to Huesca,*
> *The last fence for our pride,*
> *Think so kindly, dear, that I*
> *Sense you at my side.*
>
> *And if bad luck should lay my strength*
> *Into the shallow grave,*
> *Remember all the good you can;*
> *Don't forget my love.*[14]

The lyric was for Margot Heinemann, a Newnham College (Cambridge) graduate, research student in economics, and—inevitably for Cornford—a Communist. (His first love had also been a Communist, and the precocious pair had flouted bourgeois morals by openly living together.*) In his letters to her in Birmingham, where she had gone to teach, he tried to reconcile optimism with realism. "I don't know what's going to happen," he wrote her late in November, "but I do know we're in for a tough time. . . .

---

* They had a child shortly before drifting apart.

The losses here are heavy, but there's still a big chance of getting back alive, a big majority chance. And if I didn't we can't help that. . . ." His last letter was dated December 8. He hoped that the war would be over by summer—"and then if I'm alive I'm coming back to you."[15]

The two small British sections were attached to the Thaelmann and the *Commune de Paris* Battalions, and in mid-December deployed west of Madrid. Near the village of Boadilla losses were heavy, and the Loyalists retreated; but Nationalist losses were also heavy, and both paused to regroup. This breathing space gave the British the chance to form their own unit of 145 men, survivors drawn from Polish, German, and French units; and— with new arrivals—they were attached as "No. 1 Company" to the French *Marseillaise* Battalion of the newly formed XIVth International Brigade. (The colorful and confusing names and numbers disguised their numerical weaknesses and emphasized the international origins of the units. Rather than beginning their numbering with *one*, the Brigades started with *eleven*.)

Of the twenty-one Englishmen originally with the French battalion, only five remained to join the new British company, and, on Christmas Eve, 1936, with Cornford haggard and gray, his head still bandaged, they left by rail for the Cordova sector of the Madrid front. The five veterans were each to lead a machine gun unit in an attack meant less to take the rebel outpost of Lopera than to relieve Nationalist pressure on the capital to the north. It did neither. There were two days of confused fighting in the olive groves and about the walled villages, but the Internationals had no air support or modern weapons, and even their food and blankets somehow never reached the forward positions. Without entrenching tools, they had to resort to digging in under fire with their tin plates as shovels. After two days of heavy casualties, the company began retreating, once under fire of their own machine guns—from the disorganized French battalion. On the night of December 27–28, they withdrew from beneath the walls of Lopera, leaving their dead where they fell. One was John

Cornford. The last day of the battle had been his twenty-first birthday.

Responding to Cornford's death, Margot Heinemann wove ideology as well as emotion into a poem of her own, "Grieve in a New Way for New Losses." The obvious question—why one so young, so gifted, so beloved had to be lost—received its rationalization: the "best world" could not be achieved through the sacrifice of "wasters" and "second rates" but by the "loss of our best and bravest everywhere." Still, the cause would survive such losses—"All this is not more than we can deal with."

"I do not know," John Lehmann mused a generation later, "whether John Cornford would have seen the other side of the moon, the corruption of Stalinism, if he had lived; but I believe, on the evidence of the power of the few poems he left, in spite of their obvious moments of immaturity, that if he had written about El Alamein or the storming of Normandy as he wrote about the storming of Huesca, no other poet of action in the Second World War could have touched him: his name would be a household word today, with the more literary-minded statesmen quoting from him in their speeches for solemn occasions."[16]

Conceived in the month of Rupert Brooke's death at Skyros in the First World War, he had been christened Rupert (a name he ignored) John after the idealistic, almost legendary young poet, whose "The Soldier"* became one of the most familiar short poems in the language, one which might have been his own epitaph, and his namesake's as well. And even before Rupert

---

* If I should die, think only this of me:
That there's some corner of a foreign field
That is forever England. There shall be
In that rich earth a richer dust concealed;
A dust whom England bore, shaped, made aware,
Gave, once, her flowers to love, her ways to roam,
A body of England's, breathing English air,
Washed by the rivers, blest by suns of home.

Brooke became a soldier, or Rupert John Cornford was conceived, a young Cambridge poetess had embodied the Brooke legend in an epigrammatic—and prophetic—quatrain:

A young Apollo, golden-haired,
Stands dreaming on the verge of strife,
Magnificently unprepared
For the long littleness of life.

The celebrant of the first Rupert was to be the mother of the second—Frances Cornford.

Sommerfield dedicated his *Volunteer in Spain* "to the memory of my friend, John Cornford": "I did not see him dead; I can only remember him alive and laughing, strong, resolute and reliable." His own book, he thought, would have "only a transitory interest," although he valued it as an effort which went beyond the journalistic by-products of war. But the book stands as one of the less perishable literary experiments inspired by the Spanish experience. Yet it was an experience which apparently drained Sommerfield as a writer. He never rose to his post-Spain level again.[17]

The English Company, like other International units, had its commissar, or political officer, a Red Army practice. One of the first had been the novelist Ralph Fox—*had been*, because he was killed in the same futile fighting among the olive trees near Lopera. A dedicated Communist, he felt—so he wrote a friend—that "What is happening here is really the greatest thing since 1917. Victory means the end of Fascism everywhere sooner or later, and most likely sooner."[18] Resistance to Fascism, he insisted, however inconsequential or exasperating one's role may be, "is history, and must be effective." As a writer of history, he felt history-in-the-making where he was, and it gave him the patience to endure the rear-area boredom of Albacete, and the inefficiency of the Spanish militia, which, he felt, needed "a revolutionary

General Gordon"—something Moscow attempted to supply through various pseudonymous Red Army personages exported to Spain.

Fox's enthusiasm for the sights and sounds of Spain inevitably found expression (nonetheless sincerely) in Party jargon: the atmosphere was "revolutionary," partly because there were few signs of any "bourgeoisie"; the endlessly chattering and gesticulating crowds in Albacete were energetic "workers" who "will surely create something firm and stable in the end." But as the officer who received and indoctrinated volunteer Internationals, he had some guarded qualms about the quality of recruits the Party had shipped up to then: "We want more and quicker volunteers—no limit, but good stuff essential."

By mid-December, Fox's desultory days at Brigade head-quarters were ending. Attached to the new English unit as political commissar, he lived a catch-as-catch-can life of hasty meals and snatched sleep, acting as "general nurse, mother, teacher and commander to all the English as they pass through." When the Brigade's section that included the English Company moved into action near Madrid, Fox was with it, although he could have found reasons for remaining well to the rear. "He almost pushed himself into battle," Claud Cockburn told an interviewer long afterwards. "I saw him at the base at Albacete, where he was dodging the orders of the high political chiefs, who naturally thought it monstrous that a man like this—an internationally known, influential Communist writer—should be let to get himself in a position where he could get killed like an infantryman. . . . But Ralph's certainty was that *unless* he personally and physically fought he would cease to function fully as a writer." It was a state of mind beyond a politician's understanding—that there were individuals who "needed to take a physical part in the thing: the party talked as if the alternative to their getting killed was that they would pour out marvelous books. But it would be more likely that the writer would mentally drop dead."[19]

The enemy had advanced from Cordova, along a hilly road

which undulated among seemingly endless, symmetrical rows of olive trees. The Republican counterattack maintained its momentum as far as the bottom of a hill, where, exposed to fire from above, English troops took cover among the trees. But it was an illusory cover, for German-piloted Junkers aircraft, flying low to strafe and scatter small bombs, added an extra dimension to the Company's plight. Fox was halfway up the hill with the Company's commanding officer when the pair suddenly saw an opportunity to rush in machine gunners to sweep the Nationalists' right flank, below the crest. Hunched low to offer as small a target as possible, Fox disappeared into the rifle fire to organize a crew's move.

Through the waning day the Loyalist strategic position gradually deteriorated, making the open ground Fox had seen a no man's land crisscrossed by rifle fire and machine gun fire. But the crew Fox had gone to locate had never moved forward, for he had never arrived.

When night came, a soldier crawled out into the shambles of the olive orchard to bring in the papers from the pockets of the dead. In the collection he brought back were Fox's notebook and a letter addressed to him. A group was organized to go out the next night and identify those bodies it could not retrieve, but, before the men could go, the Company was shifted to a new sector of the front, with the one in which Cornford and Fox (among so many others) had died written off for the time as lost. Their bodies were never found.

Both men might have died other than in the sunlight of belief had they known that, in the aftermath of the engagment's failure, the megalomaniac Stalinist André Marty, Commandant of the Internationals' Albacete base, had turned up at the headquarters of General "Walter" to accuse Major Lasalle, the inept commander of the *Marsellaise* Battalion, of cowardice and spying for the Fascists. Protesting his innocence, Lasalle was court-martialed, and, protesting his innocence while shouting well-earned imprecations at Marty, he was shot. Though Lasalle may have retreated half a mile under fire, he was very likely not a spy, except to the arrogant, paranoid Marty.*

Before he died, Fox had written from Marty's base at Albacete that he had seen there a little army "of every nation," and had been inspired by the dedication of "fellows who have been soldiers nearly all their lives, happy at last to be fighting for something worth while." The Cause raised no dilemmas for its dead.†

Novelist Ralph Bates heard the news of Fox's death just before addressing a monster pro-Loyalist Madison Square Garden rally in New York. Around the beflagged platform, the banners of defiance hanging from balcony railings, the piles of military clothing and the ambulances for which the mass meeting had raised funds, the organ boomed and wailed; and while the crowd's roar surged around him, Bates thought of Fox as he had last seen him in London. Later, in a room high above Fifth Avenue, he talked with Rebecca West about the first time each had met him.

---

* A brilliant organizer, Marty had gained fame in 1919 when, as a seaman, he led the mutiny of the French Black Sea Fleet that prevented it from intervening against the struggling new Soviet Union, fighting for its life against the Western-supported "White Russian" armies. Convinced that the International Brigade was heavily infiltrated by Fascist spies, he liquidated doubtful cases rather than run the risk of "petty bourgeois indecision." When Marty was finally called upon to explain the mounting execution rate, he delivered a report to the Central Committee of the Communist Party which identified his victims as "international criminal elements," rebels and spies for Franco. Besides, he rationalized, "The executions did not go beyond 500."

† Yet A. L. Rowse, then a young history don at Oxford and a friend since Fox's days as an intense Marxist student at Magdalen College, writes, "I have the evidences, the documents . . . that before the end, Ralph Fox was through with Communism. On his very last visit to me he wanted to give up and [pleaded] for me to get him a job at Oxford, to retreat from it all. I made enquiries both at my own college and at his, but of course there wasn't a ghost of a hope. He was ordered to Spain by the Party, which wanted martyrs for the cause. The English contingent on the Cordoba front was left isolated and unsupported, in a forward position, . . . and there they were machine-gunned and cut up by . . . Nazi planes. That was where and how Ralph Fox died . . ." (*A Cornishman at Oxford* [London, 1965], p. 57). Fox's letters and other contemporary accounts do not support the story, but the war in Spain was notable for such paradoxes and contradictions.

"I expected to find him quite a young man when I first met him," she said. "After that . . . I went out and bought all his books." In his thirty-seven years he had published plays (*Captain Youth*), novels, criticism, and biography (*Lenin* and *Genghis Khan*). In his poetic-prose novel of central Asia, *Storming Heaven,* Fox's hero had said prophetically that he had "a kind of thirst. I feel I must wear my feet out seeing this world, finding out why people do what they do, why they are what they are." Fox "might have written one or two of the finest revolutionary novels of our generation," John Lehmann thought, for he had "great technical and imaginative power," and a "striking . . . , imaginative grasp of characters and events." The most substantial piece of writing Fox had left unpublished at his death was part of an unfinished novel, titled with unconscious irony by Lehmann when he printed it in one of his volumes of *New Writing,* "A Wasted Life."

One young Englishman who survived the Madrid engagement gave fleeting fame to the village of Boadilla that Cornford and Fox so briefly knew. On July 19, Esmond Romilly had read the news of the "Generals' Revolt" over breakfast with Philip Toynbee, a friend down from Oxford and visiting in Romilly's nearly bare bedsitter in Bury Place, Bloomsbury. Romilly lived by hawking advertising space for a small weekly film magazine, and before that had written (with his brother Giles) a book, rung doorbells in Kent to sell housewives silk stockings, and lasted two weeks with a small publisher. At public school (Wellington College), he had been an outspoken pacifist, refusing noisily to join the Officer's Training Corps; and, at breakfast, was alarmed and apprehensive over the news from Spain. Toynbee was excited and pleased, feeling (as a Communist) that the revolt would be crushed quickly and to the disadvantage of European fascism.

Soon afterwards, Toynbee left as a Communist roving emissary in Europe for the fellow-travelling British Student Party, and to attend a World Congress of Youth in Geneva, war-

transferred from Barcelona. Stopping at Nice between assignments, he found in the *poste restante* a weeks-old, nearly illegible post-card from Romilly. The former student-pacifist, it indicated, was on his way to fight for Spain. What Romilly had done after his friend had left was to give his landlady notice, and then have a Wednesday night party at his flat to bid farewell to all his friends in Bloomsbury. Before the night was over, he had concluded the party by auctioning away almost everything movable in the flat to raise money for travelling expenses. After he had put aside enough to pay his bills, he found himself with an unbountiful net of £9. Still, it was enough to get him on the boat train, over the Channel to Dieppe, and, in a roundabout way, south to Marseilles. Three weeks later he was at the front.

Never a Communist, Romilly, by example, had made his doctrinaire friends look ineffectual. While his commitment was a moral, rather than a political, one, Philip Toynbee, back at Oxford for the winter term of 1936, recalled:

> Soon . . . I was sunk deeper than ever in the half-life of meetings and campaigns. My chief activity now was to proliferate Spanish Defence Committees throughout the University, as a moth lays its eggs in a clothes cupboard. But although this was probably the most useful and effective of all my activities as a communist, I was con-tinually aware that Esmond's role was the nobler one. A letter arrived from him in November to tell me that he was already fighting in the outskirts of Madrid. It seemed to me very typical of his bluntness, but also of a certain inverted romanticism, that he wrote most vividly about the smell of dead Moors.
>
> The letter made me very restless, and I was half-persuaded that I too would go to Spain, join the International Brigade and smell the dead Moors.[20]

Romilly's training had been sketchy, and because of his teen-age pacifism, he had never held a gun in his life. Finally, while at the barracks in Valencia, waiting for the train to Albacete to join the Internationals, he noticed some old rifles lying about, and a few enthusiastic volunteers lifting the museum pieces up to feign aiming them. Shyly confessing his ignorance to one of the Frenchmen, he asked him "to explain the system of the thing." The old veteran showed him how to hold the rifle butt pressed against his shoulder and how to shove back and close the bolt. It was his first lesson in military science.

At Albacete an interlude in the brief training program was the summons to the political commissar to check the recruit's ideological soundness. The political commissar was a very important man in camp, Romilly discovered—very important because he also looked after clothing, food, leaves, and other things of importance to a soldier. Romilly's Commissar, a German, asked the routine introductory questions: name, age, occupation of parents, whether they knew one was in Spain, what political party one belonged to, and last, "Why have you come to Spain?" There was a poster on the wall which proclaimed, "To smash Fascism." It simplified the last answer. After a satisfactory score, the recruit was issued a rifle.

There were eighteen Englishmen (including Romilly) clustered into the English Group of the Thaelmann Battalion. About half were Marxists. They had been assured that they would receive sixteen days of training, but the Madrid situation was desperate, and the whole unit was quickly shunted to a very disorganized front. In the heat and confusion, overladen with bulky equipment and on their feet too much with insufficient rest, the exhausted Englishmen found their enthusiasm for the anti-Fascist cause waning. However, there was little time to consider the matter. Moving across a ploughed-up field in their first contact with the enemy, they heard the rustle of nearly spent bullets, then the twang of close-range fire; and they scrabbled in the furrows for cover. Ten yards away a German volunteer was hit in the thigh— first blood.

To Romilly, the fighting afterwards in the streets and buildings of Madrid's suburbs was like "an American film."[21] It was difficult for him at times to believe that what he was living through was real, for to some volunteers ideology was always more important than strategy: "All this time I had the pleasant illusion that the bombing and shelling did not actively concern us. I somehow could never really believe the enemy were occupying themselves with *us;* we were only playing at soldiers, were only amateurs . . . ; it was ridiculous that we should be doing this— who were surely concerned all the time only with seeing that we had the same food rations as the Flem[ing]s and quarrelling among ourselves and holding Group Meetings."

In the vicinity of the University of Madrid, Romilly's battalion came upon a force of Italian Fascist "volunteers" and drove them back. Sporadically, they advanced and reoccupied farmland and buildings on the outskirts of Madrid, and when the front briefly seemed stabilized Romilly and a few other Englishmen got leave to go into Madrid, interested primarily in finding a way to have a hot bath and a restaurant meal. In the peculiar situation then prevailing, one took a tram car from the front into the city, but the Englishmen found it awkward because their rifles constantly got in the way of other passengers. Halfway there, they got out and thumbed a ride in "a splendid Rolls-Royce flying an Anarchist flag." Sometimes it *was* a splendid war.

Romilly missed some of the most crucial weeks of the Madrid defense by acquiring dysentery and being sent to Barcelona to recuperate. In December he was back again, this time in villages west of Madrid. Beneath the ilex trees on the Corunna road, north of Boadilla, he met an English volunteer (attached to another battalion) whose bandaged head made recognition difficult. He had seen him before, he realized, when Romilly, at fifteen, was trying to start a public school boy's anti-war magazine.* It was John Cornford.

At Boadilla del Monte, Romilly's unit was shelled, then bombed by German tri-motored Junkers. After the artillery had dusted them with hot metal fragments, the exploding bombs covered them with dirt. "The time you are a real pacifist," Romilly

---

* It was the short-lived *Out of Bounds,* which attacked "Reaction, Militarism and Fascism in the Public Schools." Later (1935) the Romillys used the same title for their autobiographical book.

realized under fire, "is the time you know real sickening fear. That was as near as any of us got to being pacifists." Of the eighteen Englishmen in Romilly's original group, only ten remained before Boadilla. Only two survived Boadilla. (Only three of the dead were Communists, he thought.) There had been three days of bitter, useless fighting. Not only were the Government troops unable to dislodge the green-uniformed, red-capped Moors from the village, but they were forced into a disorganized withdrawal from the positions they had held themselves. Afterwards, there was the routine of night patrols into the shattered area to recover abandoned rifles and ammunition, and the bodies of the dead. None of the English could be found. On the third of January, 1937, Romilly returned to England, just as the British Battalion of Internationals (with his older brother Giles as a volunteer) was being formed. "I might have gone back and joined these men," he later mused. "But I did not go. I got married and lived happily ever after."

In his book *Boadilla*, written soon afterwards, Romilly concluded, "I am not a pacifist, though I wish it were possible to lead one's life without the intrusion of this ugly monster of force and killing—war—and its preparation. And it is not with the happiness of the convinced communist, but reluctantly that I realise that there will never be peace or any of the things I like and want, until that mixture of profit-seeking, self-interest, cheap emotion and organised brutality which is called fascism has been fought and destroyed for ever."

Romilly never lived happily ever after, as he promised himself in the closing lines of *Boadilla*. He did come come to elope— after a chaotic courtship which delighted the newspapers—with the nineteen-year-old daughter of Lord Redesdale[22] (an appropriate match for a nephew of Winston Churchill). He wrote articles about Spain, and completed his book—a work which augured a good deal for him if it were the opening of a career as a writer. It had descriptive power, narrative ease, and understated emotional force, and remains one of the few personal accounts of the Spanish War in English worth reading for other than historical purposes: not a great book, but one that promised much for its author. But there was another, and bigger, war soon to come, one inevitable after Spain. After an RAF raid over Hamburg in December, 1941, bomber pilot Esmond Romilly was listed as missing.

In spite of the Boadilla withdrawal, the Internationals had been generally effective on the Madrid front, and may have made the difference in turning back the December attempt to overrun the city. They stayed, and seeing action in the Madrid area soon after the beginning of 1937 was a new International unit—the six-hundred-man British Battalion of the XVth Brigade. All of its company officers and commissars, although not more than a majority of its enlisted men, were Communists.

Near the Jarama River on February 12, the British Battalion absorbed a ferocious artillery and machine gun assault from the crests of the hills above Pingarrón. Below, the exposed English troops had difficulty staying alive, as a survivor, John Lepper, wrote:

> *Death stalked the olive trees*
> *Picking his men.*
> *His leaden finger beckoned*
> *Again and again.*[23]

All through the day the battle continued, with one company of British even tricked into being taken prisoner by opening their trenches to a unit of Franco's Moroccans which had advanced singing the *Internationale*. On the thirteenth, the survivors fell back, but the two remaining Battalion officers rallied them, and they recaptured their positions.

With them on the twelfth had been Christopher St. John Sprigg, who was known also under the by-line of Christopher Caudwell. A jack-of-all-writing trades, he had been following the profession since, before he was fifteen, he had left the Benedictine

School at Ealing to work as a reporter on the *Yorkshire Observer.* Before he was twenty, he had become an editor with a London firm of publishers on aviation subjects, and soon afterwards a director of the company. Technically gifted, he produced five books on aeronautics and invented an infinitely variable gear, the designs for which were published in *Automotive Engineer.* Meanwhile he wrote fiction and poetry.* Before he was twenty-five he was the author of twelve books, including seven detective novels, and had published short stories and poetry as well.

In May, 1935, under the name of Christopher Caudwell, he published his first serious novel, *This My Hand.* His interests were expanding and changing, and the work indicated that one direction it was taking was toward psychology. In another direction, he had found himself fascinated by Marxism, and groped for an understanding between Marxist thought and the goals of literature. The result had been that he spent the summer of 1935 in Cornwall, reading Marx, Engels, and Lenin, the new perspectives absorbing him with the usual rapidity of all his new interests. Before then his political views were vague, and such, he considered, was proper for one who thought of himself primarily as a poet. When he came back to London, he started on his first draft of a Marxist approach to literary criticism, *Illusion and Reality,* and changed lodgings to Poplar, in the East End of London, in order to study working class conditions at first hand. There he joined the local branch of the Party—an unusual comrade among the aggressive, gregarious factory workers and dockers. Quiet and reserved, Caudwell was more likely to be a courteous listener, contributing a "Cheshire Cat grin" and, when something caught his interest, an almost imperceptible elevation of his high, intellectual brow. But the short young man who wrote books for a living was adaptable as well as independent. Quickly, he became adept at illicit placement of Party posters, street corner speaking, selling *Daily Workers* and the rest of the routine tasks. The next

---

* His poetry even echoed his technical interests, as in, for skeleton, "The white and knobbled chassis of the flesh."

year—briefly—he was secretary of the local branch, a job he inwardly disliked as much as the more petty assignments, all of which he knew restricted his personal usefulness.

To satisfy himself about the way Marxism should develop, he went to Paris to study the Popular Front movement there; and, to be able to dig more deeply into the literature of his adopted political philosophy, he began to teach himself Russian. He "had every intention," a friend later wrote of him, "of continuing to find his own line through the intellectual problems before him and consistently refused to be sidetracked into Party office or officialdom. He also had a real horror of being classed with the intellectuals of the Party, and gave them the widest possible berth, in just the same way that he had loathed and avoided all literary cliques."[24] He put in his day's work alone, at his typewriter, writing novels for a living, poetry for self-satisfaction, and literary and scientific criticism as his deeply felt professional duty. He began revising *Illusion and Reality*, completed his sharply written essays later published as *Studies in a Dying Culture*,* and started *The Crisis in Physics*, a book on the philosophy of science. When the clock struck five he would leave his paper in the typewriter and go out to the Poplar Branch to pick up his assignment to speak at an open-air meeting, or to peddle the *Daily Worker* at the corner of Crispin Street Market.

Caudwell's proletarian idyll ended with Franco's flight to Tetuán. Between July and October (the month he became 29) he

---

* A typical excerpt from the *Studies:* "The case of Shaw is . . . a proof of how stubborn is the bourgeois illusion. . . . He stands by the side of Wells, Lawrence, Proust, Huxley, Russell, Forster, Hemingway, and Galsworthy as typical of their age, men who proclaim the disillusionment of bourgeois culture with itself, men themselves disillusioned and yet not able to wish for anything better or gain any closer grasp of this bourgeois culture whose pursuit of liberty and individualism led men into the mire. . . .

"Evidently all Shaw's failings, all the things that prevented him from fulfilling the artistic and intellectual promise of his native gifts, arise . . . from his fatal choice of the bourgeois class at a period of history when the choice was wrong. From this choice springs the unreality of his plays, their lack of dramatic resolutions, the substitution of debate for dialectic, the belief in life forces and thought Utopias, the bungling treatment of human beings in love, the lack of scientific knowledge, and the queer strain of mountebank in all Shaw says. . . .'"

was one of the leading spirits in the Poplar Branch's aid-to-Spain campaign. Enough money was raised to buy and outfit an ambulance, and, in November, Caudwell himself drove it (in a convoy of trucks and ambulances) the length of France and across the border to deliver it to the Spanish Government. "You know," he wrote a friend, "how I feel about the importance of democratic freedom. The Spanish People's Army needs help badly; their struggle, if they fail, will certainly be ours tomorrow, and, believing as I do, it seems clear where my duty lies." Believing as he did, the terms *democratic freedom* and *People's Army* had a Party connotation, but their meaning was clear. Once in Spain, he stayed, and, adaptable as usual, mastered the pitifully brief Brigade basic training so well that he was made a machine gun instructor. Yet, even in Spain, the profession of letters was difficult to resist, and he took up the last of his editorships, that of the *Battalion Wall* occasional "newspaper." By February (1937) he was in action on the Jarama River front.

Although Stanhope Sprigg had been unable to stop his brother Christopher from going to Spain, he worked at trying to convince Party officials—once Caudwell had joined a fighting unit—that the new recruit was far more important to the Party as a writer than as a soldier. Christopher would not come home on his own, he appealed, but would accept Party discipline if so ordered. Since none of Caudwell's Marxist-oriented books had yet been published, it was frustratingly difficult to make a political case for a writer whose books in print were detective stories and aeronautical treatises, and who liked to be known as a poet. Besides, his independent ways and studious avoidance of prominence in the Party's intellectual and leadership circles had been so successful that no one at headquarters knew him or knew enough about him to have any strong feelings about his case. Desperately, Caudwell's brother (all of this without Christopher's knowledge) solicited the publisher, and managed to extricate an advance set of galley proofs of *Illusion and Reality: A Study of the Sources of Poetry.*

A high Party functionary agreed to read the proofs. It was (and still is) an impressive contribution to Marxist aesthetics, and, although he may have understood only a fractional amount of what he read, he was convinced of Caudwell's value as a live writer. A cable was dispatched to Spain recommending the immediate recall to England of Brigadier Christopher St. John Sprigg.

Although no one knew it yet, by the time the cable was sent, it was already too late. On his first day in battle, February 12, 1937, he had been killed, covering the retreat of his unit. "Sprigg's section," one of the survivors reported, "was holding a position on a hill crest. They got it rather badly from all ways: first artillery, then aeroplanes, then three enemy machine guns. The Moors then attacked the hill in great numbers. As there were only a few of our fellows left, including Sprigg, who had been doing great work with his machine gun, the company commander, ——,* the Dalston busman, gave the order to retire."

The last anyone saw of Caudwell, according to a wounded survivor, he was covering their retreat "with the Moors less than thirty yards away. . . . It was obvious he never managed to get off the hill."[25] The Dalston busman and a handful of the others who fell back under Caudwell's covering fire lived to fight again.

Although under the name of Sprigg he had left behind him a dozen forgettable potboilers, under the name of Caudwell— used for the work he really cared about—he had left behind him writings which would make him (in critic Stanley Edgar Hyman's phrase) probably "the most important Marxist cultural thinker of our time." Had he survived, he might have been far more than that. Some of his published and unpublished poetry, fiction, and criticism showed signs of a writer marked for greatness. His poetry alone was mature, serious, and often witty—some of the most brilliant written in the 1930's. "Even dead in his twenties," Hyman has written, "he was probably the best Marxist critic we

---

* Identity unrevealed in the source (John Strachey's introduction to Caudwell's *Studies in a Dying Culture* [London, 1938], p. vi).

have ever had," a thinker and writer of a power which went beyond
ideology. "Had he lived, we cannot even limit by imagining it
the work he might have done. The waste of his death, in intellectual
terms, is tragic beyond belief."[26] But Caudwell himself had written
of T. E. Lawrence that "A man can do no more than risk and
perhaps lose his life." And before he had gone to Spain he had
written a poem he had titled "The Art of Dying," which included
the lines,

> *For what's perfection except to be dead,*
> *Life's largest and unalterable sum,*
> *Soul's last eternal equilibrium?*[27]

The battle in the valley of the Jarama was the first in which
the British Battalion had fought as a unit, although many of its
members were already veterans of other engagements in Spain.
In command was balding, bespectacled Captain Tom Wintringham,
who had already seen much of war. Nearly twice the age of
Cornford or Romilly, Wintringham was a veteran of the First
World War and an acknowledged military expert before he came
to Spain. A "poet who had no time for poems" because of his
party activities as a Communist, he was one of the earliest to
suggest—while still with a hastily formed British medical unit
in the early weeks of the war—the combined propaganda and
military value of an international force, fostered by foreign
Communist parties (but open to all volunteers) and fighting beside
the Republican Army. By the time the British Battalion had
suffered its corporate initiation at the Jarama, Wintringham,
former editor of *Left Review,* had risen from second-in-command
because of a curious pre-battle casualty. In training, the Battalion
commander had been the more colorful Wilfred Macartney, a
radical (and notorious) journalist who acquired his position
partly because he was not a Party member and partly because
his Party sympathies were nevertheless beyond reproach. He had,
in fact, been convicted for giving military secrets to Russia, and

had served a term in prison, putting the experience to good use afterwards by writing a book about it, *Walls Have Mouths* (London, 1935). But Macartney was shot in the leg—accidentally, it seems—by political commissar Peter Kerrigan, who was cleaning his gun.

Wintringham was a tough-minded soldier who saw little difference between the strategies of warfare and those of politics. He had interrupted his studies at Balliol College, Oxford, to join the Royal Flying Corps in 1914, and returned after the war. Although he had been a Communist since the early twenties, he felt that his commitment was of even longer standing:

> Why was I here? Yes, hatred of war; to try to stamp war out as one would a forest fire, before it spreads. But more than that: all that lay behind me and, if I lived, ahead of me, led me here.
>
> Eight or nine generations back before my birth one of my ancestors, a Nonconformist hedge-preacher, had his tongue torn out by order of a royal court of justice. It was the only way to stop him [from] "carrying subversive propaganda," as we should call it today. Something of that man's attitude to life had come through to me from my parents, the most Liberal people I know. That hedge-doctor had sent me here. So, to a lesser extent, had the sickly child Tom who had started to read war histories at the age of ten, had loved battle-tales. . . . So had the poet who had no time for poems because the miseries of the world shadowed by war "were Misery and would not let him rest"—or let him be a poet. So had the lad in prison for incitement of mutiny, sedition; twenty-seven years old, waiting for April for liberty and May's General Strike.* I was here because of all I was and would be.[28]

Wintringham somehow found time for poems in the field when he had recalled having none as a political activist. Hard and unsentimental, his writing reflected unemotionally his early experience as ambulance assistant as well as his being wounded in action as an officer:

> *Hours in the night creep at you like enemy*
> *Patrols, quiet-footed: powers*

* In 1926.

And pretences that you are yourself give way
As without sound the
Splint bites tighter: there are still
Four hours to dawn. . . .[29]

His most poetically moving statement of his philosophy went beyond the ideology which often crept into his verse:

Our enemies can praise death and adore death;
For us, endurance, the sun; and now in this night
The electric torch, feeble, waning, but close-set
Follows the surgeon's fingers; we are allied with
This light.[30]

Some of Wintringham's verses tried to infuse renewed idealism into his men after one bloody reverse followed another, but the crusading spirit seems less significant after the passage of time than the fact of the composition—a Battalion Commander urging his men on to new efforts, and extolling their courage and the nobility of the cause in which it was offered, *through poetry.* It was indicative of the emotional and intellectual atmosphere in which, on one level, at least, the war was being fought. In this sense it was like few wars of the past or of the future—it had, intermittently, a soul.

After Wintringham had been wounded for the second time and had developed typhoid fever as well, Kitty, his wife, came to Communist Party headquarters in London to deliver a message from her husband to Harry Pollitt. The Party chieftain's answer was brief: "Tell him to get out of Barcelona, go up to the front line, get himself killed and give us a headline."[31] He had already suggested much the same to Stephen Spender, who had no intention of exchanging a gun he could not handle for the pen he could—". . . Go and get killed, comrade, we need a Byron in the movement."[32] No one ever accused the very efficient Pollitt— no more than people accused André Marty—of idealism. When Wintringham finally was able to leave Spain, in November, 1937, he was fifty pounds lighter than when he first arrived. Later, he left the Party.

Through no fault of his own, Wintringham's first experience of command action had been a bloody baptism for his under-manned Battalion, one from which it never really recovered. Of the 600, only 225 were alive when it ended, and barely 80 of those were unwounded. Afterwards a young Scotsman, Alex MacDade of Glasgow, who was assistant Company Commissar of the Battalion, recorded the feelings of the survivors in "Jarama Valley," a wry ballad set to the tune of "Red River Valley":

There's a valley in Spain called Jarama,
That's a place that we all know so well,
For 'tis there that we wasted our manhood
And most of our old age as well.

From this valley they tell us we're leaving,
But don't hasten to bid us adieu,
For e'en though we make our departure,
We'll be back in an hour or two.

Oh, we're proud of our British Battalion,
And the marathon record it's made,
Please do us this little favour,
And take this last word to Brigade:

You will never be happy with strangers,
They would not understand you as we,
So remember the Jarama Valley
And the old men who wait patiently.

When the veterans of the British Internationals were honored at a mass meeting in London after their departure from Spain near the close of the war, the souvenir program of the event published a less cynical, revised version of the ballad under MacDade's name:

There's a Valley in Spain called Jarama,
It's a place that we all know so well,
It is there that we gave of our Manhood,
And most of our brave comrades fell.
We are proud of our British Battalion,
And the stand for Madrid that they made,

For they fought like true Sons of the Soil,
As part of the Fifteenth Brigade.
With the rest of the International Column,
In the stand for the Freedom of Spain
We swore in that Valley of Jarama
That fascism never will reign.
Now we've left that dark valley of sorrow
And its memories we ne'er shall forget,
So before we continue this reunion
Let us stand to our glorious dead.

Too realistic to have appreciated the alterations, MacDade could not have had a hand in them. He was killed at Brunete on July 6, 1938.

The reaction to battle often froze experienced writers into mannered, insincere language. It also sometimes made poets of men who had never written verse before, and would never do so again. The whole extant poetic output of one soldier was found on his unidentifiable corpse, scribbled on the leaf of a notebook in his pocket:

Eyes of men running, falling, screaming
Eyes of men shouting, sweating, bleeding
The eyes of the fearful, those of the sad
The eyes of exhaustion, and those of the mad.

Eyes of men thinking, hoping, waiting,
Eyes of men loving, cursing, hating,
The eyes of the wounded sodden in red,
The eyes of the dying and those of the dead. . . .[33]

Equally nonpolitical was the reaction of T. A. R. Hyndman,* who was horrified by the slaughter at the Jarama, and who had not come to Spain for political reasons. In a laconic twenty-line poem, "Jarama Front," he described his trying to evade the sight and

---

* The "Jimmy Younger" of Stephen Spender's autobiography *World Within World.* See Chapter II for his relations with Spender and its effect on Spender's activities in Spain.

sounds of a dying soldier, and his failure to be able to take his eyes away from the figure under the tree in the sagging blanket:

> ... *No slogan*
> *No clenched fist*
> *Except in pain.*[34]

Charles Donnelly had gone into action on the same day as Christopher Caudwell, but had survived. In left circles at home he had already acquired a reputation as a comer, and had written for *Left Review* and for Irish periodicals. He had also achieved a wider reputation as a radical—the only way the public at large had ever heard of him—by being expelled from University College, Dublin, for refusing to deny that he was a Communist. In London he supported himself with odd jobs, and, for a time, was a barman and dishwasher while he wrote on poetry and on politics, and began a novel and a biography of Irish revolutionary James Connolly. With romantic enthusiasm he studied military science, lectured on Irish affairs at Marx House and moved up the occupation ladder into white-collar jobs. When the rebellion in Spain began he decided that it was ridiculous to talk about military science when he could defend his left-wing convictions while acquiring some military experience at first hand. Still, he waited until a company of Irishmen was being formed as an adjunct to the new American Abraham Lincoln Battalion. He could only fight beside people he knew, Donnelly told friends. Just before Christmas he went to Spain.

At least one young Irishman who was prevented from volunteering spent the months which followed feeling sorry for himself. Looking disconsolately for his family's "new" house in the Kildare Road, Dublin, Brendan Behan (later to write *The Quare Fellow* and *The Hostage*) found only "skeletoned houses, untiled roofs, unplastered walls, unglazed windows," and, to little brother Dominic rued, "Oh, Mother of the devine God! And to think that only last year me mother burned me instructions that would have taken me to Spain. Afraid I would have been hurt. Well, I can safely say I'd rather have been shot outside Madrid with the friends I know than die out in this kip alone!"[35] "Those of us who were fourteen years of age," he remembered later, "were left with the women and children, and a humiliating place it was for tough chiselers like us. We were left collecting tinned milk and packets of cocoa and bags of flour for the Food Ship, and were only consoled by street fights and rock-throwing."[36] He relieved his frustrations, too, by initiating his adult career as a writer, and by speaking as outrageously pro-Republican as he could. His opinions were blasphemous, he was warned. Sure enough, Bernard Keegan's mother had said that Father O'Flanagan would be unfrocked for declaring that he was in favor of those people in Spain. "Well," said Brendan, "if he's unfrocked twenty times a day it won't be half as many times as Bernard Keegan's mother."[37]

In 1936, he had begun writing pro-Loyalist articles for the *Irish Democrat*—"the only articles I have ever written that I was not paid for and enjoyed writing."[38] But writing was all he could contribute of himself while his countrymen were fighting in Spain.

Charles Donnelly and his company of Irishmen, meanwhile, had arrived just in time to be involved in the reorganization of the mauled Republican forces after the Jarama battle. With the Americans, the small Irish group was thrown into the counter-attack, already a week in progress, on February 23, 1937. Their jumping-off point was at the strongest sector of the Nationalists' front, in the hills from Pingarrón south to the Jarama River. Donnelly, by then, had been writing poetry again—"a great deal of verse in which his emotional and intellectual life were beginning to find fusion," his friend Montagu Slater wrote.[39] His few weeks of war had generated in him an objectivity which had freed him, in his best verse, from dated political diction. Yet his Marxist politics was of the idealistic variety, and he was contemptuous of the radical intellectual who, safe at his desk, refused to see that the difference

> *Between rebellion as a private study and the public*
> *Defiance is simple action. . . .*[40]

Few poets of any war saw it from the inside with the detachment Donnelly brought to "The Tolerance of Crows":

> *Death comes in quality from solved*
> *Problems on maps, well-ordered dispositions,*
> *Angles of elevation and direction;*
> *Comes innocent from tools children might*
> *Love, retaining under pillows,*
> *Innocently impales on any flesh.*
>
> *And with flesh falls apart the mind*
> *That trails thought from the mind that cuts*
> *Thought clearly for a waiting purpose.*
>
> *Progress of poison in the nerves and*
> *Discipline's collapse halted.*
> *Body awaits the tolerance of crows.*[41]

Of the 450 in the outgunned battalion, 120 were killed, 175 wounded. On February 27, one of the dead was Donnelly, who fell a few yards from the Nationalist trenches, in a futile charge that gutted his company. Among his papers the survivors found two compositions, "The Tolerance of Crows" and the longer "private rebellion–public defiance" verses, which he had titled merely, "Poem." They were posted on the battalion's "wall" bulletin board, outlined in black.

Donnelly would not be the last. The early battles around Madrid had been costly in many ways, and the British losses were numerically insignificant in a war which would eventually take a million lives. But the few months in Spain had already cost England half a generation's most promising poets.

By the time Julian Bell returned to England from China in March, 1937, Donnelly, Cornford, and Caudwell were dead. A "large rollicking person, endowed with a huge gusto for life, full of laughter and good fellowship, but also . . . extremely serious, sensitive and a scholar,"[42] he was Virginia Woolf's favorite nephew, son of her sister Vanessa (and art critic Clive Bell). Like Esmond Romilly, he was a former pacifist and politically un-committed, although leaning toward socialism. Increasingly fas-cinated by war, he had nevertheless edited a book of recollections by First World War conscientious objectors called *We Did Not Fight;* and, while he had ambitions of making a reputation as a poet, he had been disappointed by his lack of success as a writer, his failure to become a Fellow of King's College (Cambridge), and the unsatisfactory tangle of amorous relationships with which he had complicated his life. As a respectable escape, he sought, in the tradition of other English writers, the springboard of a uni-versity post far from London. When Bell learned of the Generals' Revolt he was already teaching English—and learning about Chinese women—at Wu Han University in central China.

To his friends, Bell seemed by then obsessed by war. "I don't mind war as killing," he had written to one, "nor as pain, nor utterly as destruction. But it means turning our minds and feelings downwards . . . : now we shall just have civil war, to the last dregs of modern invention. . . . If there must be violence, there must. But let's be thoroughly cold-blooded and unenthusiastic about it. . . . There's nothing in the world fouler than enthusiasm, the enthusiasm of a fighting group, not even jealousy or suspicion, not even open-eyed causing of misery."[43] Yet, shortly afterward, he confessed to another, "Nothing has ever really cured me of my militarist daydreams, and I hope I shall spend at least a part of my life—even the last part—on battlefields."[44]

At Cambridge, he had moved in a circle of young liberal in-tellectuals, spending the early 1930's—more years than should have been necessary—working on a thesis entitled "Some Appli-cations of Ethics to Politics." Still, political activism and social idealism were then empty gestures to Bell, who satirized them in an essay, "Open Letter to C. Day Lewis," calling the far left poets irresponsible, and in a poem, "Bypass to Utopia," labelling their behavior a betrayal of the independence of the intellect:

Who from serious tasks would turn,
Race with wind, or play with fire,
Contempt from honest men shall earn,
Emptiness in all desire.

But there was deep dissatisfaction beneath the façade. "Well, you may be thankful I'm safe in China," he wrote his mother, "for I know in England I should be feeling that the only reasonable thing is to go and fight the fascists in Spain." In another letter he admitted, "I fancy being here has salved my conscience: I know I should rather feel ashamed of myself if I'd been in England and not tried to volunteer." He confessed to being tired of the role of "an intellectual on the loose. I want something more practicable, tiresome, and involving other people. . . ." Finally, harrassed as much by amorous complications in China as by what he thought was his conscience, he found cause to volunteer in Spain: "It's impossible to let other people go and fight for what one believes in and refuse to risk oneself. . . . I should never recover from a sense of shame if I didn't go."

A new essay, "[Open] Letter to E. M. Forster, 1937," now defended the place of action in politics—that "war is a lesser evil balanced against some kinds of peace." The forces of Bloomsbury pacifism, still rigid in their 1914–1918 posture, tried to talk young Bell out of going to Spain once he had returned from China. They pointed out that it was already too late, that the tide had already turned in favor of Franco—and that Bell's inexperienced hands on a trigger would be of little use to the Loyalist cause. J. M. Keynes, David Garnett, his aunt Virginia, and his mother tried to dissuade him, eventually pressuring him into dropping the idea of volunteering as a combatant, and into joining instead a medical unit with which Richard Rees was going to Spain.

His mother's pressure was crucial. Bell's many affairs may

have been his way of resolving the oedipal feelings he and his mother seem to have unspokenly recognized. To his mother he confided his sexual intrigues, and from his mother more than anyone else he sought approval for his actions. "Dearest Nessa," he had written her from China, "I think we must leave the whole question of Spain until I get back. For one thing, it is very painful, because the only big reason to me for not doing any really dangerous thing is that it makes you unhappy, however good you are about your being reasonable and telling me that I am not to think too much of your feelings. . . ."[45] Still, all Vanessa had been able to do was divert Julian's commitment into a noncombatant direction. One way or another, he was insistent on going. He learned to drive a lorry, passed a driving test for ambulance work, and signed a statement—to acquire a passport—that he would take part in no belligerent activities in Spain. Early in June, 1937, the Medical Aid detachment left.

Although he was only to be an ambulance driver, his mother and his aunt were miserable with anxiety. Soon afterwards, Virginia Woolf—never very far from the border of a breakdown—watched a melancholy procession of Spanish refugees newly arrived in England, "impelled by machine-guns in Spanish fields," she noted in her diary, "to trudge through Tavistock Square, along Gordon Square, then where?—clasping their enamel kettles. . . ."[46] Her nephew, meanwhile, had driven with his convoy of ambulances across France, reaching the Spanish border on June 10. Within two weeks, he was on the Madrid front, his unit part of the medical support for a Loyalist counteroffensive then in preparation. From the Brunete area, on Madrid's western perimeter, he wrote his mother that he was glad he had come: "I find it perpetually entertaining and very satisfactory. And though I have begun to realize what a pleasure ordinary life will be, I don't feel I've more than touched the possibilities of this. . . . it's a better life than most I've led."[47] More realistically, at twenty-nine he was searching for a direction to his life, and thought he had found it, for his motives in going to Spain were not merely the cause of the Republic, but also "the usefulness of war experience in the future and the prestige one would gain in literature and—even more—Left politics."

Enemy fire had been fierce in Bell's sector, the Nationalists having tried for three weeks to dislodge Government troops from a strategic position they had taken. While evacuating wounded, the British Medical Unit ambulance he was driving was smashed by a bomb. With no vehicle to drive, he asked permission to go out to the front as a stretcher-bearer, and was put in charge of thirty medics in a dangerous sector of the line. By July 18, a few days later, there was a slackening in the fighting, and Bell took out a newly received truck and a party of men to fill in hazardous shell holes in the road which was the main medical evacuation route. (The repairs would help speed the wounded out of the area while making their transportation less agonizing.)

It had begun as a comparatively quiet day, but, shortly after Bell left, a Nationalist counterattack began, prefaced by artillery fire and the bombing of front line positions. In Bell's sector the artillery fire was still desultory, but one round picked out his vehicle.

Later that day, a wounded ambulance driver was brought into the Escorial hospital on a stretcher. So covered with dirt and blood that he was unrecognizable, he was ordered cleaned up by the receiving physician in order to probe for his wounds. Only then did Archie Cochrane, his old friend from King's College, recognize the patient. But as soon as he saw the shell fragment deep in Bell's chest, he knew that nothing could be done. While Cochrane tried to make his old classmate comfortable, Julian, still conscious, murmured, "Well, I always wanted a mistress and a chance to go to war, and now I've had both." Then he faded into French, quoting indistinctly lines Cochrane thought might have come from Baudelaire. Soon after he fell into a coma.[48]

Richard Rees saw Julian Bell for the last time in the hospital mortuary, covered except for his head and shoulders. No wound was exposed, and he looked "very pale and clean, almost marble-like. Very calm and peaceful, almost as if he had fallen asleep when very cold."[49]

There were others: nearly a platoon of poets from Britain served actively in Spain during the first year of the civil war, but only a few survived to the end. In the 1940's, midway through a larger conflict for which the years from 1936 to 1939 had served as overture, someone answered the question, "Where are the war poets?" with the reply, "Killed in Spain."[50] A significant segment of England's future literary voice—of the forties, fifties and sixties—had been stilled by mid-1937.

2

THE COMMITTED NONCOMBATANTS

We were not . . . a lost generation. But
we were divided between our literary voca-
tion and an urge to save the world from
Fascism. We were the Divided Generation of
Hamlets who found the world out of joint
and failed to set it right.
                Stephen Spender,
                WORLD WITHIN WORLD *(1951)*

"Poets hope too much, and their poli-
tics . . . usually stink after twenty years."
            T. E. Lawrence
            to Cecil Day Lewis, Nov. 16, 1934.

IN THE FALL of 1936 Stephen Spender returned to London from
Vienna. His book *Forward from Liberalism* had been accepted
by the Left Book Club, and the check for £300 helped modernize
his lofty studio flat in Hammersmith, which looked out toward the
Thames across a view of London rooftops. It was a period of
attending crowded Aid to Spain meetings and swallowing mis-
givings about the Popular Front alliance which had made Liberals
and Communists uneasy partners. As a result, Spender's book
was much discussed, and the enterprising Harry Pollitt invited
him for a chat at the dingy King Street offices of the Communist
Party. The talk was friendly, but the two disagreed about the

Moscow purge trials and enough other matters that Pollitt finally got down to business. The one subject they both agreed on, he began, was Spain. Why not, he suggested, admit disagreement on other matters, but join the Communist Party to help Spain? He was even willing to print Spender's heterodox points of view in a *Daily Worker* article to appear at the time the poet joined.

Spender accepted. Pollitt gave him a membership card, telling him that the Party cell in Hammersmith would contact him. Why not, he added—as if it were an afterthought—go to Spain? Spender professed no talents suitable for the International Brigade, but offered to go in a noncombatant capacity if there was some un-Byronic way to be useful. A few days later, his article appeared in the *Daily Worker,* infuriating some doctrinaire Communists in Scotland and the North of England. The Hammersmith cell never got in touch with him, and the only dues he ever paid were his original subscription at King Street.

Before Pollitt could do anything further to propel Spender to Spain, Spender's attention was re-focused there by someone else —T. A. R. Hyndman, his closest friend and the "Jimmy Younger" of his memoir *World Within World.* "Jimmy" had followed up his apparent conversion to Communism by enlisting in the International Brigade. Less a political than a personal decision, it came, Spender was sure, because he and Jimmy had parted ways, the break becoming more pronounced when Spender had married a girl he met at an Oxford Aid to Spain meeting. Soon cheerful, idealistic letters from Jimmy were arriving, and Spender's sense of guilt eased. But, after the February 12, 1937 slaughter at the Jarama, Jimmy's letters combined panic with disillusionment. (After the Jarama, Jimmy had written that he could hear the wounded moaning and calling for help as they lay between the lines.) Still, as agonized as Spender was, he could see no way of getting his friend out of the situation for which he had volunteered himself.

After Jimmy had left for Spain—it was just a few days after Spender's visit to Pollitt—the *Daily Worker* telephoned Spender

to offer him an assignment to investigate the fate of a Russian
merchant crew whose ship had been sunk in the Mediterranean
by the Italians. To send a poet out to search for the crewmen of
the *Komsomol* was an absurd errand, but Spender dutifully went,
taking along his writer friend T. C. Worsley. They flew from
Barcelona to Alicante, and on to Gibraltar, Tangiers, and Oran,
then back to Gibraltar, where they were turned away by Franco's
frontier guards when they tried to get to Cadiz. Eventually the
not-very-secret suspicion that the crew was interned at Cadiz was
confirmed when someone inquired there at the Italian Consulate,
a step which could have been taken without anyone's leaving
London. But it provided the excuse for Spender to touch at the
fringes of the war. ("Spender's adventures as an amateur intelligence agent, snooping around Gibraltar and Tangiers," his
friend Christopher Isherwood later observed, "would make a
great satirical novel, and I often beg him to write it."[1])

Wherever Spender went on the *Komsomol* mission, he was
impressed by the passion of popular involvement with the cause
of the Republic. At a rally in Tangiers he saw "a devoutness, a
sense of hope," which made him think of the crowds described
in the New Testament. Wherever he came into touch with Communist groups in Africa and Spain he was impressed not only
by their idealism and fervor, but "by their confidence and their
decency."[2] (And everywhere he found British officialdom and
business interests openly sympathetic to Franco.) En route home
he spent several days in Barcelona. As he came into the city from
the airport he saw building after building with windows crisscrossed by strips of paper—a device to suppress flying glass
splinters in case of air raids. Naïvely, he took them for a massive
political demonstration of some kind, and entered Barcelona in-
fused with a Loyalist ardor which the giant propaganda posters
and slogans along the main avenues and squares only heightened.
"The people had taken over the streets, and walked about them in
wandering crowds like heirs examining an inheritance which had
suddenly fallen to them."[3]

The infectious atmosphere convinced both Worsley and Spender that they wanted to return to Spain as soon as they could. Within weeks, Worsley was in an ambulance unit helping with the evacuation of Malaga. Spender, meanwhile, had been offered, via a letter from a Señor Thomas, a post as English broadcaster for the Socialist Party's radio station in Valencia. Remembering having heard in Barcelona "a rather languid English voice"—which he recognized with surprise as that of the poet David Gascoyne—broadcasting from loudspeakers attached to the eighth-story level of a building in the main square, he accepted.

In Valencia, Spender visited Señor Thomas, whom he told loyally, when asked how much money he wanted, that he would work for nothing. Suddenly the tone of the interview changed. Unable to stall any longer, the station manager announced that there was no longer any position open; and with un-Latin grace-lessness he indicated that the interview was at an end. Later, Spender learned that wartime "unification" of political parties had meant the abolition of party-run stations.

Brushed off but still in Spain, Spender travelled to International Brigade headquarters at Albacete to look for Jimmy. Bronzed and fit, Jimmy looked as if he were thriving on the Cause, but as soon as he found sufficient privacy he blurted to Spender, "You must get me out of here!" Not only had he decided that he no longer wanted to die for the Republic: he had become a pacifist, and wanted nothing less than to get out of Spain. Realizing that maintenance of military discipline was impossible if dispirited volunteers could demobilize themselves as easily as they had volunteered, Spender convinced Jimmy to let him intervene with the Brigade political commissar to secure a noncombatant assignment. Commissar Peter Kerrigan agreed ("We'll keep him here, but I promise he won't have to fight."), and Spender decided to go on to Madrid to have a look at the front.

The corpses in no man's land looked to Spender like "ungathered waxy fruit." They, and curious guests, were all in a day's work to the British Battalion's Captain (later Major) George

Nathan, a debonair, swagger stick-carrying hero whose bravery was already legendary.[4] "We make a point of not allowing our front-line visitors to be killed," he observed to Spender, and warned the tall poet to stoop as they toured the trenches. At one machine gun emplacement the gunner in charge insisted that Spender fire a few rounds into the Moorish lines. Praying that he would hit no one, Spender reluctantly pressed the trigger. For a visitor to intervene this way seemed to him a frivolity unworthy of the issues. Besides, he was admittedly scared: the enemy might reply in kind.

When Nathan hospitably asked Spender to stay in the line "for three or four days—perhaps a week," he declined, and went back to Madrid, where he watched Loyalist art experts cataloging and safeguarding Spanish art treasures, including an "army of stone and painted wood virgins" removed from buildings exposed to bombing or shell fire. They were, he was told wryly, "the fifth column of the blessed."[5] Later, Spender wrote an article defending the Republic against charges of looting and desecrating Spanish art. A major Fascist propaganda line at the time was that the "Red" Government not only atheistically destroyed religious art in Spain, but was systematically plundering all of the valuable art works it could find. The charge helped raise the hackles of Henry Moore, Piet Mondrian, Ben Nicholson, and the rest of the Hampstead group of artists, who felt strongly about the civil war. Conversation among them, which had been all aesthetic in 1932, was all political by 1937. Henry Moore even considered putting down his chisel and taking up politics, "but like so many progressives he found it difficult to act. He was a member of a group that planned to go to Spain during the civil war—a group that included W. H. Auden and Stephen Spender. The trip was planned as a propaganda device, its ostensible purpose to investigate Republican care of Spanish art works." But when the group applied to the Government for permission to make the trip, it was refused.[6] Both Auden and Spender had eventually gone to Spain anyway, but the artists' mission ended before it began.

Countering charges of Republican atrocities was less easy for Spender than disproving accusations about paintings and statues, for one of the more disturbing aspects of his second Spanish journey was his discovery that atrocities were committed even in the name of idealism. Brutality, he saw, resulted from violent emotions, and such emotions were not confined to one side. A *Causa*, close up, was an unsettling experience, even when it was an essentially good one.

There were other unsettling experiences. When the March, 1937 military crisis at Guadalajara had come, Peter Kerrigan, in the haste of moving Internationals up to fill breaches in the line, had forgotten his promise to Spender and sent Jimmy back to the front. And Jimmy had deserted. It took much of Spender's remaining time in Spain to get Jimmy—who was quickly located—out of the stockade and sent home. For Spender, the frenzied wire-pulling to help a recaptured deserter could only render him suspect among comrades whose loyalties to the Republic were apparently undivided. Ironically, the more real threat to his loyalties occurred afterwards back home, when he discovered how dishonest recruitment in England for the International Brigades had sometimes become. Although represented as a Popular Front collective effort, the Brigades were directed almost entirely by Communists.* But the truth would have cut down enlistments, for—as Spender began to understand—"Even the Communists realized that what made Spain an action and a symbol in this century as important as 1848 in the last, was the very fact that the Republic was *not* Communist." Although the energy and the passion for the cause came from those representing a broad spectrum of liberal values, the organization was Communist. The Communists, Spender saw, used united fronts in order to dominate

---

* Later, an English correspondent for a Communist paper agreed with Spender that he had been correct in his facts when he published an article claiming that there was Communist deception in recruitment for the Brigades. But, nonetheless, said the correspondent, the article should not have been written, for Spender should have considered not only the facts, but the result of making the facts public. The truth, he argued, lay in the cause itself (*World Within World*, p. 222).

them from within, and forced men of good will who began to recognize the fact "into a struggle of conscience which caused a deep division amongst the supporters of the Republic." It became a literarily significant struggle: the tensions of the committed liberal conscience come to grips with an increasingly complex Cause were clearly more the substance of drama than the rigid orthodoxy of party-line Communism. "The best books of the War," Spender thought later, "—those by Malraux, Hemingway, Koestler and Orwell—describe the Spanish tragedy from the liberal point of view, and they bear witness against the Communists."[7] (He might in fairness have added that they bore witness even more strongly against the Fascists.)

Spender's commitment to the cause of the Republic remained relatively unshaken, although his mood had become anti-heroic and despairing. His look at the line and the affair of Jimmy had induced some poetic ferment, and on the train to Valencia cynical lines popped into his head about a war in which no one on either side is given leave, "except the dead, and wounded," and in which exposure to cold and fear and hunger have so erased an army's enthusiasm

> *That each man hates the cause and distant words*
> *Which brought him here, more terribly than bullets.*

The dehumanization of the trenches had made enemy and comrade equal, united by common suffering:

> *Finally, they cease to hate: for although hate*
> *Bursts from the air and whips the earth like hail*
> *Or pours it up like fountains to marvel at,*
> *And although hundreds fall, who can connect*
> *The inexhaustible anger of the guns*
> *With the dumb patience of these tormented animals?*
> *Clean silence drops at night when a little walk*
> *Divides the sleeping armies, each*
> *Huddled in linen woven by remote hands.*
> *When the machines are stilled, a common suffering*
> *Whitens the air with breath and makes both one*
>   *As though these enemies slept in each other's arms.*[8]

The war was still so young by the end of Spender's second Spanish journey that the early glow of political idealism was only beginning to fade; but Spender still found it difficult to strike—let alone sustain—a heroic military note. Later, in discussing his wartime poems he defended supporting the Republican side by making the plea "that the small truth of immediate experience does not contradict the larger cause if the cause itself be true."[9] Still, his own immediate experience, but for the first impact of Loyalist strongholds like Barcelona, was that whatever the truth of the cause for which it was fought, war was shabby, brutalizing and wasteful. He developed the theme in an ironic poem in which the economic resources needed to kill a "too young and too silly" soldier only important in that he is the Enemy are compared to the victim:

> *Consider his life which was valueless*
> *In terms of employment, hotel ledgers, news files.*
> *Consider. One bullet in ten thousand kills a man.*
> *Ask. Was so much expenditure justified*
> *On the death of one so young, and so silly*
> *Lying under the olive trees, O world, O death?*[10]

The poem ("Ultima Ratio Regum") which had ended in death had begun with the lighthearted enthusiasm with which the dead boy had taken up the cause:

> *O too lightly he threw down his cap*
> *One day when the breeze threw petals from the trees. . . .*

Poignantly, Spender had encapsulated the experience of the young volunteers on both sides. Spain had prompted the lines, but it was a poem for all nations and all wars.

When Spender tried to go to Spain again in the early summer of 1937, to be a delegate at a Writers' Congress in Madrid—the beseiged city deliberately chosen to emphasize the devotion of intellectuals to the Republic—the British Foreign Office refused to grant him a visa. In order to cross the Spanish border, Spender obtained through André Malraux a fraudulent passport which described him as a Spanish citizen unimaginatively named Ramos Ramos. Malraux amused himself at the frontier by explaining that "Ramos Ramos" was an unusual kind of Spaniard—fair-haired and blue-eyed, and speaking a northern mountain dialect indistinguishable from English. The delegates drove from Barcelona to Valencia, and then to Madrid, in a convoy of Government cars, enthusiastically greeted everywhere by people who felt their faith in the Republic justified because the presence of *"los intellectuales"* was evidence that the free world was on their side. On the trip to Madrid, Spender travelled with Malraux, who in mid-1937 "had the air of a battered youth," walked with a nervous slouch, and wore a rough tweed suit which slouched independently. As literary personality as well as hero of the Malraux Squadron, he dominated the proceedings, aided by an attention-focussing nervous sniff and tic. Observing these mannerisms, Hemingway joked to Spender, "I wonder what Malraux did to get that tic? It must have been at well over ten thousand feet."

For ten days in Valencia and Madrid that July, European writers—many of them émigrés—discussed the relationship of the writer toward the Spanish war. Such meetings inspired no literature, but were an opportunity for writers to meet writers, and gave an impression of Republican solidarity which had its morale and propaganda values. But this one resulted in an unexpected attack upon the pro-Communist orthodoxy of the conference sponsors. The noisiest discussion arose over André Gide's book, *Retour de l'U.R.S.S.,* in which the backsliding Communist confessed to having become disenchanted with Russia as a result of his tour there. Except for the usual irrelevant attacks on Trotsky, the Gide affair was the only issue to arouse any interest on the part of the Russian delegates, who assailed the Frenchman as a "Fascist Monster," and as a "self-confessed decadent bourgeois." It turned the Congress away from idealistic slogans and resolutions, and into embarrassing name-calling.

Spender later recalled the whole "circus of intellectuals" as a grotesque facet of the reality of war. The beautiful scenery as backdrop to war-ruined towns, the banquets and the staged peasant dances, the hortatory speeches and the champagne, were "a thick hedge" dividing them from reality. Once, though, the reality made itself felt not by the blazing upper stories of the shell-struck Ministry of the Interior, but by a peasant woman on the Valencia-Madrid road who seized Spender's arm and appealed, "Sir, can you stop the *pájaros negros* machine-gunning our husbands as they work in the fields?" The blackbirds were the Fascist planes, and the villagers of Minglanilla in their innocence looked upon *los intellectuales* as a source of salvation.

One of the most grotesque episodes to Spender was the "kind of hysterical conceitedness" which had seized some of the delegates who had seen more of the war than the tourist-writers:

An English Communist novelist, who had some connection with the Republican Army, gave the English delegates a lecture on its organization. "The Republican Army is full of anomalies," he began. "For example, take my uniform. You will notice that I am dressed as a private, but really I have a rank corresponding to that of a general." He was a nice, sincere, simple and genuinely cultivated man, interesting when describing his working-class youth or when speaking of the craftsmanship in Catalan ironwork. His public activities revealed a less sympathetic side of his nature. One day he told me that, in his role of political commissar, he had been asked to decide the fortunes of a member of the Brigade who was a coward. He had had a long talk with the young man and persuaded him that he should go back into the fighting. Secretly he had arranged that he should be sent to a place where he was certain to be killed. "I have just had a message to say that he is dead," he said rather pompously. "Of course, I am a little upset, but the matter does not weigh on my conscience. For I know that I did right." There was a pause. Then, looking at me he added: "I am telling you this because there is a moral for you in the story." What made this more frivolous (though really, of course, much better) was that I did not think that he had the authority to make such a decision. His telling was the showing off of a literary man who had tasted a little power.[11]

In John Lehmann's *New Writing* No. 4, Spender published his account of the Congress—a personality sketch of Malraux,

and capsule descriptions of the meetings, at which the only dis-
cordant note appeared to be a Soviet writer's attack on Trotsky.
The Gide affair came to the surface only in a description of a
conversation with a Gide critic, the President of the Congress,
José Bergamín, whom Spender described as having "a mind of
even greater honesty, a mind which sees not merely the truth of
isolated facts which Gide observed in the USSR, but the far
more important truth of the *effect* which Gide's book is going to
have." Like the Communist writer Spender described as having
criticized him for his *New Statesman* article exposing Brigade
recruitment tactics, Spender had apparently seen the truth not
in the facts of the Congress, but in the cause it represented. A
generation afterward, in his autobiography, and in *The God That
Failed,* he was more cynical about what he then called the "Spoiled
Children's Party." Only Malraux came off unscathed. The names
belatedly under attack had been discreetly removed, and there
were the accounts of a braggart English novelist in the Brigades,
a hypocritically gracious and self-indulgent English (and Communist) lady novelist, and a pompous French Communist writer
who left Madrid when frightened by shelling, explaining that his
death might precipitate a world war, for his country would have
had no other course but to avenge him. And Gide was exposed
as the "hidden theme" of the Congress, one well-hidden in
Spender's original account. A critic, noting the discrepancies between the two versions, wondered whether "there [has] been
another time in the past hundred years when a writer of Spender's
quality could have brought himself to believe that the truth one
saw with one's own eyes should be suppressed." It may have
been, he suggested, "an outrage to Spender's own nature."[12]
At any rate, Spender never returned to Spain, although when
back in England he again took up—somewhat less devotedly—
Popular Front activities.

At the Cambridge Union, just as 1938 began, Spender de-
bated "Art Must Be Political" with writer-politician Harold
Nicolson, and took the affirmative. Afterwards the students bal-

loted, and declared Nicolson the victor by 230 votes. Less witty in his delivery than his M.P. opponent, Spender had amused his audience by conceding, "I fear I cannot make an amusing speech. I have just been reading a book which says that 'all geniuses are devoid of humour.'" More seriously, afterwards, in spite of his debating stance, he confessed to Nicolson that he was worried about the young men who were still joining the International Brigade. "They go out there with deep faith in communism and in a few weeks they lose all their faith and illusions. But they have to stay and be butchered for a cause they do not believe in."[13]

The only outward sign of Spender's withdrawal from the causes which first brought him to Spain—other than his public disenchantment with the Communist role in the Brigades—was the continuing desolate note of his pro-Loyalist poetry. He had never written platitudes about freedom or anti-Fascism in his verse, which made the alteration in his mood an almost invisible one. But he himself thought that there had been a reaction in his own poetry—a withdrawal into a preoccupation with the problems of the isolated self. He had defended what he thought was a good cause against a bad one, and W. H. Auden remarked to him at the end of the 1930's that he had been "political" for the same reason —he thought something could and should be done. To do it blatantly, Spender mused later, was not to enlarge the scale of his contribution any more than to refuse to be "political" was to ignore the issues: "A pastoral poem in 1936 was not just a pastoral poem; it was also a non-political poem." His own poetry nevertheless refused to ignore the doomed cause. Through the early months of 1939, the last months of the Republic, he continued to publish despairing verses about Spain, each underlining his own inability to forget.

After Spender's final Spanish journey he and his wife had rented a small house near the Kentish coast for the rest of the summer. There Auden came to visit and to write, and the two poets discussed the just concluded Writers' Congress and the attacks on Gide. Auden found no dilemma in the affair. Em-

phatically, he insisted that political exigencies were no justifica-
tion for lies. Yet the talk skirted the problem of Spain, although
Auden had been there too, earlier in the year.

In January, 1937, Auden had offered his services as a
stretcher-bearer in the British Ambulance Unit, and had gone off
in the cause of the Republic. Madrid at the time appeared saved,
and the enemy, if not being rolled back, was at least being held
in some places. Revolutionary enthusiasm was no counterbalance
to Franco's firepower, but (as Spender had discovered) it was
infectious, and captured Auden almost as soon as he arrived.
In Valencia, he admired the striking propaganda posters, and the
effectiveness of the bereted, pistol-on-hip Anarchists who handled
much of the municipal services in the refugee Republican capital,
"doing all those things that the gentry cannot believe will be
properly done unless they are there to keep on eye on them.
This is the Anarchy of the bourgeois cartoon, the end of civilization from which Hitler has sworn to deliver Europe."[14] Eight
driving hours away were the battered gates of Madrid and
beseiged Teruel was only 150 kilometers distant; but Valencia
itself, sunny and warm in the afternoons like a fine English May,
radiated a whistling-by-the-graveyard optimism.

Cabarets closed at nine, but crowds drank to the unity of the
war effort elsewhere, and, on the night of the twenty-fifth, Auden
found himself at a party in the Hotel Victoria. It was a cosmopolitan group—*Pravda* correspondent Mikhail Koltzov, a game-
legged Romanian pilot from the Malraux Squadron, Norwegian
journalist Gerda Grepp, Hungarian (but "English") correspondent
Arthur Koestler, and others. The atmosphere was oppressive, and,
as everyone grew drunk, the wounded pilot hopped about excitedly, insisting that he was going to die, and finally had to be
carried off to bed. When Auden and Koestler met again a dozen
years later they traded memories of that night in Valencia and
discovered that they were the only two from the party who were
still alive.[15]

Auden's poetic celebration of his weeks in Spain was to have the strangely elegiac tone of an already-lost cause. In the main square of Valencia, he had seen an enormous poster-map of squarish amputated Spain, illustrated in relief not only with the country's hills and valleys but with symbolic scenes. Badajoz, scene of the notorious bullring mass executions, was represented by a Fascist firing squad; a hanged man swayed from a gibbet at Huelva; a toy-sized train and truck brought supplies to besieged Madrid; at Seville, radio-happy Nationalist General Queipo was "frozen in an eternal broadcast."[16]

The Valencia map may have helped suggest some Shakespearian-sounding lines midway through Auden's poem:

On that arid square, that fragment nipped off from hot
Africa, soldered so crudely to inventive Europe,
    On that tableland scored by rivers,
Our fever's menacing shapes are precise and alive.

Tomorrow, perhaps, the future: the research on fatigue
And the movements of packers, the gradual exploring of all the
    Octaves of radiation;
Tomorrow the enlarging of consciousness by diet and breathing.

Tomorrow the rediscovery of romantic love;
The photographing of ravens, all the fun under
    Liberty's masterful shadow;
Tomorrow the hour of the pageant-master and the musician.

Tomorrow, for the young, the poets exploding like bombs,
The walks by the lake, the winter of perfect communion;
    Tomorrow the bicycle races
Through the suburbs on summer evenings: but today the struggle.

Today the deliberate increase in the chances of death;
The conscious acceptance of guilt in the necessary murder;
    Today the expending of powers
On the flat ephemeral pamphlet and the boring meeting.

Today the makeshift consolations; the shared cigarette;
The cards in the candle-lit barn and the scraping concert,
    The masculine jokes; today the
Fumbled and unsatisfactory embrace before hurting.

The stars are dead; the animals will not look;
We are left alone with our day, and the time is short and
*   History to the defeated*
*May say Alas but cannot help or pardon.**

The struggle, Auden had declared, was necessary—if there were to be a tomorrow worth living for, a tomorrow when poets would explode into poetry, rather than be exploded by bombs. Thus, earlier in his poem he had accepted, for his generation, the Civil War in Spain as symbol:

What's your proposal? To build the Just City? I will.
I agree. Or is it the suicide pact, the romantic
*   Death? Very well, I accept, for*
I am your choice, your decision: yes, I am Spain.

It was a paper commitment, a metaphorical acceptance, for although Auden had created the central poem of the war around it, he had already left Spain.

Even in his first few weeks as a volunteer, Auden had seemed impatient to leave Spain. What he saw of internal rivalries, particularly of Stalinist attempts to suppress any other political approaches to Marxism, was disturbing; and the brutality toward churches and priests further alienated him. By March, he was back in England, unwilling to talk about his experiences except through the long poem he had been working on. What he had done in Spain he left to conjecture, but it was clear that he had discovered that physical action was best left to those better at it than he was. As Claud Cockburn later put it, "Quite a lot of the literary people of the '30's had an exaggerated idea of physical

---

* Of the poem—and particularly its last lines—Auden told an inquirer in 1966, "I dislike it very much and consider the last stanza inexcusably false" (Letter to J. M. Muste, March 3, 1966). Long before that he had altered "necessary murder" in later printings to the unpolitical "fact of murder."

Auden had changed his mind by then in other ways about the writer's involvement in politics. "His views," he thought in 1967, "have no more authority than those of any reasonably well-educated citizen. Indeed, when read in bulk, the statements made by writers, including the greatest, would seem to indicate that literary talent and political common sense are rarely found together." It was a point one was more likely to reflect upon at sixty than at thirty.

action. They discovered in Spain that every Tom, Dick and Harry who knew the innards of a bren-gun was better at it than them; then came disillusionment. . . . They were [at first] always thinking I must *act*, I must *do* something, but the poets' effectiveness, in their political actions, was nil." According to Cockburn, Auden at the beginning of the war in Spain "had the feeling that life could not be carried on at all without some kind of union with the party. So he came out to Spain; of course, what we really wanted him for was to go to the front, write some pieces saying hurrah for the Republic, and then go away and write some poems, also saying hurrah for the Republic; and that would be his job in the war—and bloody important at that. Instead of which, unfortunately, he took the whole thing terribly seriously; he wanted to *do* something."

Cockburn, then one of the most effective Communist propagandists active in the war area, arranged to divert the poet's enthusiasms. "When Auden came out," Cockburn said later, "we got a car laid on for him and everything. We thought we'd whisk him to Madrid and that the whole thing would be a matter of a week before the end-product started firing. But not at all: the bloody man went off and got a donkey, a mule really, and announced that he was going to walk through Spain with the creature. From Valencia to the Front. He got six miles from Valencia before the mule kicked him or something and only then did he return and get in the car to do his proper job."[17]

Whether the blow he received in Spain was from an intractable mule or a cause which had disturbing implications when examined at close range, Auden nevertheless quickly fulfilled his writing commitment. His enthusiastic impressions of Valencia appeared in a *New Statesman* article while he was still in Spain, and his long celebratory poem was completed only a few weeks after he returned to England. In May, 1937, "Spain" was published by Faber, the proceeds of its sale designated for the British Medical Unit with which Auden had intended to serve. He had done "his proper job." Whatever the extent of his disillusionment, it had not prevented him from offering in the service of the Cause perhaps the best poem the Civil War had inspired. Still, its dubiously confident, obviously clever elements later caused George Orwell's gibe that if Auden had fought, he would never have written the poem.

"Spain" was the climax, but not the end, of Auden's political involvement. He had worked out his intellectual position toward Spain, and afterwards wrote little on political matters. He had done what he thought had reached the theoretical limits which politics could have upon his art. "Poetry," he had said in 1935, "is not concerned with telling people what to do, but with extending our knowledge of good and evil, perhaps making the necessity for action more urgent and its nature more clear, but only leading us to the point where it is possible for us to make a rational and moral choice."[18]

Two years later, when the cause in Spain was completely lost, there was a *Ballad of Heroes,* set to music by Benjamin Britten, performed in honor of the fallen of the British Battalion. The first movement had words by Randall Swingler, full of posturing nobility, and the second was a setting of Auden's "Danse Macabre," which had been published in 1937 with the title "Song for the New Year" ("It's farewell to the drawing-room's civilized cry," it began). The last movement, "Recitative and Choral," had words by Swingler as well as the final chorus of Auden's *On the Frontier.* Auden's place in the program was deceptive: he had already left England and settled in the United States, and had nothing to do with the program. With Christopher Isherwood he had first travelled to another conflict in China, and their grim *Journey to a War* (1938) viewed a world war as inevitable, for appeasement was eroding the independence of one nation after another. The choice whether to act or accept had not changed and, he realized, "the liberty to be and weep has never been sufficient."

But Auden wept. From America he watched the Cause of Spain fade, and the bells toll for some of the activists he admired, among them refugee poet-playwright Ernst Toller, a despondent suicide after the fall of Madrid. The dead writer, Auden mourned, would now

> ... *lie shadowless at last among*
> *The other campaigners who existed till they'd done*
> *Something that was an example to the young.*[19]

The third personality in the "Auden-Spender-Day Lewis" school of Oxford poets* was the only one of the trio to venture amateurishly into politics, in spite of good advice to leave it alone. "Poets are always (and have been always) savagely political: and the real politician, the politician-by-trade, always carts them properly," T. E. Lawrence—still Private Shaw—had cautioned Cecil Day Lewis late in 1934, adding prophetically, "Poets hope too much, and their politics . . . usually stink after twenty years."[20] He was warning Day Lewis to spend more time on poetry and less time on Communist activity, and on squeezing ideology into his poetic theory and practice. In another letter, he had underlined the point, as well as his distaste for Marxist materialism: "The trouble with Communism is that it accepts too much of today's furniture. I hate furniture."[21]

It was a year and a half before the Revolt of the Generals, but the advice, Day Lewis later confessed ruefully, had only a delayed action upon him, for it was not easy to leave politics to the politicians of the thirties when the results of doing so "were all too disastrously in evidence all around us." A schoolmaster in Cheltenham, he had been a committed Marxist since 1933, wrote for Communist fringe publications, and accepted other assignments for the Party which took him away from writing. Yet, he found time not only for poetry and criticism but discovered in 1935 that he could earn—as "Nicholas Blake"—a liberating income as a writer of detective stories. Still, like Christopher Caudwell, he continued to distribute leaflets, sell the *Daily Worker*, and organize political rallies. He dreaded speaking at public

---

* The triple incantation dear to thirties critics who declared the three a "Movement" had nothing to do with reality: the trio met under the same roof for the first time as late as 1947.

meetings, but steeled himself to do that, too, especially after he became chairman of the British section of the Communist-directed International Association of Writers for the Defense of Culture. It was still a time, he thought, when "it seemed possible to hope, to choose, to act, as individuals but for a common end."

Spain put a heavy weight on his conscience, already burdened with guilt at not being able (or, subconsciously, willing) to meet all the Party demands upon his energies. He believed that he ought to volunteer for the International Brigade, but "lacked the courage to do so." He redoubled his energies in other directions, contributing to *Left Review*, editing a book of essays by leftist writers, *The Mind in Chains*, and writing Party pamphlets. The work brought him into contact with Party intellectuals, a few of whom he admired; but—again, like Caudwell—he never felt at ease with the rest of them, "not because they were Communists but because they were intellectuals."[22] He wrote some poetry inspired by Spain, a prophetic description he titled "Bombers," and an idealistic "The Volunteer"—a sort of penance for his own remaining at home.*

Day Lewis's major contribution as a writer was "The Nabara" (1938), one of the better modern narrative poems, the long stanzas singing of the courage of Basque fishermen over whose "obstinate bones" the "tides of Biscay" afterwards flowed. Based on an incident of March 5, 1937, it was first celebrated in G. L. Steer's *The Tree of Gernika* (1938). The battle pitted a Basque codfish boat (and auxiliary warship), the *Nabara*, against the rebel cruiser *Canarias*, "a giant in metal," which had intercepted an Estonian freighter loaded with Soviet arms for the Republic. Three of the Basque trawlers, one of them the *Nabara*, had created a diversion to wrest away the supply ship (which continued toward Bilbao) and, five miles off shore, forced the *Canarias* to do battle with them.

A hopeless fight for the three little ships, they were shot to pieces from a distance out of range of their own puny guns.

* The first eight lines of "The Volunteer" may be found on the last page of Chapter 5.

Only one of the estimated ninety to one hundred shots from the *Nabara* actually reached the *Canarias*, killing a midshipman in the hold; and even that shell failed to explode. Refusing to surrender, the *Nabara*, last ship of the three to remain afloat, settled into the water in flames, its handful of survivors resisting to the end, taking to a "matchwood boat" (in the words of the poem) and hurling hand grenades at a launch sent out by the *Canarias* to capture them.

Like the brutal levelling of Guernica, the hopeless agony of the *Nabara* awakened world sympathy for the tragedy of the doomed Basque people; and Day Lewis's long poem sustained the tragic image with memorable lines, beginning:

> *Freedom is more than a word, more than the base coinage*
> *Of statesmen, the tyrant's dishonoured cheque, or the dreamer's mad*
> *Inflated currency. She is mortal, we know, and made*
> *In the image of simple men who have no taste for carnage*
> *But sooner kill and are killed than see that image betrayed.*[23]

A symbol of simple, freedom-loving humanity, uncomplicated by ideologies or parties, the Basques were the perfect subject to outlast topicality. They were, the poet wrote,

> *Simple men who asked of their life no mythical splendour,*
> *They loved its familiar ways so well that they preferred*
> *In the rudeness of their heart to die rather than surrender. . . .*
> *Mortal these words and the deed they remember, but cast a seed*
> *Shall flower for an age when freedom is man's creative word.*
>
> .   .   .   .
>
> *For these I have told of, freedom was flesh and blood—a mortal*
> *Body, the gun-breech hot to the touch; yet the battle's height*
> *Raised it to love's meridian and held it awhile immortal;*
> *And its light through time still slashes like a star's that's turned*
>   *to ashes,*
> *Long after* Nabara's *passion was quenched in the sea's heart.*

The poem has had its detractors as well as its admirers, one critic seeing in it a "sort of archaic mock-pastoral narrative style," a "patronizing tone" and "an embarrassing sea-shanty heartiness"[24]—all very likely the result of the romantic embroidering of the *Nabara* incident. But Day Lewis's Marxism *was* romantic, and as long as it remained that way for him it was real—until, one night in 1938, while addressing a large anti-Fascist audience at Queen's Hall, he sensed that what he was saying, however true and for a good cause, had suddenly receded into insignificance for him. "It just won't do."[25] He had been, he realized, defending "the bad against the worse."[26] After the meeting was over, he left politics to the politicians.

An older poet, once a young officer in a larger war, steadfastly refused to leave politics to the professionals. Herbert Read had written some of the best verse of the First World War in *Naked Warriors* (1919) and *The End of a War* (1933), and one of its most moving memoirs (*In Retreat,* 1925). He had seen enough of war from the trenches, resented the "glory camouflage" in which it was usually celebrated, and found no conventional solutions to prevent another war, from Liberalism to Communism. "I do not see why intellectuals like myself, who are not politicians," he wrote during the Spanish War, ". . . should not openly declare ourselves for the only political doctrine which is consistent with the love of justice and our need for freedom."[27] He was referring to Anarchism, which had been briefly triumphant in Catalonia, and had been as well a powerful force in saving Madrid in the early weeks of the war. He saw in Catalonia (as Auden had observed in Valencia) the proof that Anarchist collectives could function efficiently—"whatever may be the merits and demerits of the anarcho-syndicalist system, it can and does work."[28] Long bereft of human dignity, the Spanish people, he felt, "once roused to a sense of its human rights," would never again "submit to a medieval tyranny," nor would they, with the examples of Russia and Germany before them, "pass from a medieval to a *modern tyranny.*" He put his faith in the possibilities of "human humility and individual grace,"[29] and sang a song for the Spanish Anarchists, as humble and austere as the people:

The golden lemon is not made
 but grows on a green tree:
A strong man and his crystal eyes
 is a man born free.

The oxen pass under the yoke
 and the blind are led at will:
But a man born free has a path of his own
 and a house on the hill.

And men are men who till the land
 and women are women who weave:
Fifty men own the lemon grove
 and no man is a slave.[30]

His mood grew darker as the Anarchist cause became hope-less, and he wrote a sad description of children who had become bombing casualties ("Doll's faces are rosier but these were children. . ."), and an elegy which characterized Spain as a per-sonal loss. By then the fate of the Republic had been sealed, and his despair was a cry from the heart. "I who have fought my battles / keep these in a sheath," he said, more emotionally than accurately. All he heard was "the sobbing fall" of a cause which had neither end nor beginning:

Lorca was killed, singing,
and Fox who was my friend.
The rhythm returns: the song
which has no end.[31]

Equally bitter, but satiric, rather than bleak, was Edgell Rickword, critic and *Left Review* editor (and a veteran of World War I trench warfare), one of the few to substitute satire for anger or despair. "To the Wife of Any Non-Intervention Statesman" was Rickword's imaginary entrance into the boudoir to direct a dramatic monologue at the well-to-do wife of any of the English politicians who had played into Fascist hands by permitting non-intervention to become a means of keeping arms from the Republic while Hitler and Mussolini supplied Franco:

Traitor and fool's a combination
To lower wifely estimation,
Although there's not an Act in force
Making it grounds for a divorce:
But canon law forbids at least
Co-habitation with a beast.

Mercilessly, Rickword detailed the acts of omission and commission which, to him, justified the equating of non-intervention with bestiality—the arming of rebels, the denial of aid to the legitimate Government, the bombing of defenseless cities, the inevitable future war for which the British statesmen had awarded Germany and Italy time to prepare. Then his satire closed mordantly,

Would not a thinking wife condemn
The sneaking hand that held the pen
And with a flourish signed the deed
Whence all these hearts and bodies bleed?
Would not those fingers freeze the breast
    Where the young life should feed and rest?
Would not his breath reek of the tomb
And would cold horror seal her womb?
Could a true woman bear his brat?
The millions wouldn't
    Thanks, my hat.[32]

It was a fallow period for Rickword, and it took massive indignation to generate in him any urge to write poetry. "Apart from the Spanish War poem," he recalled later, "I wrote practically no verse between 1920 and 1956. . . . I did not refuse any 'inspiration' because none came."[33]

    With sadder—yet savage—indignation, Rex Warner treated the same subject in "Arms for Spain":

So that men might remain slaves, and
    that the little good
they hoped for might be turned all bad
    and the iron lie

stamped and clamped on growing tender
  and vigorous truth,
These machine-guns were despatched from Italy.

So that the drunken General and the
  Christian millionaire
might continue blindly to rule in complete darkness,
that on rape and ruin order might be
  founded firm,
these guns were sent to save civilization.

Lest the hand should be held at last more
  valuable than paper,
lest man's body and mind should be
  counted more than gold,
lest love should blossom, not shells, and
  break in the land
these machine-guns came from Christian Italy.

And to root reason, lest hope he held in it,
to turn love inward into corroding hate,
lest men should be men, for the banknotes
  and the mystery
these guns, these tanks, these gentlemanly words.[34]

Like much pro-Loyalist writing, both "non-intervention" poems had first appeared in *Left Review,* and were afterwards collected—in the last phases of the war—into the Stephen Spender–John Lehmann anthology *Poems for Spain* (which also reprinted material that had first appeared in Lehmann's *New Writing*). *Poems for Spain* published "name" poets as well as writers whose better-known work had been in other areas. J. Bronowski, a scientist and philosopher of science, contributed "Guadalajara," in which he regretted that he gave little more to the cause of Spain than his pity:

What is my pity worth? I fret
no frozen body, but my mind;
and if I tremble, all my rage
weighs nothing in the bite of wind.

Sylvia Townsend Warner, a novelist who had been in Spain more than once, contributed two poems, as well as reports from Spain to *Left Review*. The *Review* was the focus of Loyalist literary effort in England, and attempted to demonstrate broad Popular Front support. In June, 1937, Randall Swingler replaced Rickword as editor, and became the victim of increasing Communist Party control over its policy. By mid-1938 the *Review* had folded, leaving the field to the Left Book Club and its *Left News*, and the more moderate *New Writing*.

Connected with both the Left Book Club and *Left Review*, Jack Lindsay, a prolific writer in nearly every genre, was asked by Edgell Rickword when the war in Spain began to do a long rhetorical poem for the *Left Review* in the mass-declamation style (borrowed from America) which Lindsay had employed successfully before. Lindsay produced *On Guard for Spain*. It was even more successful than his earlier *Who Are the English?* and was done all over England by the left-wing Unity Theatre and amateur acting groups affiliated with the Left Book Club. It was performed at indoor rallies and outdoor rallies, including one in Trafalgar Square, fulfilling exuberantly the goal of mass-declamation to restore "the traditional link between poetry and the people." The typical English meeting in support of the Spanish Republic—at least those organized openly or under subterfuges from King Street—hardened into a regular format. There were speeches by Party Secretary Pollitt, Left Book Club director Victor Gollancz and the "Red" Duchess of Atholl, followed by a performance of *On Guard for Spain*. After one emotional meeting Harry Pollitt, felt impelled to write Lindsay that he had never, in a long career of exhortation, seen an audience so powerfully affected as by *On Guard*.

Unquestionably, Lindsay's mass-declamation had a powerful impact on an already committed audience, with its lines about "fascist vultures gathering / to pick the bones of Spanish cities," and its appeal to "Workers of the world" to "unite for us / that bear the burden of all." Sometimes laborers afterwards left un-opened pay envelopes at the collection.

Lindsay himself felt guilty at not having joined the Inter-national Brigade, but assuaged his conscience by joining the Communist Party and getting on with his writing. "The map of Spain / bleeds under my fingers. . . ," he wrote. "I lean towards Spain over the sundering waters."[35] "To join the C.P.," he con-fessed later, "was to me tantamount to going into the International Brigade—though in fact after the deaths of Fox, Cornford and Caudwell, every barrier was put in the way of intellectuals sacrificing themselves."[36] The Party had been seeing its most articulate spokesmen put their lives where their convictions were, and had real cause for fear about its dwindling cadre of intel-lectuals, dead on the field or beginning to loosen their ties of commitment. One of the latter was Spender, who attacked *On Guard for Spain*'s taste, and Lindsay blamed "the element of whole-hearted acceptance" which had made the poem so effective with working class audiences for making him "suspect with the intellectuals." It was always Lindsay's fate, he rued, to suffer inadequate recognition, and perhaps Spender's attack was the worst blow of all, for it came at the same time that the *Daily Worker* had run a story (with photographs) of a great Trafalgar Square performance of *On Guard for Spain*—and omitted Lind-say's name.

There were other writers in England who felt the cause of Spain in less political terms. George Barker, in a long, introspec-tive poem, heard "the women weeping in Irún's ruins," and wondered about the dilemma of the writer who sincerely wanted to leave politics alone:

> ... *How can he cease*
> *From a political fight, how can his word sleep in his hand,*
> *When a dark time in a dark time*
> *Inundates and annihilates the mind?*

It was not particularly good poetry, but through the long work, *Calamiterror* (1938), he kept remembering "the women weeping in Irún's ruins," symbols to him of a world gone rotten in the heart. Barker composed two other poems in the dying days of the Republic, both elegiac—a sonnet titled "O Hero Akimbo on the Mountains of To-morrow," and an "Elegy on Spain," dedicated to "the photograph of a child killed in an air-raid on Barcelona." Holding her photograph, the poet held "the crime of the bloody time in my hand. . . ." Again, Spain was the fallen hero, but the few deeply felt lines were lost in Barker's failure to prove in verse what some of his colleagues who had died in Spain had learned: *Hitler* and *Mussolini* were impossibly unpoetic words. Some of the last lines were more effectively elegiac:

> *Fly the flag low, and fold over those hands*
> *Cramped to a gun: gather the child's remains*
> *Staining the wall and cluttering the drains;*
> *Troop down the red to the black and the brown;*
> *Go homeward with tears to water the ground. . . .*[37]

Young left-wing poets in mid-thirties London—like George Barker—found their political mood shaped less by King Street, where Harry Pollitt's pragmatism held sway, than by Parton Street, in Holborn, just off Red Lion Square. It was a crescent of shabby three-story Georgian houses with shops or offices on the street level and seedy rooms to let above. There were the offices of Lawrence and Wishart, who published Communist and left-leaning writings, and, next to them, Archer's bookshop, stocked with slender volumes of poetry and ponderous volumes of Marxist theory, and noisy, cheerful—and mostly non-buying—browsers. Across the street was Meg's Café, where earnest discussions would continue after the shop had closed. David Archer, co-proprietor of the bookshop (with Ralph Abercrombie), was a general's son and graduate of Wellington and Cambridge—his background the epitome of the values he had rejected. He not only sold the literature of the left (or loaned it to the impecunious), he abetted its production. When Esmond Romilly had run away from school to issue *Out of Bounds*, it emanated from an unfurnished room above the bookshop. When Philip Toynbee had run away from Rugby, he fled to Parton Street. When sixteen-year-old David Gascoyne was looking for a way to publish his first volume of surrealist poems, Archer found a way. When Barker, at twenty, sought a publisher for his first book of verse, Archer published it. Before Spain, John Cornford, unshaven and sometimes un-washed, would turn up there, and also young—and equally grubby—Dylan Thomas, whose *18 Poems* Archer helped publish in the last days of 1934. When Cornford had left for Spain, it was with a copy of *18 Poems* in his pocket.

Valuing his "one-and-only body," Thomas left politics alone and stayed home; but—his biographer Constantine FitzGibbon has written—"during the winter of 1936–1937 his vision of 'the poet' was deeply influenced by the Spanish Civil War. Quite a number of his friends and contemporaries had gone to Spain to fight. Some, such as John Cornford, . . . had already died there. Dylan had no intention of following their example, but he was pas-sionately on the side of the Republic."[38] It reinforced his rejection of bourgeois values, but specifically political overtones never en-tered his poetry. At various times, he had called himself a Com-munist or a Socialist, but, as early as 1934, he had written a friend, "As a Socialist myself, though a very unconventional one, I like to read good propoganda [his spelling] but the most recent poems of Auden and Day Lewis seem to me neither good poetry nor propaganda."[39] Incoherent about politics all his life, he once stood up at a meeting of a writers' organization in Communist Prague in 1949 and shouted, "I am a Communist, but am I also a bloody fool?"[40]

Recalling the libertarian atmosphere of Archer's twenty years later, George Barker wondered, "I do not know how many juvenile revolutionaries were temporarily harboured on the top floor of this bookshop, but they came and went like a rotation of furious tiger-moths, always at night. Mothers arrived, weeping, in taxi-cabs. Did all the conspirators die, I wonder, in Spain?"[41]

Living and writing away from England, poet-publisher John Lehmann felt a commitment to the Spanish cause, but fulfilled it neither as correspondent, ambulance driver, or soldier, although many of his friends had done all three, and one of the more aloof ones, Christopher Isherwood, "with his insatiable passion for directing the destinies of his friends as if he were allotting the parts in a play, . . . had immediately begun to invent roles" in the war for the two of them. Lehmann chose to remain in Austria through to the already foreseeable end there, and edit *New Writing* from Vienna, leaning heavily upon material by writers in Spain. Not being in Paris or Madrid (or even London) helped him, he thought, "maintain a balance against the encroachments of politics into literature," for *New Writing* never turned into a tract. Absorbed as he was in the oncoming tragedy in Central Europe, he nevertheless followed the movements of his friends Spender and Auden, mourned the deaths of others like Fox, Bell, and Cornford, and was fascinated by the drama of the new underground railway through Europe which carried volunteers for the Internationals over mountain passes and by water to Spain.

Lehmann's novelist sister Rosamund (*The Ballad and the Source, The Echoing Grove*) was equally absorbed by Spain, and she added to his news about writer-activists. Her husband, Wogan Phillips, had been wounded while with the British Ambulance Unit, and her letters communicated some of the despair of a wife of a volunteer in Spain for a cause her government was helping to send down to defeat. As late as January, 1939, she was still campaigning indignantly but forlornly against the self-deceiving English policy of non-intervention, writing to her brother about what may have been the last of the official demonstrations sponsored by the Labor Party and the Trade Union Council:

> Yesterday I took part in a deputation to the P.M. [Neville Chamberlain], Attlee, Sinclair, Alfred Barnes. Attlee . . . spoke of 'exploring every avenue' etc. etc. This roused a Welsh delegate to a fine frenzy of vituperation—and we all felt worse than ever. . . . To my pained surprise I found myself committed to walking in a pro-

cession down Whitehall, holding a placard, with Dame Adelaide Livingstone in a fur toque and eyeveil in front of me, Amabel (Williams-Ellis) beside me, and various T.U.C. delegates at the back and before. 200 strong! We were stopped at No. 10, delivered a protest by letter to a flunkey, and were bidden to stand on the corner and shout 'Arms for Spain!'—when I escaped, and jumped into a taxi and came home. The policeman on duty suggested we should all go home quietly, which no doubt we did.

An even more hopeless observation closed the letter: "It's snowing here, and I await the fall of Barcelona with feelings to match the leaden skies."[42]

Many of the deeply committed English noncombatant writers, following the Auden-Spender example, had gone to Spain out of curiosity, loyalty, or to get some insight into the Republic's agony. Novelist-poet Rex Warner described the dilemma of the tourist in Spain who wondered whether what he considered the reality of Spain—the holy virgins in the churches, the groves of oranges, the pompous processions, the flowers and the dancing— had disappeared because of the war. There was a greater reality, he concluded, unsurprisingly, for Spain had "torn the veil of Europe," and it could now be seen that "In Spain is Europe. England also is in Spain." The tourist would not be able to enjoy a landscape anywhere without guilt, for

Near Bilbao are buried the vanguard of our army.
It is us too they defended who defended Madrid.[43]

Warner, like many other writers, was sure that in Spain he was "witnessing a singularly callous and hypocritical performance on the part of the 'democracies,' " and also that there was "fast disappearing the last hope of avoiding a second world war." Putting his convictions on the line, he volunteered "as an ambulance or any other type of driver," and was interviewed by "some rather solemn Communists" about his suitability. In the process he made what was intended to be a witty remark about "Russian gold." The interviewers' faces registered even graver solemnity, and Warner was informed afterwards that his services would not be needed.[44] Still, he supported the Republic through speeches and writing, unwilling to condemn a cause he thought a good one because of the nature of some of its promoters.

A real eve-of-war tourist fitting Warner's description had been Louis MacNeice, who had been at Oxford at the same time as Auden, Spender, and Day Lewis. In 1936, MacNeice, who had just moved to Bedford College for Women in London as a lecturer in Greek, made an Easter trip to pre-war Spain, half ignoring the already "haunted faces" and the "writing on the walls— / Hammer and Sickle, *Boicot, Viva, Muera. . . .*" For the "tripper" there were complaints about the rain, the beggars, the slovenly soldiers, the garbage in the streets, the peeling posters, the disappointingly clumsy bullfight, the poor Spanish cigarettes which came to pieces in one's hands. He remembered ignoring the Cambridge don who predicted "trouble shortly in this country," thinking "the papers a lark / With their party politics and blank invective," and seeing little significance in "the mob in flower at Algeciras / Outside a church bereft / Of its images and its aura. . . ."

> *And next day took the boat*
> *   For home, forgetting Spain, not realizing*
> *That Spain would soon denote*
> *   Our grief, our aspirations;*
> *Not knowing that our blunt*
> *   Ideals would find their whetstone, that our spirit*
> *Would find its frontier on the Spanish front,*
> *   Its body in a rag-tag army.*[45]

When the war had first begun, MacNeice was again a tripper, this time with Auden in Iceland when

> *Down in Europe Seville fell,*
> *Nations germinating hell. . . .*[46]

In a satiric "Last Will and Testament" in their *Letters from Iceland*, Auden and MacNeice left—"as a Christmas token"—

"all the lives by Franco gently stopped," and to Europe's dictators, guilty of those lives, they offered to leave

> The midnight hours, the soft wind
>   from the sweeping wing
> Of madness, and the intolerable tightening
>   of the mesh
> Of history.[47]

Still, MacNeice, returning, did not follow Auden to Spain, confessing that his sympathies "On paper and in the soul," were left, "but not in my heart or guts." Disarmingly honest, he admitted that he lamented "the passing of class . . . [and] a man for me is still largely characterized by what he buys."[48] But the appeal of Spain was too great to resist, and the pre-war tourist returned in the last, desperate days of Barcelona, from December 29, 1938 to January 9, 1939. The Spanish Consulate in London had been skeptical about his visa, suggesting that he was going only to "show off." MacNeice retorted (he wrote in his post-humously published autobiography) "that it was rather late in the day to show off in this way, as nearly all literary London had long ago done the rounds of the trenches in Madrid and hobnobbed with the Republican celebrities. I admitted, however, that my motives were egotistical; I was sensation-hunting, testing myself, eager to add a notch to my own history."

To MacNeice the quiet, beleaguered city after dark was "like limbo but crowded"—two and a half million in a space which before Franco had held only a million. To London's *Spectator* he submitted a report so confident about Barcelona's future that it could only have come from one overwhelmingly making an eleventh-hour case. He had found his cause in the permanence of basic human values that war had not undermined in what remained of the Republic:

> . . . These people's lives have become very much simplified and assimilated to one another; the topics of conversation are few and

universal, money has lost its diversifying force, and everyone, one feels, is by necessity in the same boat. For this reason one feels very much at home in the dark streets of Barcelona. There may be bitter dissensions among the politicians, but the people in the streets, one feels, have become a family party—or, if you prefer it, are in on the same racket—united by material necessities, by hunger, by the fear of sudden death which enhances the values of life. I have never been anywhere where these values were so patent. It would be difficult to be a Hamlet in Barcelona.

. . . Facts in a city at war are necessarily uncertain; how can one know the truth about the Front or unravel the paradoxical knots of Spanish party politics or sort out truth from propaganda? One fact, however, is as clear—and as refreshing—as daylight: the extraordinary morale of these people—their courage, good-humour and generosity.

. . . Again, while a people must obviously adapt themselves to war conditions, it does not seem altogether desirable that war should become quite so much a habit as it has in Barcelona; one feels the people have almost forgotten about peace and might not know what to do with it if it came. Yet without this confidence and adaptation to circumstances, Barcelona no doubt would have already given way to Goliath. Her people are essentially non-defeatist; no one this New Year admitted for a moment that Franco's present offensive might succeed.[49]

Barcelona fell on January 25, five days after MacNeice's report was published.

The poem he based on the visit to Catalonia—a part of his *Autumn Journal* and, in fact, a verse adaptation of the *Spectator* piece—did not appear until the cause had been entirely lost; but the theme was a tireless one, that "human values remain,"

Life being more, it seems, than merely the bare
Permission to keep alive and receive orders,
Humanity being more than a mechanism
To be oiled and greased and for ever unaware
Of the work it is turning out, of why the wheels keep turning;
Here at least the soul has found its voice
Though not indeed by choice. . . .[50]

The rest of his poem tried not to be an elegy at the bier of Spain, for MacNeice felt that "to be wisely sad" was of no use,

> *For here and now the new valkyries ride*
> *The Spanish constellations*
> *As over the Plaza Cataluña*
> *Orion lolls on his side. . . .*

The importance for him lay in the apolitical realization that not governments, but people, contained truth, "whatever / Their nominal façade." The most characteristic sound in Barcelona, he had found in those days before the city fell, had been the crowing of cocks, which people kept on their window balconies. In the last lines of his poem that observation had furnished him with a symbol:

> *Listen: a whirr, a challenge, an aubade—*
> *It is the cock crowing in Barcelona.*[51]

If the writer was at all political, MacNeice observed afterwards, he had the obligation to preserve his critical faculty and not see events in terms of political blacks and whites. "Thus in the Spanish Civil War some English poets were torn between writing good propaganda (dishonest poetry) and honest poetry (poor propaganda). I believe firmly that in Spain the balance of right was on the side of the government; propaganda, however, demands either angels or devils. This means that in the long run a poet must choose between being politically ineffectual and politically false."[52] It was an idealistic, but inaccurate conclusion. However true it was that literature intended as propaganda hazarded not being literature at all, there was still—for "poets hope too much"—honest writing which turned out to behave in a manner befitting good propaganda.

3

HOMAGE TO UTOPIA
Orwell in Catalonia

There was much in it that I did not understand, in some ways I did not even like it, but I recognized it immediately as a state of affairs worth fighting for.
George Orwell,
HOMAGE TO CATALONIA *(London, 1938)*

ARMED WITH AN ADVANCE from Secker and Warburg for a book, and intentions to write magazine and newspaper stories about the Civil War, a gaunt Englishman named Eric Blair came to Spain in December, 1936. As Eton-educated Englishmen went, Blair was highly untypical. Although he wrote journalism, it was often for splinter left-leaning publications, and he had recently run a combination pub and village shop at Wallington in Essex. But earlier he had lived as a tramp in Paris and London (and wrote a book about it) and tried his hand at fiction with little more success. And even if his name *had* become a household word in the mid-thirties (as it did some dozen years later), it would not have identified the private man, for he wrote under the by-line of George Orwell.

Never one to do anything in an orthodox way, Orwell brought his newlywed wife Eileen with him to Spain, but then almost immediately volunteered for the militia—because, he later wrote,[1] "at that time and in that atmosphere it seemed the only conceivable thing to do." He had just finished *The Road to Wigan Pier* on assignment for the Left Book Club. It was a commission the Club directors had regretted, for the completed book left them even unhappier than the research on it had left Orwell. *Wigan Pier* was a cheerless picture of how industrial workers in the depressed North of England lived, and an indictment of the left-wing political blundering which offered them little hope. Almost everywhere— including England, Orwell implied—he saw Socialists in retreat before Fascism, "and events are moving with terrible speed. As I write this the Spanish Fascist forces are bombarding Madrid, and it is quite likely that before the book is printed we shall have another Fascist country to add to the list."

Like some of the young writers from the universities, Orwell saw utopian possibilities in contacts between the working classes— to whom the future theoretically belonged—and middle class poets and artists. Mixing with the workers in their pubs was one attractive, yet politically virtuous method; but it did not, Constantine FitzGibbon has written, work out that way. "The club-and-class traditions of the English prevented any but the most superficial mingling. The . . . old regulars might at best tolerate, at worst resent, this influx of young men and women into their local. They went on going there because it was their pub, but there was very little mixing—perhaps a game of darts now and then, perhaps a beer offered and accepted, very little real contact. The young men and women who were interested in the arts formed a group or groups of their own which tended to grow larger as more such people, some of them neither young nor poor, went to these few pubs in search of company. And George Orwell, who desperately longed for real contact with the working class and who had therefore left the over-bourgeoisified Fitzroy [Tavern] for the simpler Wheatsheaf soon found that there too he was hearing nothing at his end of the bar but Oxford voices talking to one another, and he departed for the deeper disillusions, the profounder disappointments of a workers' war in Spain."[2]

The night train from Paris to the Pyrenees was a slow one,

almost as if it were straining under the load of Czechs, Germans, Frenchmen and others, all bound for the Spanish border, and all in the same cause. "Up and down the train you could hear one phrase repeated over and over again, in the accents of all the languages of Europe—*là-bas* (down there). My third-class carriage was full of very young, fair-haired, underfed Germans in suits of incredible shoddiness—the first *ersatz* cloth I had ever seen—who rushed out at every stopping place to buy cheap wine and later fell asleep in a sort of pyramid on the floor of the carriage. About halfway down France the ordinary passengers dropped off." Possibly because it was the year of the great sit-in strikes in Paris, the Popular Front, and the war to the South, the French peasants reacted to the train in something more than their usual phlegmatic way. It was "practically a troop train, and the countryside knew it. In the morning, as we crawled along southern France, every peasant working in the fields turned round, stood solemnly upright, and gave the anti-Fascist salute. They were like a guard of honour, greeting the train mile after mile."[3]

It was a far different reaction than he had experienced in Paris, where he had stopped off to pay a visit to the reigning prince of the literary avant-garde, Henry Miller. Orwell had been fascinated as well as depressed by Miller's irresponsibility toward everything but what he conceived as his "art." Miller had said that he understood anyone going to Spain "for purely selfish motives, out of curiosity for instance, but to mix oneself up in such things *from a sense of obligation* was sheer stupidity. In any case, my ideas about combating fascism, defending democracy, etc., were all baloney. Our civilization was destined to be swept away and replaced by something so different that we should scarcely regard it as human—a prospect that did not bother him."[4]

From Orwell's arguments with Henry Miller it was clear that his decision to go to Spain had more complex beginnings than a simple yearning to merge his soul with the working class; yet it was true that he found the Socialism he saw preached in England inherently distasteful. It was intellectual and theoretical,

while Orwell's politics and economics—particularly before Spain
—were sentimental. English Socialism smugly claimed "historic
necessity" both as chief virtue and as explanation of its inevitable
success, while its rival adherents were busy postponing that in-
evitability by undercutting each other. Partly, Orwell thought,
it was due to "the mistaken Communist tactic of sabotaging
democracy, i.e. sawing off the branch you are sitting on," but still
more it offended his libertarian outlook. Marxist propaganda, he
felt, proceeded "on the assumption that man has no soul," and
thus was narrowly attuned to economic principles, stressing the
"goal of a materialistic utopia" rather than justice and liberty.
No wonder that the impact upon him was so profound when suddenly, in Spain at the very time Victor Gollancz was providing
Left Book subscribers with a remarkable foreword to *Wigan Pier*
in which he argued with his author's findings, Orwell was discovering justice and liberty and other goals he valued exploding
surprisingly into existence. Still, Orwell's corner of Spain—
Catalonia—was not a Marxist utopia, but an Anarchist one:

> When one came straight from England the aspect of Barcelona
> was something startling and overwhelming. It was the first time I
> had ever been in a town where the working class was in the saddle.
> Practically every building of any size had been seized by the workers
> and was draped with red flags or with the red and black flag of the
> Anarchists; every wall was scrawled with the hammer and sickle and
> with the initials of the revolutionary parties; almost every church
> had been gutted and its images burnt. Churches here and there were
> being systematically demolished by gangs of workmen. Every shop
> and cafe had an inscription saying that it had been collectivized;
> even the boot-blacks had been collectivized and their boxes painted
> red and black. Waiters and shopwalkers looked you in the face and
> treated you as an equal. Servile and even ceremonial forms of speech
> had temporarily disappeared. . . . And it was the aspect of the
> crowds that was the queerest thing of all. In outward appearance it
> was a town in which the wealthy classes had practically ceased to
> exist. Except for a small number of women and foreigners there were
> no "well-dressed" people at all. Practically everyone wore rough
> working-class clothes, or blue overalls or some variant of the militia

uniform. All this was queer and moving. There was much in it that I did not understand, in some ways I did not even like it, but I recognized it immediately as a state of affairs worth fighting for.

Separatist-minded Catalonia, with its traditional independence, its homogeneity of land and language, was really, as an English journal characterized it at the time, "the world's newest nation." In the first weeks of the Anarchist revolution, it had satisfied—violently—its long-standing grudges against large landholders and Catholic churches, and basked afterwards in a sense of moral elevation fed by patriotic (but Catalan, more than Spanish) war fever and revolutionary faith. The forms revolutionary expression took were often impractical and unreal. The Anarchist on the train from Barcelona, declaring to the ticket taker, "I am a Valencian going to Valencia. That is my ticket," would be applauded by the other passengers,[5] but trains could not keep running on such revolutionary economics. Stirring, too, were the propaganda posters all over Barcelona, brilliantly colored and dramatic. One needed to know no Catalan to appreciate the scene of a peasant's rope-soled foot descending upon a cracked swastika in a cobbled street.

It was Orwell's way, one of his biographers has observed, "to do any moment the thing he found most important."[6] And it had suddenly become more important to fight in the Spanish war than investigate it. In the newly renamed Lenin Barracks in Barcelona, Orwell checked on how to join the militia. Before him, in front of the officers' table, was a tough-looking young soldier in his middle twenties, with reddish-yellow hair and broad shoulders, and a peaked leather cap pulled down over one eye. The puzzled frown with which he examined a map open on the table in front of him convinced Orwell that the soldier was illiterate, and that he regarded map reading as a stupendous intellectual feat which rendered those who mastered it worthy of great reverence. Talk across the table brought out the fact that Orwell was a foreigner, and the militiaman raised his head. *"Italiano?"* he asked.

"No, Ingles. Y tu?"

"Italiano."

As they both were leaving the room the *Italiano* stepped over and gripped Orwell's hand very hard. The gesture moved Orwell deeply ("Queer, the affection you can feel for a stranger!"), and he never forgot the Italian militiaman's fierce, pathetic face, although he never saw him again. In him the Englishman sensed the unique atmosphere of the time, and, later, long after Orwell had left Spain, the Civil War still going on but the cause for which both he and the Italian both fought by then hopelessly lost, Orwell—no poet—felt compelled to write some verses in his memory:

The Italian soldier shook my hand
Beside the guard-room table;
The strong hand and the subtle hand
Whose palms are only able

To meet within the sound of guns,
But oh! what a peace I knew then
In gazing on his battered face
Purer than any woman's!

For the flyblown words that make me spew
Still in his ears were holy,
And he was born knowing what I had learned
Out of books and slowly. . . .

Good luck go with you, Italian soldier!
But luck is not for the brave;
What would the world give back to you?
Always less than you gave. . . .

For where is Manuel Gonzalez,
And where is Pedro Aquilar,
And where is Ramon Fenellosa?
The earthworms know where they are.

Your name and your deeds were forgotten
Before your bones were dry,
And the lie that you slew is buried
Under a deeper lie;

But the thing that I saw in your face
No power can disenherit:
No bomb that ever burst
Shatters the crystal spirit.[7]

The deliberate indiscipline of the Anarchists made them difficult for a non-Catalan to understand, but their quixotic idealism appealed to that crystal spirit Orwell saw, rather than to the jaded, slogan-suffocated intellect. In the semi-Trotskyist (or, at least, anti-Stalinist) POUM militia, Orwell had found a Barcelona-based group independent of the Anarchists but with roughly the same Utopian aspirations. With his wife Eileen established in a job in the POUM party offices, Orwell, who had had some military training at school and therefore knew more than his barrackmates, itched for immediate fighting orders. When he enlisted, he had been told that he would be sent to the front the next day. Instead, he was sent to the Lenin Barracks to await the raising of a fresh *centuria*. His quarters was a group of splendid stone stables, empty since the animals had been seized and moved to the front, but still smelling of "horse-piss and rotten oats." The morning parades in the wintry sunshine were comic affairs under the veneer of revolutionary ardor, for no uniform—"multiform" would have been more accurate, Orwell suggested—was like any other, and no soldier marched like any other. Clothes were issued as the factories rushed them out, and were assigned piecemeal, so that few soldiers had an entire "uniform" even when they were ready for the front. Most wore zipper jackets, and some kind of a cap adorned with a party badge; and most wore a red, or red-and-black, handkerchief around their throats. Infected by the pervasive Anarchist atmosphere as well as by normal teen-age contrariness, the recruits, mostly boys of sixteen or seventeen, refused to stand in line, or march in step. If a man disliked an order he would often step out of the ranks and argue fiercely with his officer—a practice made easier by the fact that there was theoretical social equality between the ranks. When a politically unindoctrinated recruit addressed the officer as "Señor," the lieutenant cried out, "What! Señor! Who is calling me Señor? Are we not all comrades?" Orwell might have written, too, about the time—on another front—when a platoon ran out of ammunition and sent the local children back for it and the children brought it back and then refused to give it up. Twenty soldiers had to chase down the children before they could do battle with the enemy. Or the story of the lieutenant who refused to give up his three bars for the one due him as a newly made captain. "What, give up three for one! Nothing doing." (Of course, like the men he commanded, he could neither read nor write.)[8]

For a time, in the egalitarian exhiliration of hoped for victory, people and parties were comrades, however suspicious they remained of each other; but Orwell quickly—and reluctantly —sensed the pathetic reality behind the idealism. Military training consisted not of weapons instruction and tactics but of antiquated parade-ground drill and slogans. It took going into action later for Orwell to realize that the reason there had been no lessons in how to use weapons was that there were none to be had. (In the POUM militia the shortage of rifles was at first so desperate that troops in the line on being relieved handed their replacements their own rifles and grenades.) After one public parade, the rabble quickstepped to a grocer's to imbibe some cheap wine, and Orwell took the opportunity to corner his lieutenant and plead for some machine gun instruction, using rapid glances at his dictionary to find the right words: *"Yo se manejar fusil. No se manejar ametralladora. Quiero apprender ametralladora. Quando vamos apprender ametralladora?* No dictionary was needed to understand the answer: *"Mañana."* He never saw a machine gun until he was in the line; but once an armed *Carabiñero* was sighted by Orwell's section, and permitted the militiamen to inspect his rifle. Only Orwell—who had learned at fifteen—knew how to aim it or load it.

One afternoon, at two hours' notice, the *centuria* was ordered to the front. The train was due to leave at eight, and in typical Spanish fashion the men were finally marshalled in the barracks square at eight-ten. Then, with red flags flapping in the torchlight, and amid a clatter of boots and pannikins, and a confusion of knapsacks and rolled blankets, the weary militiamen were stood to listen to a political exhortation in Catalan before being marched three or four miles—by the longest route, to show them to the whole town—to the station. Finally, the train crawled out of Catalonia and onto the plateau of Aragon; and, at Barbastro, in the January cold, the journey continued by truck, past bleak, bullet-marked houses. Eventually—the driver lost his way in the winter mists—the company was bedded down in darkness on the chaff-covered floor of a mule-stable in Alcubierre. Only in the morning light, after a sound sleep, did they discover that the chaff was full of breadcrusts, torn newspapers, bones, dead rats, and jagged milk tins. They knew they were near the front because the characteristic smell of war was everywhere—not decaying bodies, but decaying food and excrement. Even in peacetime the squalid Aragonese villages were only a collection of mud-and-stone houses huddled around a church. Now the church, like the stubbled fields, was a latrine, and the ragged chickens forever wandering about the beds of mule dung had to exercise great caution in order to keep alive.

On the third morning, Orwell's *centuria* received its rifles—a dismaying collection of museum pieces. The newest—only ten years old—was issued to a dull-witted teen-ager known as *maricon* (fairy). Orwell's weapon was a rusty, damaged German Mauser rifle dated 1896. Most of the rifles were dangerous to fire, and the first casualties were accidentally self-inflicted wounds caused by bursting bolts and similar hazards of handling anti-quated arms with improper cartridges and five minutes' loading instruction. With this awesome firepower the POUM militia was to defend the low sierra east of the enemy stronghold of Zaragoza. Overwhelmed with horror and disillusion, Orwell watched the enthusiasm of his rabble grow as it slopped along toward the front. Half of them were children no more than sixteen, which explained why they were happy and excited about what they thought lay ahead. Later, Orwell recalled with a shudder that when they neared the line "the boys round the red flag in front began to utter shouts of 'Visca P.O.U.M.!' 'Fascistas-maricones!' and so forth—shouts which were meant to be war-like and menacing, but which, from those childish throats, sounded as pathetic as the cries of kittens. It seemed dreadful that the defenders of the Republic should be this mob of ragged children carrying worn-out rifles which they did not know how to use."

Although Orwell was "profoundly disgusted," he discovered that nothing made much difference on a stationary front, for the chief enemies were boredom and discomfort, rather than bullets and artillery. Fascists and Loyalists alike, ragged and dirty, struggled to keep warm while meaningless bullets wandered sporadically across the empty valleys. In October, there had been bloody fighting for each hilltop, but winter mud and lack of heavy weapons stalemated operations, and the "front" zigzagged from spur to spur, with each Loyalist militia element (POUM, PSUC, Anarchists) flying its own flag. The vista, with the monster peaks of the snowcapped Pyrenees floating in the far distance over the dead, bare country, "was stupendous, if you could forget that every mountain-top was occupied by troops and was therefore littered with tin cans and crusted with dung. . . . The hills opposite us were grey and wrinkled like the skins of elephants. Almost always the sky was empty of birds."

In the cold mists and the mud, patrols crossed and re-crossed the dark valleys, supposedly to feel out the enemy's defenses and keep on the alert. But there was no way, Orwell found, to keep his *centuria* alert—and it had become his particular problem because as soon as they had reached the front he had been made a *cabo*, or corporal, in charge of a dozen "men." The "wretched children" of his section slept whenever they could—leaning against the wall of a trench, or standing up "on guard." There were nights when it seemed to *Cabo* Orwell that his position could have been successfully stormed "by twenty Boy Scouts armed with air-guns, or twenty Girl Guides armed with battledores. . . ."

Fortunately, enemy activity congealed in the mud of late winter and early spring, and Georges Kopp, his company commander, would say, "This is not a war. It is a comic opera with an occasional death."

Life at the front, however squalid and dehumanizing, failed to wipe away all the quixotic vestiges of utopian equality bred in the revolutionary atmosphere of Catalonia. When one of Orwell's men suddenly refused an order to take up sentry duty at a post which he said was exposed to enemy fire, Orwell angrily began dragging the feeble, frightened creature towards his post. But the other men in the section ringed Orwell and shouted at him, "Fascist! Fascist! Let that man go! This isn't a bourgeois army. Fascist! . . ." In halting Spanish, Orwell shouted back that orders had to be obeyed, "and the row developed into one of those enormous arguments by means of which discipline is gradually hammered out in revolutionary armies." Eventually some took Orwell's side, others maintained just as stoutly that he was wrong. But a brown-faced, Arab-looking boy Orwell had inadvertently humiliated while still back at the barracks in Barcelona sprang into the ring to defend Orwell. With impassioned gestures as his exclamation marks he insisted, *"No hay cabo como el!"* (He's the best corporal we've got!") Order was restored, the men apparently feeling that they had made their revolutionary point. It was the kind of situation which had caused the Communist-sympathizing Christopher Caudwell earlier to repeat the old joke as to the Anarchist's code:

"Para. 1. There shall be no order at all.

"Para. 2. No one shall be obliged to comply with the preceding paragraph."[9]

Only the residue of revolutionary discipline—the understanding that there were political reasons why orders had to be obeyed—kept even the worst drafts of militia molded into responsive units, groups which held the line, or at least stayed in the field, although there were often compelling physical reasons for them to have melted away with the snows. The thermometer hovered just above freezing, and the sun warmed only with the assistance of firewood. But the hills had long since been picked clear of everything but dried reeds, and those only within range of Fascist machine gunners. Still, if to draw firewood one had to draw fire as well, then one drew the singing bullets which chipped the limestone outcrops, and gathered the precious twigs and reeds. Nothing was as Orwell had anticipated from his public school officers' training corps. The vital concerns of trench warfare on a stalemated front were "firewood, food, tobacco, candles and the enemy. In winter on the Zaragoza front they were important in that order, with the enemy a bad last."

For the Zaragoza sector of the front the entire artillery consisted of four trench mortars with fifteen rounds for each gun. The ammunition was much too precious to be fired, so the mortars were kept to the rear, in Alcubierre. There were no helmets, no bayonets, a few over-volatile grenades, no maps or charts, no signal flares, no field glasses or telescopes, no wire cutters. But there were plenty of passwords to learn—generally of a political or revolutionary nature—and double-passwords to answer each of them. *Cultura* received the response of *progresso,* and *seremos* was answered with *invencibles.* For Orwell's uneducated, often illiterate, sentries, the political passwords were often too elevated to be meaningful. One night, for example, the response to *Cataluña* was to be *eroica,* and Jaime, a peasant boy, asked for an explanation. It meant the same as *valiente,* Orwell replied, helpfully. A little later, as Jaime stumbled along the trench in the darkness he was challenged by *"Alto! Cataluña!"*

"Valiente," Jaime yelled, and the sentry's gun went off. Fortunately, he missed, as usual.

After three weeks on the line, Orwell and another Englishman were shifted several miles west to join a contingent of a couple of dozen men sent from England by the I.L.P. Within sight, twelve miles further southwest, was Zaragoza, and at night they could see the lights of the city, and of the supply trucks winding forward from there. A dozen Spanish machine gunners augmented the English unit and managed communications in spite of the language barrier. All Spaniards, Orwell claimed to have discovered, knew two English expressions. The helpful one was "O.K., baby." The other was used by Barcelona whores in their dealings with English sailors.

Orwell's sector of the front had no defensive aircraft cover, but neither did the enemy consider the Aragonese barrens worth many air strikes. Instead, the cities, and the Madrid front in general, absorbed the air pounding, giving him the small consolation of a wry prophecy. "Sometimes it is a comfort to me," he thought, "that the aeroplane is altering the conditions of war. Perhaps when the next great war comes we may see that sight unprecedented in all history, a jingo with a bullet in him."

There was still no fighting. Only a few random bullets flew from the Loyalist side, and Fascist machine gun fire sometimes raked exposed positions. In service of the cause, Orwell found when he checked his cartridge supply on transferring, he had fired exactly three shots at the enemy in three weeks. It was cheaper—and no less effective—to shout at the enemy. Via megaphones, shouted propaganda carried well over the hills in the clear, cold air. Shouting-duty generally consisted of broadcasting, from a forward position, a set piece which "explained" to the enemy troops that they were the hirelings of international capitalism and were fighting against their own class. The operation failed to fit in with the English view of how wars were to be fought, and the "Don't fight against your own class!" slogan aimed through the darkness at cold, equally miserable Fascist conscripts and recruits "dismayed all of us; it made us feel that the Spaniards were not taking this war of theirs sufficiently seriously." As if to confirm their suspicions, the PSUC megaphonist sometimes tried to encourage defections from across the lonely valley not with political slogans but with a highly imaginative "Buttered toast! We're just sitting down to buttered toast over here! Lovely slices of buttered toast!" It even made Orwell's mouth water, although he knew it was a lie.

Because the Fascists were winning, their propaganda could take a different form—as when Orwell's unit was bombed by a lone plane carrying copies of a Fascist newspaper, the *Heraldo de Aragon,* which headlined the fall of Malaga. For a few days, the Loyalist press and radio continued to report beating off tremendous Fascist tank and cavalry attacks, and Orwell put down the report in the *Heraldo* as a lie; but soon the disgraceful story of the flight from Malaga (when not a shot was fired at the invading Italians) leaked out, and up and down the line militiamen blamed the outcome on some kind of treachery, on the divided aims of the tenuously allied Loyalist groups. For the first time, Orwell had doubts about a war in which up to then the rights and wrongs seemed so beautifully simple. It taught him, too, to read the war news in the newspapers with a more disbelieving eye, a lesson he later applied imaginatively, as he did many of the lessons he learned in Spain, in a novel he would title *1984.* As he wrote six years later in "Looking Back on the Spanish War," he saw "great battles reported where there had been no fighting and complete silence where hundreds of brave men were killed." And he saw "troops who had been fighting bravely denounced as cowards and traitors; and others who had never seen a shot fired hailed as the heroes of imaginary victories." What he had seen, he realized, was "history being written not in terms of what happened but of what ought to have happened according to various 'party lines.' " He had discovered what he felt was a characteristic unique to the age in which he lived—"the abandonment of the idea that history *could* be truthfully written." Eventually, he thought, anticipating *1984,* it would lead to a "nightmare world in which the Leader, or some ruling clique, controls not only the future, but *the past.*"

In mid-February all the POUM troops in the Zaragoza sector were redeployed fifty miles across the bare plains to become part of the Government army vainly besieging Huesca. If anything, the war there was even drearier, and the chief excitement among the troops came in March when it was suddenly warm enough for lice. Musing wryly over the experience of *"resident* vermin" he wrote, "Glory of war, indeed! In war *all* soldiers are lousy, at least when it is warm enough. The men who fought at Verdun, at Waterloo, at Flodden, at Senlac, at Thermopylae—every one of them had lice crawling over his testicles."

The ironies of the unheroic war were seldom humorous. Supplies of everything were scarce, and men whose boots were no longer wearable had to wear rope-soled sandals and—for lack of firewood—sometimes warmed their toes by dug-out fires of worn-out boots. For Orwell, supply shortages were eased by his wife in Barcelona, from where Eileen sometimes contrived to send her husband tea, chocolate, and tobacco.

Outside Huesca, the opposing lines of trenches were about three hundred yards apart, at which range the aged Loyalist rifles could not fire accurately. In order to return Fascist sniping, POUM militia would sneak out in darkness to cover about a hundred yards from the enemy, and—with luck—get a shot at a Fascist through a gap in a parapet. Cover, unfortunately, consisted of a few ditches in an otherwise flat beet field. One day, when Orwell was out sniping, his group was caught by the dawn, with two hundred yards of bare fields to cross. While pausing to nerve themselves for the dash back to their own lines, they heard an uproar and a blowing of warning whistles in the enemy trench in front of them. Some of the rare, and rarely seen, Loyalist aircraft were apparently about to come over. In the midst of the commotion a soldier—probably a messenger—leaped out of the trench and, silhouetted fully against the dawn sky, began running along the top of the parapet. To Orwell's further surprise, the man was only half-dressed, and was holding up his trousers with both hands as he ran.

He was a clear target, within easy range, but no one fired. Years afterward, Orwell rationalized that he was too poor a shot to hit a running man at a hundred yards, and that his mind was more upon how to get back to his own lines while Fascist attention was, happily, distracted by the air raid warning. "Still," he had to admit, "I did not shoot partly because of that detail about the trousers. I had come here to shoot at 'Fascists'; but a man who is holding up his trousers isn't a 'Fascist'; he is visibly a fellow-creature, similar to yourself, and you don't feel like shooting at him."[10] It was the kind of thing which happens in all wars: a man holding up his trousers as he runs represents no inimical cause—he is mankind.*

The blur of desultory activity ended in April when POUM troops advanced about a thousand yards as a diversion to assist an Anarchist attack. It was a stretch of some sixty or seventy hours without sleep, in numbing cold; and it was a feat of organization accomplished quietly and smoothly until Fascist fire caused the first extensive casualties Orwell had experienced. His arm in bandages from an infection which had been lanced, Orwell sat out the worst of the action on the damp clay of a trench bottom, reading a detective story—*The Missing Moneylender*. But the final attack on the Fascist redoubt assigned to the POUM militia was temporarily called off, and Orwell was out of his bandages in time to become one of the fifteen volunteers. Each of the fifteen prepared meticulously for the surprise attack, and, a little before midnight, Kopp, in English and Spanish, explained the assault plan. Assailed by sheets of rain which filled the irrigation ditches to brimming, they were assembled in a farmyard, in darkness.

There were to be several groups of attackers. To prevent them from inadvertently shooting at each other, all were to wear white armlets, an ingenious plan rendered useless almost immediately by the arrival of a messenger who reported that there were no armlets available. Out of the rain and darkness a voice of a volunteer piped up: "Couldn't we arrange for the Fascists to wear white armlets instead?"

* Another literary man, in another war, tells a similar story. Robert Graves, in *Goodbye to All That* (London, 1929) records a trench-war incident from the First World War: "I only once refrained from shooting a German I saw. . . . While sniping from a knoll in the support line, where we had a concealed loophole, I saw a German, perhaps seven hundred yards away, through my telescopic sights. He was taking a bath in the German third line. I disliked the idea of shooting a naked man, so I handed the rifle to the sergeant with me. 'Here take this. You're a better shot than I am.' He got him; but I had not stayed to watch."

They crept through the ooze into no man's land, snipped aside the two lines of enemy barbed wire, and crept on. When they were only a few yards from the Fascist parapet, the defensive firing began, and men hastily tossed their bombs short of the redoubt. Fright, thought Orwell, had spoiled his aim, too, and only brought him an enemy bomb in return. It exploded close enough for him to feel the heat. He flung himself flat into the mud, and in the din heard an English voice behind him say quietly, "I'm hit." Rising to his knees, Orwell heaved his second bomb, then ran across the line of fire to where the leader of his group was signalling. Terrified of being hit in the face, he naïvely clapped his left hand over his cheek as he ran. Then, kneeling beside the others, he pulled the pin out of his third bomb and watched it disappear and explode inside the corner of the parapet.

The return fire slackened, then died; and the militiamen scrambled into the parapet to take it over and see what precious weapons might have been left behind. Where the machine gun had been, only the tripod remained. They poked about, and discovered an enormous telescope, but the triumph of acquisition was short-lived: the enemy was counterattacking, and had brought up a machine gun and a mortar. Dragging a captured box of ammunition and several rifles, Orwell and his group stumbled back to their own lines. The attack had been called off. It was nearly dawn, and nothing had been gained except to add to the number of wounded and missing, and provide Orwell with another chance to volunteer. (A party of five was to go out to look for the missing men.) In the half-light, Orwell crept out to the first strand of barbed wire after his four comrades retreated in terror from a new Fascist volley. There was no sign of life, and he crawled back, only to find that the two men they had been searching for had turned up at an aid station.

When Orwell's unit went on leave in the April heat, it had been in the line one hundred and fifteen days, the most futile period in his life, he assumed at the time. Later he thought of the months as an interregnum in his life—the only time at which he was isolated among people who instinctively lived out their revolutionary doctrine of the equality of man.

> Of course such a state of affairs could not last. It was simply a temporary and local phase in an enormous game that is being played over the whole surface of the earth. But it lasted long enough to have its effect upon anyone who experienced it. However much one cursed at the time, one realized afterwards that one had been in contact with something strange and valuable. One had been in a community where hope was more normal than apathy or cynicism, where the word 'comrade' stood for comradeship and not, as in most countries, for humbug.

By mid-afternoon of the twenty-sixth of April, Orwell was back in Barcelona, hoping to see his wife, buy some boots and clothes, and possibly a pistol. The city was a shock. The revolutionary tide had receded, and with it the egalitarian atmosphere. The well-to-do were well-dressed again, and had lost interest in the war; and the poor were, if anything, poorer and more poorly dressed than before. At the front, he had been insulated from the civilian indifference typical of all wars, whether fought for righteous causes or submitted to with apathy. Conditions in Barcelona were a return to the normality Orwell resented. Smartly dressed people filled the smart hotels and restaurants and were served by deferential waiters in boiled shirts, while in working class districts food supplies were shorter and queues longer. Under the surface-gaiety, political rivalries were festering. Party militias desperately were trying to preserve their own identities, and a sense autonomy, while on paper they had been incorporated in the Communist-dominated Popular Army. Without their militia units, the Anarchists and Trotskyites had no chance of committing Catalonia to continuing their social revolution; while, on the other hand, the Communist attitude—accepted by more conservative groups in the Government—was that there could be no order (and no victory) unless the workers' units were disarmed or integrated. As a result, Orwell spent much of his leave early in May as a POUM sentry, sitting in intolerable boredom on a Barcelona rooftop overlooking an Assault Guards stronghold established in the Café Moka. An armistice followed, then more street warfare, again followed by an armistice, and the pressures of food short-ages each day eroded further whatever Catalonian autonomy re-mained. Sitting, useless rifle in his hand, on a steaming roof, while his stomach grumbled with hunger, all Orwell could think about was that as soon as the shooting was over he was due to return to the front to fight for a cause which had soured.

The fighting in Barcelona gave the Valencia Government the excuses it needed to take over more effective civil control of Catalonia (which in effect was a secessionist ally) and break up the workers' militias. The POUM was declared to be a disguised Fascist organization whose fifth-column rising had been checked by loyal troops, and Orwell, dismayed by the Communist propa-ganda and the atmosphere of suspicion and hostility, changed his mind about wanting to go to Madrid to join the International Brigade. He was furious about the Government's hostility to the Catalans, seeing only the naïve idealism of the Anarchists and the POUM and ignoring the fact that the Catalans were using the opportunity of the civil war to break free from the rest of Spain, whatever common cause they were then making against Franco. What Orwell was learning in Spain was the real difference be-tween the Communists and other elements of the Left. Although such groups as the Anarchists were vague about their principles, and even more vague about how to put them into execution if a government were to operate according to their philosophy, their hatred of injustice and privilege was genuine. But while the Anarchists were quixotically attempting to carry out their revolu-tion in the midst of civil war, the Communists dispensed with liberty and equality in favor of centralism and efficiency—more practical guidelines in getting on with the war. That, after all, was the important issue: without victory no social revolution could survive, or be put into practice. But Government propa-ganda, mostly Communist-inspired, was vicious, suggesting that the POUM—an organization at the worst only eccentric—was in the pay of Franco and Hitler, and the Anarchists run by Trotsky from exile. In the *New Republic,* Ralph Bates, just returned from service in Spain, declared that not only was the war effort "retarded by the political problem of Barcelona, [but] three days before the Twelfth International Brigade, under Lukacz, attacked Huesca in an attempt to help Bilbao, the POUM troops were playing football with the fascists in no man's land."[11] Three days after the squalid battles in Barcelona, Orwell was back in the POUM sector of the front. It bore little resemblance to the fun-and-games allegation, which exasperated him when he read about it, months later.

In the line opposite Huesca again, Orwell discovered that he was now a *teniente* (second lieutenant) in command of thirty men, English and Spanish. The front was quiet except for sniper activity on both sides, and, after ten days of presenting himself as a target, Orwell was hit. It happened at five in the morning, with the dawn at his back, when he was talking with a sentry before the changing of the guard. With his characteristic detachment and understatement, Orwell later wrote, "The whole experience of being hit by a bullet is very interesting and I think it is worth describing in detail." The shock crumpled him to the ground, but he felt no pain. Quickly, the usual fuss began, as concerned militiamen started forward to lift him up and find out where he was hit. Conscious and not in pain, he felt a vague satisfaction—that it would please his wife to have him invalided out of the line rather than killed in the next big push. Then it occurred to him to wonder where he had been hit, and he managed to get the question out in a faint squeak. A bullet had gone clean through the throat, he was told—something he realized soon enough when, in being lifted, he watched a gush of blood pour out of his mouth.

Orwell took it for granted that he was finished. He had never heard of anyone surviving his kind of wound, and wondered how long one lasted after the carotid artery was severed. Things blurred, and he thought he was dead:

And that was interesting—I mean it is interesting to know what your thoughts would be at such a time. My first thought, conventionally enough, was for my wife. My second was a violent resentment at having to leave this world which, when all is said and done, suits me so well. . . . The stupid mischance infuriated me. The meaningless of it! To be bumped off, not even in battle, but in this stale corner of the trenches, thanks to a moment's carelessness! I thought, too, of the man who had shot me—wondered what he was like, whether he was a Spaniard or a foreigner. . . . I could not feel any resentment against him. . . .

As he was lifted onto a stretcher the arm he had fallen upon began to hurt excruciatingly, and it suddenly reassured him that he was not dying, for his senses would be failing, rather than becoming more acute. No longer feeling sorry for himself, he began feeling sorry instead for the four exhausted stretcher-bearers who were sweating their burden the mile-and-a-half to an ambulance. There were silver poplars fringing the trenches here and there; their leaves brushed his face and he thought "what a good thing it was to be alive where silver poplars grow." But the pain in his arm made him swear aloud, much as he tried to suppress his outcries, for each time he breathed an oath the blood bubbled out of his mouth.

Groggy from morphine which, nevertheless, failed to smother his pain, he managed, when he arrived at the hospital in Siétamo, to prevent a "nurse" from force-feeding him the regulation Spanish hospital meal of soup, eggs, and greasy stew. Soon, two of his comrades turned up to ask for his watch, pistol and flashlight —before they were stolen during the evacuation process. They were precious objects at the front, and the men were as delighted to see that he still had them as they were that he was still alive.

By evening, arm in splint, he was bounced to Barbastro in an ambulance. None of the wounded had been lashed to their stretchers, and, while one helpless wretch was spilled on the floor and a walking case was jostled into vomiting, Orwell hung on with his good, left arm. The hospital train at Barbastro took him to another ward in Lérida, about which his most indelible memory afterwards was of the sad faces of the wounded singing a song with a refrain that ended:

> *Una resolucion,*
> *Luchar hast' al fin. . . .*[12]

Lérida was only a way station for him en route to Barcelona, he was told, but when the Barcelona-bound train started, it was casually announced that the train would go to Tarragona instead. When Orwell complained that he had already telegraphed his wife to meet him in Barcelona, the train was held up while he sent another telegram. It was all very Spanish, he thought, particularly the fact that the corrective telegram never arrived, anyway. But the train did, as the sun dropped low in the sky, gilding a train leaving Tarragona in the opposite direction. It was crowded with men from the International Column, and topped off with field guns fixed to the open cars, and clustered about with more International. As they glided past, silhouetted against a turquoise sea, the wounded in the other train who were well enough to stand came to the windows to cheer the *estranjeros*. "A crutch waved out of the window; bandaged forearms made the Red Salute. It was like an allegorical picture of war; the trainload of fresh men gliding proudly up the line, the maimed men sliding slowly down, and all the while the guns on the open trucks making one's heart leap as guns always do, and reviving that pernicious feeling, so difficult to get rid of, that war *is* glorious after all."*

Finally, eight or nine days after the Fascist bullet had passed through his neck, a doctor ripped off the field-affixed bandages and examined the wound, tugging at Orwell's tongue until the bleeding began again in his throat, and his eyes watered with agony. Finally, he told Orwell that one vocal cord was paralyzed.

---

* These troops were part of the reorganized Catalan army, which had been under Government control since the May riots in Barcelona, and Italians of the Garibaldi Brigade, many of them singing *Bandiera Rossa* (Hugh Thomas, *The Spanish Civil War*, p. 443).

Naïvely Orwell croaked, "When shall I get my voice back?"

"Your voice?" he said cheerfully. "Oh, you'll never get your voice back."

Orwell had apparently traded a vocal cord for his life, for another fraction of an inch in any direction might have severed a vital artery or vein. But the doctor turned out to be partly wrong. For about two months, Orwell could not speak above a raw whisper, and then the other vocal cord "compensated" for the lost one, giving his voice a cracked quality it never lost. The neck wound had caused the pains in the arm too, it appeared, for a bundle of nerves affecting the arm had been pierced; and, for a month, the pain kept him tossing in restless sleep. Yet he could write to Cyril Connolly while convalescing, "I have seen wonderful things, and at last really believe in socialism, which I never did before."[13] Barely removed from it, he was already filled with nostalgia for the working model he had seen of the libertarian society.

When he emerged from the hospital and returned to Barcelona with Eileen,* Orwell found the atmosphere unconducive to recuperation. The street battles in May had left an uneasy feeling in the air, for the mutual suspicions and hatreds refused to evaporate. Rumors of sellouts, coups, and conspiracies flew amid the defeatism, and, by ones and twos, Anarchists and POUM adherents—including some of Orwell's friends—disappeared into jails at the request, apparently, of Stalin's local agents; and Orwell was himself warned not to show his POUM militiaman's card, but only his passport and hospital pass. Splinter party news-

---

* Richard Rees, who had been editor of *The Adelphi*, publishing some of Orwell's early essays, and was then an ambulance driver in Spain, passed through Barcelona in April, 1937, just before the street fighting, and called on Eileen at the POUM offices. It struck him that she was in "a very strange mental state. She seemed absentminded, preoccupied, and dazed. As Orwell was at the front I assumed that it was worry about him that was responsible for her curious manner. But when she began talking about the risk, for me, of being seen in the street with her, that explanation no longer seemed to fit. In reality, of course, as I realised afterwards, she was the first person in whom I had witnessed the effects of living under a political terror" (Sir Richard Rees, *George Orwell* [London, 1961], p. 147).

papers like *La Batalla* and *Solidaridad* appeared only after heavy censorship, and Orwell marvelled at a new regulation that censored portions of a newspaper could not be left blank but had to be filled up with other matter in order to make it impossible to tell when something had been cut out. It stuck in his mind.

Writing *Homage to Catalonia* five months afterwards, Orwell observed, "It is not easy to convey the nightmare atmosphere of that time—the peculiar uneasiness produced by rumors that were always changing, by censored newspapers and the constant presence of armed men. It is not easy to convey it because, at the moment, the thing essential to such an atmosphere does not exist in England. In England political intolerance is not yet taken for granted. . . . It seemed only too natural in Barcelona. The 'Stalinists' were in the saddle, and therefore it was a matter of course that every 'Trotskyist' was in danger." In Spain, Trotsky was only as mythical a bogeyman as "Goldstein," his equivalent in *1984,* but the suspicions and the dangers were no less dismaying, and the Orwells determined to leave for England as soon as they could. Medically unfit to fight again, voice almost gone, and short in funds, Orwell had to begin earning money again—and had to extricate himself from the possibility of arrest—a paradoxical but common fate for soldiers in service of a once—but no longer— common cause.

Once he had the safety of a discharge from the politically suspect 29th (POUM) Division, and a "declared useless" certificate from the Monzón Hospital at Barbastro, Orwell returned to Barcelona, to the Hotel Continental, where he had been staying with his wife. She was sitting in the lounge, and got up to greet him smilingly in a demonstratively unconcerned manner. Putting her arm around his neck, she whispered, *"Get out!"* While Orwell sputtered questions in confusion, she led him down the stairs, but before they reached bottom a Frenchman friend going in the other direction looked at them concernedly and warned, "Listen! You mustn't come in here. Get out quickly and hide yourself before they ring up the police." And, at the bottom of the stairs, one of the hotel staff furtively gave him, in broken English, the same advice. While Orwell had been away to get his medical discharge, the POUM had been declared an illegal organization, and not only its leaders clapped in prison, but wounded 29th Division militiamen as well, dragged out of hospitals. Already arrested when he came to the Continental to fetch his kit-bags was Georges Kopp, Orwell's friend and superior officer, "a man who had sacrificed everything—family, nationality, livelihood—simply to come to Spain and fight against Fascism," who had been at the front since October, 1936, and who had risen from recruit to major, and who had been wounded in action.

Plainclothes police had already searched Orwell's room, and had taken his diaries and letters—and a pile of press cuttings and a bundle of dirty laundry. Going back to the hotel was unsafe, and, for the rest of his stay in Spain, Orwell wearily lived on the run while his wife went back to the hotel to pretend he had not yet returned. That first night as a fugitive he slept fitfully in the ruins of a church which had been gutted and burned in the early days of the Catalan revolution. It was a weird existence, because he was in danger of arrest only at night, and, during the day, could lose himself in the city's crowds. Eileen insisted before they parted that he destroy everything he possibly could which might connect him with groups in disfavor. One of the most dangerous possessions he had was a photograph of a group of militiamen, for in the background was a POUM flag. Reluctantly, he tore it up. (That was the kind of thing that got you arrested. . . .") After that went his militiaman's identification card—it had POUM on it in big letters. His discharge papers bore only the seal of the 29th Division, but he had to take his chances that it would not be recognized in a hasty search as the POUM Division, for without it he could be jailed as a deserter.

Meeting Eileen at the British Consulate in the safety of daylight, Orwell got his passport in order for departure, but then risked his scarred neck by going to visit Kopp in prison, and appealing in various directions for his release. The prison atmosphere was thick with hopelessness, but Kopp shrugged cheerfully, "Well, I suppose we shall all be shot." But Orwell's faith in human decency was still uncomplicated, and he failed to interpret Kopp's remark as a signal that it was already too late.

Orwell's inquiries had quickly brought out his confession that both he and Major Kopp were POUM militiamen, and the response of the Spanish official to the terrible word was such shocked alarm that Orwell thought all was finished for him too. At police headquarters, where he and the official stood among the "narks, informers and spies of every kind" who hung about, the only possible answer was supplied: They would see about it—the proper inquiries would be made. Amid the hopelessness, "There was no more to be said; it was time to part. Both of us bowed slightly. And then there happened a strange and moving thing. The little officer hesitated a moment, then stepped forward and shook hands with me." It was almost impossible, Orwell felt, "to bring home to you how deeply that action touched me." As Laurence Brander has written, "It was the gesture of the world to the English eccentric. Orwell could not feel as the little officer felt about his courageous action for his friend. He was under the compulsion of his character and training."[14] Although Orwell saw the incident as reflecting "a generosity, a species of nobility" among Spaniards "that do not belong to the twentieth century," it was very likely the little Spanish official's recognition of those qualities in the unselfish Orwell.

The next night, three fugitives—Orwell and two English friends slept in the tall grass of an abandoned building lot, and, in daylight, again adopted—after shaves in a barbershop—the pose of somewhat seedy English tourists. Only once in five nights was Orwell able to sleep with his clothes off, when a sympathetic restaurant keeper offered him a room and promised not to submit the usual report of new guests to the police. The morning after, Orwell's wife slipped out of the Continental and met him at the train which—although an agonizing hour late in starting—took them across the border into France. When he had first arrived in Barcelona, to look bourgeois was out of place; now it was the only way to allay suspicion. Nevertheless, at the frontier passport office, government officials looked up the Orwells in their growing list of suspects to be apprehended; but, due to the Spanish inefficiency he had met so often before, the list of names in which he surely would have appeared had not yet arrived. They were searched from head to foot, and their baggage as well, and then passed through into France. As Orwell put it in a letter to Rayner Heppenstall, "We started off by being heroic defenders of democracy and ended by slipping over the border with the police panting on our heels."[15]

In England, Orwell found less misunderstanding of the situation in Spain than unwillingness to contemplate the future. And the refusal to look at the facts was no more a crime of the Right than of the Left. To those who knew what was going on in the Russia of the nightmarish staged trials, or who knew what the Stalinist Communists were doing to the withering Spanish Republic, any action less than open denunciation of Communism was to Orwell "to have the mentality of a whore." But the Popular Front concept—the feeling that the whole political spectrum of the Left had to live together and cooperate, or be submerged by Fascism—left no room for idealistic Orwellian extremism, which sounded as treacherous to the cause of the Republic as the propaganda of the Right. Nevertheless, Orwell persisted, and set about preparing a series of blistering articles attacking the Spanish Government for permitting itself such a degree of domination from Moscow,* and offered them to Kingsley Martin, the editor. Martin had gone to Spain himself twice during the war:

> he talked with Republican leaders and he saw what one could see. Orwell on the other hand, saw what one was not supposed to see and what most men could not see: that imperialism is imperialism whether its bosses are Russian Communists or British adventurers or

---

* Orwell evaded the practical issue in favor of the ethical: the Republic was receiving less military aid from Russia than it wanted, and more strings attached to it; but it received *nothing* from the non-communist West.

American bankers. It was in Spain that he conceived his loathing for Party-line Communism. He perceived, what, by the way, any experienced British trade unionist could have told him, that if Russian Communism was at war with Fascism it was much more whole-heartedly at war with Social Democracy, with any kind of Leftism which did not entail toeing the Party line; above all with the pure Communism of the Trotskyist World Revolutionaries. And as the Communist Party had got control of the Spanish Government, assisted by the fact that Negrín's Government could look to no power but Russia for arms, it was able to wreak its will on its supposed allies. . . . Kingsley Martin did not disbelieve what Orwell had written, but he decided against publishing it. In Spain there was a fight between Fascism and Democracy and the latter must be supported; if neither triumphed, but Communism came out victorious over both, even that would be better than a Fascist victory. In short, the *New Statesman* had become a "committed" paper while recognizing that, Fascism defeated, we might then have to fight for our principles against the worst elements in Communism.[16]

As a sop to Orwell for not publishing his pieces on Spain, the *New Statesman* offered him a new book on Spain to review, Franz Borkenau's *The Spanish Cockpit*. Even the review was too hot to handle. It was "against editorial policy," and was paid for, but not printed. And there were similar difficulties about the book Orwell wanted to write. As soon as his publisher heard that he had been associated with the POUM and the Anarchists, and had been through the May riots in Barcelona, "he said he did not think he would be able to publish my book, though not a word of it was written yet."[17] Nevertheless, Orwell began it, and Warburg finally agreed to publish it.

Writing his book in the seclusion of Wallington, the war still going on, but going ever more badly for the Spanish Republic, Orwell still wished it well, and confessed that, although so many memories with which he was left were evil, he was grateful that he had participated, however ineffectually. The result, he concluded, was "not necessarily disillusionment and cynicism," for he had gained additional faith in the decency of human beings, and had been awakened, he wrote prophetically—a year before a larger and far more bloody war began—from the "deep, deep sleep of England, from which I sometimes fear that we shall never wake till we are jerked out of it by the roar of bombs."

Certainly the publication of *Homage to Catalonia* awakened few Englishmen, and fewer Americans. The best-written non-fiction book to come out of the war, it was also one of the worst-selling. Of the 1,500 copies printed, only 900 had been sold by the time of Orwell's death more than ten years later; and it was not published in America until 1952. But it was one he *had* to write, and it became the first of the books which Arthur Koestler thought would cause "future historians of literature" to regard Orwell "as a kind of missing link between Kafka and Swift."[18] Orwell had lived through the Kafkaesque elements of the war, from seeing reports of battles where there had been no fighting, and finding silence where there had been slaughter, to reading Barcelona newspapers filled with non-news only inserted to conceal the blanks left by the censor's scissors. If nothing else, the nightmare in Barcelona and the Aragon helped form such *1984* concepts as *Newspeak, doublethink*,* *thoughtcrime*, and the rectification of newspapers in the "Ministry of Truth." For the adjective *Orwellian* we owe ironic homage to Catalonia.

In other ways, too, the Catalonian experience altered Orwell's outlook, for the heady atmosphere of the microcosmic Marxist utopia he had found in Barcelona faded slowly. As England later stumbled into its second year of the Second World War, Orwell published his *The Lion and the Unicorn*, his appeal for a wartime social revolution which would inspire the lethargic working classes by giving them something more than patriotism to fight for. It was a group, he conceded, which "never thought or acted internationally. For two and a half years they watched their comrades

---

* "Applied to a Party member, it means a loyal willingness to say that black is white when Party discipline demands this. But it means also the ability to *believe* that black is white, and, more, to *know* that black is white, and to forget that one has ever believed the contrary. This demands a continuous alteration of the past, made possible by the system of thought which really embraces all the rest, and which is known in Newspeak as *doublethink*" (*1984*).

in Spain slowly strangled, and never aided them by even a single strike." It was true, he was quick to add, that they raised money for Spain, but the sums collected "would not equal 5 per cent of the turnover of the Football Pools during the same period." The idea of a vast social transformation in the midst of a war appealed to few people. Survival seemed more important than socialism, and Orwell was further disillusioned. "Almost certainly," George Woodcock has written, "the idea arose out of his experiences . . . when he became attached to the losing faction in the internal struggle on the Republican side, the faction which contended that to defeat Franco one must carry out the revolution of social justice behind the government lines and so unleash a great flow of dynamic enthusiasm on the part of the poverty-stricken masses of Spain. As Orwell watched England, at the time when *The Lion and the Unicorn* was written, only slowly emerging from the apathy of the days of the 'phony war,' he remembered Spain, and it seemed to him that nothing but a radical change in the social structure, an immediate establishment of economic justice, would galvanize the people into action. He deceived himself into believing that this was just what the majority of English people would want once they knew their own minds. . . ."[19]

"The things we had seen in Spain," Orwell wrote afterwards, "did not recede and fall into proportion now that we were away from them; instead they rushed back upon us and were far more vivid than before. We thought, talked, dreamed incessantly of Spain." Later, he felt that the Spanish war had "turned the scale" for him ("thereafter I knew where I stood"), and that "every line of serious work" he wrote after 1936 was a result of those experiences.[20] It was true in part even for a novel of between-the-wars English life Orwell wrote after *Homage to Catalonia, Coming up for Air* (1939), about a plump, middle-aged insurance salesman in a small country town. The saga of George Bowling, with his revisiting an urbanized town he had remembered only as the idyllic village in which he grew up, is almost a comically novelized treatment of the indictment he had put into

Wigan Pier—except for a vivid memory transferred from Spain. A bomb (perhaps a warning of what was in store for an England that still slept) accidentally falls on "Lower Binfield," and shears away the front of a house, leaving its furniture exposed but undisturbed, like the open side of a doll's house. It was a phenomenon sometimes visible in Spanish towns, although not seen as often as the less neat rearrangement a bomb usually occasioned. Even the nightmare images of stamping boots and smashed faces, with their origin in the bold and colorful Catalan posters, began appearing in Orwellian fiction as early as *Coming up for Air*.* As afterwards, Orwell spared neither side. Political brutality could belong to any party.

Coming up for Air went through several printings. As remorselessly objective and satirical as *Homage to Catalonia*, it did not have the fatal flaw (for sales) of being a political book which could appeal neither to Right nor to Left. Candidly, Orwell always admitted that *Homage* was a "frankly political book," but it was written, he insisted, with "a certain detachment and regard for form. I did try very hard in it to tell the whole truth without violating my literary instincts." Still, he had included chapters of apologetics for the Anarchist and POUM Catalans, which were bound to fade in interest in time, and, even when technically alive as fresh reportage, slowed the book to a standstill. A critic he respected raised the question: "Why did you put in all that stuff? You've turned what might have been a good book into journalism."

---

* George Bowling, attending a Left Book Club meeting in a London suburb, suddenly imagines himself into the mind of the glib anti-Fascist speaker: "I saw the vision that he was seeing. . . . It's the picture of himself smashing people's faces in with a spanner. Fascist faces, of course. I *know* that's what he's seeing. It was what I saw myself for the second or two that I was inside him. Smash! Right in the middle! The bones cave in like an egg-shell and what was face a minute ago is just a great big blob of strawberry jam. Smash! There goes another! That's what's in his mind, waking and sleeping, and the more he thinks of it, the more he likes it. And it's all O.K. because the smashed faces belong to Fascists. You could hear all that in the tone of his voice."

Afterwards the image of the boot on the face represents the terror through which the Inner Party (and its dehumanized spokesman O'Brien) dominates the people of Oceania in *1984*.

Orwell admitted it, but insisted that he had known at the time what few persons in England knew, that innocent, idealistic men in Spain—like the murdered Georges Kopp—were becoming victims of a cause which somehow had become warped into turning upon itself. If, he later thought, he had not been burning with anger over such bitter memories (and the despairing realization that most, if not all, revolutions inevitably move to the Right, or collapse), he would have never written the book. But the act of writing it proved no catharsis: in other forms—in his essays and later memoirs, in *Animal Farm,* and in *1984*—he rewrote it the rest of his life.

4

THE ADOPTED ENGLISHMAN:
Koestler

*"When, in June, 1937, thanks to the in-
tervention of the British Government, I was
unexpectedly set free [from a Franco condemned cell], . . . I had made the acquaintance of a different kind of reality, which had
altered my outlook and values, and altered
them . . . profoundly and unconsciously. . . ."*
Arthur Koestler,
THE GOD THAT FAILED *(London, 1950)*

THE PROPAGANDA GENIUS of the thirties may have been not the
shrill Joseph Goebbels, but Willi Muenzenberg, head of the Comintern's propaganda activities in Western Europe. Inadvertently,
he was also the means by which Arthur Koestler became an
adopted Englishman. Koestler, a Hungarian émigré Communist,
and a writer in Muenzenberg's pay at the time of the General's
Revolt, found himself unable to keep his mind on his work while
the situation in Spain deteriorated. Returning to Paris from
Ostend, he asked Willi's help in joining the Spanish Republican
Army. Willi was full of ideas, but soldiering for Koestler was not
one of them; and he was in the process of forming the Committee
for War Relief for Republican Spain, the Spanish Milk Fund,
the Committee of Inquiry into Foreign Intervention in the Spanish
War, and other Communist-front organizations to be supported

in good faith by sincere men and women while operated behind the scenes on instructions from Moscow. A philanthropic or intellectual cover for Comintern political operations was Willi's specialty—he "produced Committees as a conjurer produces rabbits out of his hat; his genius consisted in a unique combination of the conjurer's wiles with the crusader's dedication."[1] Koestler had brought along his Hungarian passport to expedite arrangements for Spain, and Willi thoughtfully fingered it, clearly unenthusiastic about writers wasting themselves digging trenches when there was so much useful propaganda to be manufactured out of events.

In the passport folder, providentially, was Koestler's press card as correspondent in Paris for the Budapest *Pester Lloyd*. Willi's eyes brightened. The *Pester Lloyd*'s Paris correspondent had never written a line from there for the paper, and only possessed the press card as a favor from old Veszi, the editor, to help acquire occasional theater passes and to display in any dealings with the *Préfecture de police*. "Why don't you rather make a trip to Franco's headquarters for the *Pester Lloyd?*" Willi suggested. "Hungary is a semi-Fascist country. Franco will welcome you with open arms." Koestler acted interested, but both realized that the *Pester Lloyd* would never send him, however good a cover assignment it was. That difficulty was solved easily by deciding not to inform the newspaper, and hoping that, in the confusion of the war, no one would try to verify the accreditation. Since the Nationalists were refusing entry to reporters from left-wing newspapers, Koestler's press card from an ultra-conservative paper solved the problem of how to get someone to the enemy side to collect evidence proving German and Italian intervention: Koestler, Willi thought, could "have a good look around."

To make the journey more plausible required finding a parallel assignment for the *Pester Lloyd*'s correspondent, since the Hungarian paper's sending a special correspondent rather than relying on press agency reports might have given rise to suspicion.

Willi turned to his second-in-command, Otto Katz,* who made a telephone call to London and arranged with friends on the Liberal, anti-Franco *News Chronicle* (the only connection he had) for a second accreditation. Within an hour, it was arranged that Koestler would pick up the necessary papers at the *News Chronicle*'s Paris office. The second blind required preparation of a story in which Koestler would mention the English newspaper only if a press colleague or Fascist official should show signs of suspicion: "In this case, I would confidentially admit that, though my sympathies were the same as the god-fearing *Pester Lloyd*'s, I had been forced for financial reasons to accept a second assignment. . . ." There was a second risk—that he would be recognized for what he was. But that was a chance he had to take. As for travelling expenses, the "Committee" would pay that, Katz said; and when Willi inquired how much would be needed, Katz suggested, "Lots. To start with, if Arturo is going to be a Fascist, he needs a decent suit."

In the service of the twin Causes of Republican Spain and the Committee, Koestler entered Franco Spain as an undercover agent via Southampton and Lisbon. Through an unsuspicious Honorary Hungarian Consul in Lisbon, he was armed with a safe conduct signed by Nicolás Franco, the General's brother, and a personal letter of recommendation from Gil Robles to the commander of the garrison at Seville, General Queipo de Llano. Whether or not Koestler was technically a spy, he felt like one, and was, at the least, a paid agent travelling under false pretenses. For the next four years of risks and dangers, he lived "in a chronic anxiety-neurosis in the clinical meaning of the term." The first span was the most brief. On the second day in Seville, he was recognized and denounced as a Communist.

---

* Otto Katz, alias André Simone, wrote the original German manuscript of *The Nazi Conspiracy in Spain*. Katz had earlier been the anonymous author of the *Brown Book of the Hitler Terror* (1933) which played such an important part in the Reichstag fire trial, as well as other books of propaganda. Ironically, in 1952's Stalinist purges, he was one of the nine accused in the Slansky-Clementis trial in Czechoslovakia and, having been found guilty of the unlikely charges of being "a British spy, a saboteur and a Zionist agent," was executed. A loyal comrade to the end, he even "confessed."

As short as his sojourn was, it was highly successful, and only boomeranged later in an incredible coincidence. In his two days, he saw the German pilots and aircraft which constituted the core of Franco's air force, and obtained an exclusive interview with the voluble Queipo, who, thanks to the warmth of Gil Robles' introductory letter, was helpfully indiscreet about foreign aid. With the civil war only entering its second month, and Nazi and Italian non-intervention still a carefully maintained fiction, Koestler already had as much information as he needed.

It was in the lounge of the Hotel Christina, patronized by uniformed Nazi fliers, that Koestler was recognized. He tried to bluff his way out, but an officer who introduced himself as "von Bernhardt," wore a swastika on his blouse, and spoke in German, insisted that he had the right "as an officer of the Spanish Army" to ask any suspicious character to identify himself. It was an appropriate time, Koestler thought, to disclose his status as a war correspondent of the London *News Chronicle*, accredited with Captain Luis Bolín, head of Franco's Press Department. England seemed like a more powerful nation than Admiral Horthy's land-locked Hungary to impress the Germans with the implied threat of diplomatic complications. But then Captain Bolín walked in, and the first thing Koestler could think of doing was to act noisily indignant, in order to prevent any reasoned argument. It worked. Bolín reminded them that there was a war on, told them all to go to hell, then stalked out. It gave Koestler the opportunity to walk out in a pretended huff. Quickly, he went to Queipo's head-quarters, announced that he had been urgently recalled by his London office, and left with an exit permit. An hour before the warrant for his arrest was issued in Seville, he crossed the frontier into Gibraltar, safe in the territory of his hastily adopted nation.

In Seville, Bolín was helpless with rage, and vowed "to shoot Koestler like a mad dog," if he ever got hold of him. Five months later, when the Nationalists took Málaga, it was Captain Bolín who arrested him.

On his way back to Paris from Gibraltar, Koestler stopped

for a day in London, and visited, for the first time, the *News Chronicle* building in Bouverie Street. The newspaper had put his dispatches from Gibraltar about Franco Spain on the front page —his earliest work to be originally written in English[2]—and Norman Cliff, the foreign editor, gave him a friendly welcome. Returning to Paris, he went directly to Muenzenberg's office on the Boulevard Montparnasse. There his hero's welcome was short, for Otto Katz had just been placed on the British Home Office's blacklist, and could no longer get visas approved for England. Koestler's destiny was to be more and more associated with England. Ordering him back across the Channel as the new liaison, Willi barked, "The English comrades suffer from sleeping sickness." Nevertheless, the first English mission had to be abbreviated, for a skilled political journalist was needed to go to Madrid. Otto Katz had quickly insinuated himself into becoming the Spanish Republic's unofficial chief propagandist in Western Europe, and had already been called upon by Republican Foreign Minister Álvarez del Vayo to get someone to search the correspondence and private papers left behind in Madrid by fleeing Rightist politicians —to look for evidence linking the Nazis with the Franco rising, and make propaganda hay out of whatever was found. It had to be an outside expert, del Vayo explained, because party rivalries and jealousies in Spain had made the job impossible for a Spaniard.

For nearly a month, Koestler improved his weak Spanish by searching through letters and documents, including a mass of passionate and perfumed correspondence between an elderly former prime minister and various señoritas as much as fifty years younger. (Otto later discovered to his disappointment that Koestler had discarded them. A little sexing-up of the war, he mused, regretfully, could do no harm.) By the first week in November, when Largo Caballero's Government was fleeing Madrid for Valencia, and the capital was written off as lost, Koestler had all the useful material available loaded into two suitcases. Panicky that the letterheads emblazoned with swastikas and Falangist arrows would be misinterpreted by illiterate Anarchist patrols, or correctly interpreted by a rebel advance unit, he made an uneasy after-dark departure from Madrid, accompanied—as a façade—by three French volunteer pilots of the Malraux Squadron. In Paris, those documents not rendered obsolete by events, or previous publication, were slapped together by Otto into a book published in England as *The Nazi Conspiracy in Spain*. It would be published by Victor Gollancz as a Left Book Club choice, as was planned for the complementary book Koestler was to write, based upon his own experiences.

Willi Muenzenberg was impatient to get the book in print, and would visit Koestler's flat in Paris to urge more speed, for the Spanish war had become for him, as well as for many others, a personal obsession beyond mere Party obligations. He would pick up sheets of typescript and scan them disapprovingly, shouting, "Too weak. Too objective. Hit them! Hit them hard! Tell the world how they run over their prisoners with tanks, how they pour petrol over them and burn them alive. Make the world gasp with horror. Hammer it into their heads. Make them *wake up*. . . ." He hammered on the table with his fists.

Among Willi's complaints was the paucity of atrocity propaganda in the book, and, over Koestler's protests, he insisted on adding an insert of glossy horror photographs. In the text itself, Koestler guiltily limited the atrocity material to a dozen pages, some of it from doubtful or unidentified sources, but passed on by Willi, who argued reasonably that the accuracy of the details hardly mattered since the allegations were generally true. The important thing, Koestler realized, was to make people *feel* about Spain: "If those who have at their command printing machines and printer's ink for the expression of their opinions remain neutral and objective in the face of such bestiality, then Europe is lost, and it is time for Western civilisation to say good night."

There were to be German, French, and English editions of the book. The French version (*L'Espagne Ensanglantée*) was in press when Koestler was ordered to Spain for the last time, as correspondent on the Southern front for the "Spanish News Agency," a Loyalist Government organization midwifed not un-expectedly by Otto Katz.

Less squeamish than Koestler over the Muenzenberg-Katz doctoring of events was Claud Cockburn, who wrote for the Party as "Frank Pitcairn" and as a journalist had written more fiction than most novelists. The first pages of his saga were Orwellian —unlike Koestler, he was able to volunteer for the militia in the early days of the war, and joined a green Spanish unit at a time when "it was considered . . . a long training if you had more than twelve hours of it." Cockburn fought in the early defense of Madrid, retreating across the rocky, nearly treeless Guadarrama Hills in blinding summer sun and heat. By October, 1936, his account of the war—written, under Harry Pollitt's orders, in a week—was in print (as *Reporter in Spain*, by "Frank Pitcairn"), and he was in Paris working for Otto Katz. What he needed, said the chief of the *Agence Espagne*, was "a tip-top, smashing, eye-witness account of the great anti-Franco revolt which occurred yesterday at Tetuán, the news of it having hitherto been suppressed by censorship." "Pitcairn" confessed that he had never been in Tetuán, and had not heard of the revolt. "Not the point at all," said Otto. "Nor have I heard of any such thing." He explained that the French were reluctant to let an arms shipment through, worried that the Republic was sure to be defeated, and their aid to it would then jeopardize relations with the Nationalist victors-to-be. But if Franco's hold began to appear shaky, the prudent French might release the arms. What more spectacular place for such an anti-Franco uprising, suggested Otto, than the very city in Spanish Morocco where the Fascist rebellion had begun? When they set to work concocting their scoop, Cockburn confided later,

> Our chief anxiety was that, with nothing to go on but the plans in the guidebooks, which were without contours, we might have democrats and fascists firing at one another from either end of an avenue which some travelled night-editor might know had a hump in the middle. The fighting, accordingly, took place in very short

streets and open squares. . . . Katz was insistent that we use a lot of names, of both heroes and villains, but express uncertainty over some of them—thus in the confusion of the struggle outside the barracks it had been impossible to ascertain whether the Captain Murillo who died so gallantly was the same Captain Murillo who, a few months ago in Madrid. . . . In the end it emerged as one of the most factual, inspiring, and at the same time sober pieces of war reporting I ever saw.[3]

French Premier Léon Blum read the dispatch and was impressed with its significance. The arms were permitted to go through.

When Koestler left for Spain as correspondent for Katz's ubiquitous *Agence Espagne,* again he carried with him a handy additional assignment from the *News Chronicle.* January, 1937, found him in Valencia with another Spanish News Agency reporter, William Forrest, also a comrade, both sleeping overnight in the overcrowded refugee capital on the floor of Mikhail Koltzov's hotel room. When Koltzov—the correspondent of *Pravda*—had turned out the lights, the other two heard his voice, strangely flat in the darkness: *"Attenzione, Agence Espagne.* Tomorrow, in Moscow, starts the trial of Piatakov, Radek, Sokolnikov, Muralov, and accomplices; we are all expected to report the reactions of the Spanish working class." Koestler, emotionally involved as he was with the cause of Spain, was already in a state of suppressed disenchantment with Communism, and the news of the continuing purge must have reminded him, whether he realized it or not, that the "dialectically correct attitude was to remain inside [the Party], shut your mouth tight, swallow your bile. . . ."[4]

By January 27, he was reporting the war from Málaga, a town nearly cut off from supplies and all but theoretically defenseless. To check on the situation, Koestler went out in a steady drizzle to inspect the most exposed front, the coastal road to the south from Málaga to Gibraltar. There was nothing. He saw no trenches, no fortifications—nothing but a handful of militiamen casually smoking cigarettes a mile from the forward enemy positions. After all, he thought, if this was a war, there ought to be soldiers defending the only strategic road in the area. "Where are your troops?" he asked one of the sentries.

"Somewhere in the barracks. If the rebels were to attack, we should see them and have plenty of time to warn our men. Why should they sit out in the rain?"

They had no tanks to confront the enemy, the Captain in charge of the handful confided to Koestler; but, quickly, he added, "We shall strangle them with our naked hands."[5] When the moment of truth came, they made no resistance at all, and fled, leaving the *Causa* to Koestler. On February 8, the town fell without a battle. Koestler was still there. The Málaga area, Cyril Connolly observed soon afterwards, once had been considered an "escapist" place to live, "till 1936, when the centre of actuality shifted, and Sir Peter Chalmers-Mitchell who had retired to end his days in the sun, found himself, for a few hours in Málaga, in the intenser glare of History."[6] Sir Peter, a retired zoologist, was seventy-two, and lived at the Villa Santa Lucia, overlooking the sea. Koestler had tried to get him to leave for friendlier territory, as Sir Peter had been outspoken in his Loyalist sympathies; but he refused to go, insisting that since all the foreign consuls had fled, some responsible neutral observer should remain. Instead, Sir Peter warned Koestler to leave, but Koestler thought he detected in Sir Peter's voice an undertone of hope that he would not have to face the ordeal alone. The conviction that an elderly British citizen might have a restraining influence on the Nationalists was naïve; the feeling that Koestler was safe under the British flag, although he had been declared *persona non grata* six months before in Seville, was irrational. If he stayed, Sir Peter argued, the Nationalists might shoot only forty thousand people in Málaga, instead of fifty thousand. (The actual figure may have been as high as four thousand.)

As the Loyalist troops left the city without firing a shot, the chaos and panic had its effect on Koestler, and he headed in the direction of the stream of refugees, leaving his typewriter and papers behind in the Villa. But as he came to the edge of the city he changed his mind and returned. Analyzing his motives later, he thought that what had brought him back was "inverted cowardice, the fear of being afraid." Had he known all there would be to fear, he might not have come back after all, in spite of his later theories about "the tortuous ways of the death-wish."

The first of General Queipo's troops to come upon Koestler in Málaga—in the supposed sanctuary of Sir Peter's house—was Captain Bolín. Sir Peter carefully identified him as "the correspondent of a London newspaper, and . . . my guest." Bolín was unconvinced, and covered Koestler with his pistol.

"He is a spy; I know all about him. . . ."

Both Sir Peter and Koestler were arrested. Shortly afterwards, Sir Peter was released and expelled from Nationalist Spain. Koestler, wrists bound, was marched off at gunpoint to the Málaga prison, where he was held incommunicado for four days, each day expecting to be shot. Instead, he was transferred to the Central Prison of Seville. He had no official word, but plenty of unofficial hints, that the first three months he spent there in solitary confinement were lived under sentence of death. The vague and confusing information he did get convinced him that the executions, which were carried out three or four times a week between midnight and two a.m., would include him. After April 13, he lost count, having worked out a technique of sleeping through the critical hours when dazed prisoners, unforewarned, were led past the spyhole of his cell. One night—Thursday, April 15—the inmates of cells 39, 41, and 42 on his left and right were all removed to be stood against the cemetery wall, and his own cell was spared only after the warder had inserted his key in the lock, perhaps in error, and then had withdrawn it.

The torture was entirely mental—the loneliness of solitary confinement, the atmosphere of nightmare, and the uncertainty of when, if ever, one would be shot. Nevertheless, Otto Katz produced some baseless stories about Koestler's ill treatment in prison

("Koestler kept in chains in dark underground dungeon. . . .")
as part of an immense propaganda campaign which had some
Communist help but quickly gathered a momentum beyond Communist control. The sense of outrage in England was based on
Koestler's position as legitimate correspondent of a Liberal
English newspaper; the indignation might have been far different
had he been described instead—more accurately—as a German-
speaking Hungarian-Jewish émigré agent of the Communist Party
in France.

His fate in prison would have been different, too. Realizing
that he had to keep up appearances as *"Ingles—periodista"*—the
way he was classified in prison—once he began to inscribe a crude
diary on the wall of his cell with a piece of wire from his bed,
he wrote in English, to avoid calling the Gestapo's attention to
him.[7] When he was finally given a stump of pencil and some
sheets of paper, it was with explicit instructions that the paper
was not for writing letters but to "compose," for the Governor
felt that if he were allowed to "compose" again, it might "lighten"
his heart. (He had been on a hunger strike to test prison rigidity.)
His diary dated from that day, with earlier events reconstructed
from memory, and from the wire-scratchings on the white wall.
When he was released, he managed to smuggle the diary out with
him, having in effect written his first book in English.

While Koestler began a new and surreptitious fast (to simu-
late heart trouble, in hopes of gaining release that way), fifty-
eight Members of Parliament, nearly half of them Conservatives,
were sending letters of protest to Franco. Associations of English
authors and journalists protested, as did various English political,
cultural, and religious organizations. The British Government
itself forwarded stern representations to Franco on behalf of a
correspondent for one of the nation's newspapers. (As a dis-
cordant note, an official protest even came over-helpfully from
Budapest.)

Emotional superstructures were being built over events which would have had little meaning or impact in England had they been reported correctly, a fact which caused George Orwell to remark to Koestler afterwards—both of them thinking of the Spanish war—"History stopped in 1936." History was not being reported or written in terms of what happened, he thought, but in terms of what ought to have happened according to various "party lines." Current history, Orwell thought, would be written that way for a long time afterward.[8]

Late one afternoon, Koestler saw the first evidence of outside interest in him. A smiling young woman in Falangist uniform, accompanied by two elegant young officers, rattled the lock on his cell and let themselves in. The woman announced that she worked part-time as correspondent for the Hearst Press, and asked if Koestler spoke English. Then she wanted to know whether he was a Communist. He had to reply in the negative, and did, but it was not entirely a lie. A friendly warder had asked him how he had got mixed up with the *rojos*, and Koestler had answered, "But I no longer am a *rojo*." He had spoken the truth, he later realized, but with the intention of telling a lie. His hours by the recessed window of Cell 40 had already caused his inward break with Communism.

General Franco, the young *Falangista* said, had been asked by the *News Chronicle* and by Mr. William Randolph Hearst to spare his life. Hearst's newspaper empire had come out against the "Communist dictatorship in Spain" and for the "so-called rebellion," his newspapers, using Spanish-American War methods, habitually branding the Republic as "the Reds" and the rebels as "the Nationalists." (In an editorial entitled "Red Savages of Spain," Hearst's *Los Angeles Examiner* declared that out of a total of 33,500 priests in Spain, 14,000 had already been murdered by "Reds," and even Franklin Roosevelt had found that it was difficult to ignore Hearst-chain stories of Republican tortures of priests and church burnings. "You are right about the distortion of the news," the President had written to Ambassador Bowers in

Spain. ". . . Over here the Hearst papers are playing up all kinds of atrocities on the part of what they call the Reds.") The Muenzenberg-Katz operation had formidable adversaries, and was far from clean itself, but his new guardian angel, Koestler thought, was a poor lot.

During the long days and nights of solitary confinement, he felt intermittent anxiety and despair, but, for the most part, a newly discovered peace and happiness—a paradox he later attempted to explain "as the effect of a satisfied craving for punishment. The neurotic type of anxiety is the irrational anticipation of an unknown punishment for an unknown crime. Now retribution had come in a concrete, tangible form for a concrete, tangible offence. . . . Whether I was technically guilty of espionage or any other crime before the law was beside the point; I had gained entry to the enemy camp through deception, and I had done everything in my power to damage their cause. My condition was thus a logical consequence of a consciously taken risk, the whole situation was clean, proper and equitable." He found contentment, too, in scratching mathematical problems on the cell wall with a piece of bedspring, and solving them; and, in the solitude, his mind sometimes relaxed into mystical introspection. Being (he thought) beyond earthly hopes simplified life when all of the outside world he saw was a narrow patch of blue Andalusian sky. "I feel that I have never been so free as I was then," he mused afterwards. "Often when I wake at night I am homesick for my cell in the death-house in Seville. . . ."[9]

After sixty-four days in his cell, he was permitted out for exercise for the first time, and began making contacts with other prisoners. It was a result of the burgeoning campaign in England to secure his release, but he knew nothing of it. He still knew nothing of it when, towards the end of his imprisonment, he was visited by the British Consul in Seville. To him, Koestler stuck to his cover story that he was a *bona fide* correspondent for the *News Chronicle,* imprisoned because his dispatches indicated

Loyalist sympathies. His propaganda book on Spain had not yet been published in England, but the Consul brought up the subject of *L'Espagne Ensanglantée*, and asked whether Koestler had proof of all the accusations in it. Limply, he could only answer that some of the atrocity material was of doubtful authenticity. At that the Consul said nothing, but, after a few minutes of desultory conversation, he ended the interview with a few murmured words of perfunctory encouragement and a limp handshake. His silent revulsion was obvious. Koestler could see no further advantage ever accruing to him from his faint claim of being an "English" newspaperman.

The campaign to secure Koestler's release had begun when Sir Peter, released to the British destroyer *Basilisk* in Málaga and allowed to go on to Gibraltar, had radioed the *News Chronicle* of its correspondent's arrest. In England, most of the people who voiced indignation over Koestler's detention had never heard of him, and no book under his name had yet been published in English. The *News Chronicle*, in which Koestler had published only half a dozen dispatches, helped mobilize public opinion, and his estranged wife Dorothy (expenses paid by Muenzenberg's funds) went to England, a country in which she had never been before, to help collect signatures on petitions and protest resolutions. Harold Nicolson noted in his diary for April 21, 1937, "Mrs. Koestler, whose husband has disappeared in Spain, came to see me [in the House of Commons] and sat upon the bench with tears pouring down her cheeks. The Consul at Seville has been assured that Mr. Koestler is 'alive and well.' If that were so, he would certainly have communicated with his wife, and I very much fear that he has been shot. I talked to [Sir Robert] Vansittart [of the Foreign Office] about it, and he promised to take the matter up tomorrow and insist on a reply."

"Her tongue-tied manner," Koestler thought, "achieved more in England than eloquence could ever have done; her sincerity was instantaneously convincing; the fact that she spoke as the distressed wife of a husband in prison was more effective than any political argument."* Inevitably, the issue came to the floor of the House, where Anthony Eden, the Foreign Secretary, replied that the British Government was intervening on Koestler's behalf "in spite of the fact that he is a Czechoslovak citizen." He was right that Koestler was only an Englishman on the slimmest of technical grounds, but he produced the wrong national label. It made little difference, for the larger issue was the freedom of the English press: not even Hitler or Mussolini had jailed a foreign correspondent, both resorting to nothing more serious than expulsion. Koestler had inadvertently become symbol of an issue dear to Englishmen.

Finally, through the pressure from England and the good offices of the International Red Cross, Koestler was exchanged for the wife of a prominent Nationalist air force officer who had been held hostage in Valencia; and the officer himself flew Koestler from Seville to the Gibraltar frontier town of La Linea. The *Guardia Civil* escorted him to the border. His hair had not grayed, his features had not changed, and he had not acquired any religious mania, but he had "made the acquaintance of a different kind of reality," one which altered his outlook and his values "so profoundly and unconsciously" that during the first days of his unexpected freedom he was not even aware of it.[10] As his first free act in Gibraltar—unaware that he was no longer a *rojo*—he cabled his Party chiefs about his release. His first line was a symbolic quotation from Goethe: *"Seid umschlungen, Millionen"* —"I embrace thee, ye millions." Although he later considered it an even stranger act, he added the words "am cured of all belly-aches." "Belly-ache" was Communist slang for qualms about the Party line,[11] and the very fact that he felt compelled to report his "cure" indicated, whether he knew it or not, that the illness had already set in.

---

* After Koestler's release, he and Dorothy, for the sake of appearances, lived together again for a few months, but the marriage still would not work, and the pair separated again without rancor.

Koestler spent much of the next year in England, first working at keeping up appearances as a Liberal journalist. To begin with, there was the account of his prison experiences to be serialized in the hospitable *News Chronicle* and then to appear as *Dialogue with Death*, both carefully drawn to be as honest as was possible without revealing the various deceptions involved in his having been in Spain in the first place. Early the next year, his Left Book Club choice was published—*Spanish Testament*, incorporating *Dialogue with Death* and the least odious chapters of *L'Espagne Ensanglantée*. It was a commercial success, and Koestler at thirty-three was launched as an English writer. Although he still required collaboration with translators from 1938 to 1940, more than half of *Spanish Testament* (including *Dialogue with Death*) was originally written in English, based upon his diaries and dispatches to the *News Chronicle*,[12] some of it dictated directly onto the typewriter in his first few months in England. But his dilemmas as to how to proceed as a writer were complicated and considerable. He could not return to Loyalist Spain for the *News Chronicle* or the Spanish News Agency, because, as a condition of his release, he had signed an agreement not to return to Spain for the duration of the war. At first, he had a Middle East assignment for the *News Chronicle*, then a four weeks' lecture tour on the situation in Spain for the Left Book Club, which had just published his book.* The lecture tour strained his allegiance to the Party line, because, inevitably, his questioners brought up the subject of the POUM. The correct response was to label the militiamen of the POUM Trotskyite or Francoist traitors, but Koestler neglected that line in favor of mildly disagreeing with POUM principles, while insisting that its members were undoubtedly acting in good faith, and that a more vicious interpretation was a desecration of their war dead. Very often, an uneasy silence

---

* *Spanish Testament* has since been out of print, Koestler refusing to permit republication of the propaganda sections he had written for Muenzenberg. *Dialogue with Death*, published separately in the U.S. and elsewhere, was later reissued in England under that title.

followed. The embarrassed chairman would then ask for the next question.

Koestler's break with the Party was only a matter of time, but he had no desire to attack it publicly while Communists were helping to keep Republican Spain alive. During the spring of 1938, he gave a talk in Paris before several hundred refugee intellectuals, members of the German Émigré Writers Association. Many, he knew, were Communists. Before the talk, a representative of the Party *apparat* asked him to insert a passage denouncing the POUM as agents of Franco. Koestler refused. Shrugging, he then asked Koestler to let him see the text of the speech and to "discuss it informally." Again, Koestler refused. The speech contained no overt criticism of the Party or of Russia, and was entirely on the situation in Spain. But it closed with three seemingly innocuous statements, all of which were actually Party heresy: "No movement, party or person can claim the privilege of infallibility. . . . Appeasing the enemy is as foolish as persecuting the friend who pursues your aim by another road. . . . A harmful truth is better than a useful lie." The last was a quotation from Thomas Mann; the second was (to the Communists in the audience, at least) a clear denunciation of the Party line on the POUM. When he finished, the non-Communist half of the audience applauded. The Communists sat in silence, many of them with demonstratively folded arms. A few days later, Koestler decided that it was foolish to prolong the agony of waiting for the Party to expel him. He wrote a letter of resignation to its Central Committee.

For Koestler, the experience of the Spanish prison and the experience of the Communist system had become one, and in the years which followed he wrote a number of books in which he "attempted to assimilate the experiences" of Cell 40. Two-thirds of his novel *The Gladiators* was written "after Seville." In the prison, he had observed how easy it was to develop a slave mentality once one was in the position of a slave. Before Spain, he had been puzzled by the failure of Roman slaves to turn on their

masters, despite their overwhelming superiority in numbers. After
Seville, he understood why. Suddenly, it appeared to be "one of
the most natural things in the world for the oppressed to regard
the privileges of their masters as part of a divine order."[13] The
novel was finished in July, 1938, four years after he had begun
it. It was his first novel to appear in print, under contract with
Jonathan Cape of London. Without the experience of Málaga and
Seville, and his having become a *cause célèbre* in England, the
novel might neither have been completed nor published. Now he
thought of himself as a professional writer, where before the
"creative" side of his writing had been "occupational therapy"
while he worked for the Party.

Although he had not yet realized it, Koestler had chosen
more than to leave the Party: he had chosen a writing career,
and he had chosen England over the Continent (although he was
still to spend some months in France). He had found it difficult to
take the average English Communist seriously as a Communist, although he had met some fiercely dedicated ones. Their "Blimpish"
qualities caused them to put decency before dialectics, and they
indulged in diversionary humor and eccentricity, rather than
insisting unrelentingly upon the class struggle. They were closer
to the Pickwick Club, he thought, than the Comintern, and he
found the contrast as refreshing as it appeared at first bewildering.
It reminded him, as he lectured to staid Left Book Club gatherings,
of a story about Lenin. He had been shown a newspaper dispatch
about a strike in England, which reported that the police and the
strikers had played a soccer match, and that the strikers had
won. Lenin's reaction was to immediately cut the subsidy of the
British Communist Party, declaring that the English were obviously incapable of making a revolution. The realization apparently helped Koestler choose, although the events which brought
him into contact with England had triggered the choice. "In plain
language," he later wrote, ". . . if I have to choose between living
under a Political Commissar or a Blimp, I unhestitatingly choose
Blimp. He will treat me as an annoying kind of oddity and push

me about from sheer lack of imagination: the imaginative Commissar will politely shoot me because I disagree with him. In other historical situations on the upward grade, Blimp might again become the enemy of progress. For the next decades, his muddled decency and clinging to traditional values (even if it is partly pretence) will be a great asset. . . ."[14]

For his English publisher of *The Gladiators*, Koestler also prepared a synopsis of another novel he planned to write. Not surprisingly after his experience, it would be about several people in prison in a totalitarian country, under sentence of death. The Soviet purge trials had been going on, and the "stored memories of seven years" in the Party apparatus were to provide the material for character and plot; for background and atmosphere he needed only go back to Seville. Begun in October, 1938, at the time of Munich, it took him until April, 1940, to complete it. As a suspected Communist and alien in France when war with Germany began, he was clapped into Le Vernet, a concentration camp on the French side of the Pyrenees. When he finally escaped into England, he was arrested again and put into Pentonville Prison. When *Darkness at Noon* was published by Cape, Koestler was still in an English cell.

Through all of his troubles a manuscript of the book somehow survived. It was not always the same manuscript, for the German original of the novel disappeared in France; but by that time he had rewritten it in English with the collaboration of Daphne Hardy, a young English sculptress who had escaped from France ahead of him. After 1940 all of his books were written directly in English.[15] By the end of World War II, he had made England his "permanent home, wrote in English, thought in English, and . . . had applied for British citizenship. . . ."* His life had been "a phantom-chase after the arrow in the blue, the

* V. S. Pritchett, uneasy with Koestler as an English writer, found a literary reason: "Koestler has a voice, an urgent voice, vital, voluble and lively, above all never boring—a voice, but an arid and mechanical style. On the face of it this is an unkind criticism to make of a displaced writer who is not writing in his own tongue, who has to shift to write our own and has mastered it. But we suspect that no language

perfect cause, the blueprint of a streamlined Utopia." After Spain, he had adopted "a country where arrows are only used on dart-boards, suspicious of all causes, contemptuous of systems, bored by ideologies, sceptical about Utopias, rejecting all blueprints, enamoured of its leisurely muddle, incautious about the future, devoted to its past. A country neither of Yogis nor of Commissars, but of potterers-in-the-garden and stickers-in-the-mud, where strikers played soccer with the police and Socialists wore peers' crowns." When he was absent from England, he felt "conscious of living *abroad*." He had gone through the process of changing languages twice—from Hungarian to German, then from German to English. It was only fitting that the title of *Darkness at Noon* (a suggestion from Daphne Hardy) come from English literature —John Milton's "Oh dark, dark, dark, amid the blaze of noon."

Darkness at Noon was Koestler's attempt "to come to intellectual terms with the intuitive glimpses gained during the 'hours by the window' " in Seville. One element in his perspective came later, when he learned about the campaign, mounted in England for the most part, to extricate him from his Spanish prison. It was the paradox in the mentality of the liberal public to whom he owed his life. These were men and women of good will whose sincere commitment to the fight against Fascism was so total that they were blind or indifferent to another totalitarianism as long as it appeared to remain anti-Fascist. Yet, when Koestler compared the fuss that had been made over him to the silently accepted imprisonments and executions in Russia (the Great Purge had already swallowed up wholesale many of his friends), he became "increasingly aware of a crushing debt that must somehow be repaid. *Darkness at Noon* . . . was the first instalment towards it." It was a chapter of what a critic later called Koestler's "pilgrim's regress from revolution."[16]

---

is an inconvenience to him; language is a machine; not even in his own language, we feel, has he any love for words or any sense of their precision and grace. . . . Koestler uses words as thought-saving gadgets . . . and draws especially on the vocabulary of science and economics . . ." ("The Art of Koestler," in *Books in General* [London, 1953], p. 159).

In the novel, Koestler could draw on his own experience in Seville for the psychology of the condemned and the atmosphere of hysteria in which men under sentence of death lived. Sometimes, other elements of his stay in cell 40 found their way—he thought—into the book subconsciously. When he had been interrogated by the Falange-uniformed Hearst correspondent, he had been asked whether he might like to make a statement to her newspaper with regard to his feelings toward General Franco. The General, she had said, in charmingly low-pressure conversational tones, had condemned him to death, but he "might possibly" grant a commutation. "Well, life-long imprisonment. But there is always hope of an amnesty, you know." From his iron prison bedstead, where she was sitting, she flashed him a knowing smile.

It was an irresistible temptation. After days of waiting for torture and death, days when he often thanked God silently that the day had only twenty-four hours, rather than twenty-five or thirty, he found that he did not have the moral strength to resist. Although he did not know Franco personally, he explained to her by way of answering the request, he felt that the General must be a man of humanitarian outlook, one he could trust. Pleased, the American *Falangista* wrote it down. When she then asked him to sign it, it suddenly occurred to him that he was signing his own moral death sentence. Rather than complete the self-betrayal, he crossed out what she had written and dictated another statement:

> I do not know General Franco personally, nor he me; and so, if he grants me a commutation of my sentence I can only suppose that it is mainly from political considerations.
>
> Nevertheless, I could not but be personally grateful to him, just as any man is grateful to another who saves his life. But I believe in the Socialist conception of the future of humanity, and shall never cease to believe in it.

This statement he signed, and patted himself inwardly on the back for having resisted completing the betrayal.[17]

The motive of a potential betrayal which is never consummated and remains known only to the subject himself appeared in two later Koestler novels. Again, the author credited the incidents to the subterranean hold upon him of the incident in Seville. In *Darkness at Noon*, the interrogator Gletkin tells how, when he was a prisoner of the enemy, a burning wick was placed on his shaven skull to extort information from him. A few hours later, his comrades, having recaptured the position, found him unconscious. The wick had burned down to the end, but Gletkin had remained silent. "That's all bunk," he explains. "I did not give in because I fainted. If I had stayed conscious another minute, I would have spoken. . . . When I came to, I was actually convinced that I *had* spoken. But the other prisoners established that this was not the case. So I got a decoration." In *Arrival and Departure*, Koestler thought, there was a similar incident. In both cases, he was unaware of their inspiration at the time the novels were written.[18]

Like Koestler in the Seville prison, the Rubashov of *Darkness at Noon* has plenty of time in prison to reevaluate a relationship to the Party which has gone sour. Like Koestler, Rubashov keeps a prison diary, is starved for reading matter and outside news, and learns the stealthy means of intercell communication. The routine of the cell block for the condemned, the perpetual fear of torture and death, the disintegration of the ego under questioning, the inexorable isolation that distorts moral and ideological complexities into abstract terms, and even causes the victim to look at himself abstractly, the sudden agony of sympathy for each prisoner marched out of his cell for execution—these were insights Koestler might have arrived at through reading and research, or through his own work in the web of the *apparat;* but the hundred days in Spain under sentence of death were creatively vital to him in *Darkness at Noon*, as well as later books. It was an experience so intense that it required exorcism through gradual attenuation over years of writing.

Like several other immediately post-Spain major works by participants in the Spanish Civil War, *Darkness at Noon* has survived topicality. Its obsessive power, its understanding of human motives, its near-Shavian ability (as in the Inquisitor's scene in *Saint Joan*) to project a defense of the official line as powerful and as persuasive as the attack upon it, have made it a modern classic. It was a masterpiece, Orwell thought, partly because Koestler's "life style" permitted him a pity and an irony in handling his theme beyond the experience of an English or American writer. It reached "the stature of tragedy" because Koestler's unique background (for an author working in the English language) enabled him to digest his material and "treat it on the aesthetic level," rather than as a "polemical tract."[19] Although it was usually considered Koestler's celebration of his rejection of Communism, the most significant act of his life, it may be hardly less a by-product of the war in Spain than Orwell's own *Homage to Catalonia* (although Spain is mentioned only once in Koestler's novel).

Later, there were other Koestler novels which continued to reflect the experience of Spain—*Arrival and Departure* (1943) and *The Age of Longing* (1951). In the latter book, Julien's limp and scar were results of wounds at Teruel in 1937. Like so many other intellectuals, he had gone to Spain with enthusiasm and hope that he was fighting for a better world. Now he realized it was a tragic farce—"the climax and apotheosis of the great buffoonery which preceded the Fall. . . . I was in the hospital when I read in the paper that the last Mohicans of the [Russian] Revolution had all confessed to be spies, and were whimpering for a bullet into the backs of their necks as a man in pain whimpers for morphia."

Earlier, in *The Yogi and the Commissar* (1943), Koestler had tried to digest, this time in the form of essays, "the essential meaning of solitary dialogue of cell No. 40." It was a book, he thought, which finally "closed the cycle" begun in Seville: "It had taken five years to digest the hours by the window." But Koestler was wrong: the grip of Spain had been more tenacious than that. It had taken nearly fifteen.

5

THE ALOOF OLYMPIANS

*I still feel convinced that it is best that at
least a few men of letters should remain isolated, and take no part in these collective
activities.*

T. S. Eliot

*Spain must choose for itself: it is really not
our business. . . .*

Bernard Shaw
AUTHORS TAKE SIDES *(1937)*

"IT IS IMPOSSIBLE to be angry with Picasso," Arthur Koestler
once wrote, "for believing that Stalin was the greatest benefactor
of mankind, for one feels that his error is the result of a naïve and
warmhearted passion. But it is not easy to forgive . . . the ironically
dispassionate Olympian."[1] Above the Spanish battle stood several
literary Olympians, their beliefs far removed from those of a
writer they would not have recognized as one of them. "I cannot
excite myself over nations and causes and creeds," Norman
Douglas observed; "my contempt for humanity is too great. Individuals are the only things that interest me. If Spaniards like
to cut each other's throats and get Germans and Russians to help
them—why not let them? It's not my affair. If they eat each
other up to the last man, like Kilkenny cats, let them! . . . Nobody
is going to compel me to 'take sides.' To hell with sides."[2]

When Bernard Shaw left England on a round-the-world cruise early in 1936, there had been no reason to take sides. But there was trouble enough in Europe, with Hitler gathering strength, Mussolini gathering new colonies, and the impotent Geneva-based League of Nations reflecting the vacillation of the West. On board ship, somewhere in the vicinity of the Panama Canal, Shaw found the necessary distance from the European scene* to begin a play intending to satirize the League—in particular, its adjunct Intellectual Cooperation Committee. When it had been founded, Shaw recalled, European intellectuals were delighted, and the most eminent of them offered their names for its shop window. A Frenchman gave a million francs to endow the Committee, but the depression deflated the francs into uselessness, and the Committee survived in a little office somewhere, where a secretary performed some busy-work; intellectually, however, it sank into what Shaw called "a profound catalepsy."

With that history in mind, Shaw began writing, inventing an office in Geneva for Begonia Brown, his secretary in the play, and a group of representative Europeans to bring grievances to her—an Anglican bishop who complains about Communism in his diocese, a Russian commissar who complains about activities in Russia of the Society for Propagation of the Bible in Foreign Parts, a Jew complaining of oppression, an anti-Semitic Catholic widow, and others. Some of the complaints were to find their way eventually to the International Court of Justice, where Shaw would satirize the ineffectiveness of League machinery through a *tour de force* exhibition of caricatures of Hitler and Mussolini,

---

* When Shaw's ship stopped at Honolulu, he was interviewed on world affairs by racially casual Hawaiians particularly interested in his views on Hitler's anti-Semitic drive to purify the German people. Laughingly, Shaw said that he believed that Hitler would have a better biological result if he summoned all Jews to Germany and then punished all Jews who married Jews in preference to Germans and all Germans who married Germans in preference to Jews. "A pure bred dog," he joked, "is not good for anything but a dog show" (*Honolulu Advertiser*, February 25, pp. 1, 5). This showed an unfortunate tendency of Shaw's in the thirties to take serious matters increasingly lightly—a way of disguising his own confusion about what stand to take, if any, on Europe's dictators and democrats.

among others. But no play of Shaw's had so much difficulty keeping up with events as did *Geneva,* and, by early in 1938, when he finally decided to finish the play, events in Spain required not only that his Mr. Battler (Hitler) and Signor Bombardone (Mussolini) be flanked by General Flanco de Fortinbras, but that Flanco be one of the pivots of the discussion.

By the time Shaw had gone that far, it was clear that the war in Spain was straining and confusing his loyalties. A staunch Marxist since his twenties, he might have been expected to support the cause of the Left, yet his growing feeling that parliamentary democracy was weak and inefficient and would give way to benevolent (but efficient) autocracy caused him to lean toward the Right. He was finding Hitler somewhat indigestible, but Mussolini had not yet become the Fuehrer's junior partner, and Italian trains were reputed to run on time. The result was that he was found at lunch one afternoon declaring in a discussion about Spain that civil war was the only excusable form of war.[3]* When the *Left Review* asked him to "take sides," he stalled, then answered at the last moment:

> In Spain both the Right and the Left so thoroughly disgraced them-selves in the turns they took in trying to govern their country before the Right revolted, that it is impossible to say which of them is the more incompetent. Spain must choose for itself: it is really not our business, though of course our Capitalist Government has done every-thing it possibly could to help General Franco. I as a Communist am generally on the Left; but that does not commit me to support the British Party Parliament system, and its continental imitations, of which I have the lowest opinion.
>
> At present the Capitalist powers seem to have secured a victory over the General by what they call their non-interference, meaning their very active interference on his side; but it is unlikely that the last word will be with him. Meanwhile I shall not shout about it.[4]

In a BBC speech on short wave to the empire, Shaw did his only shouting, outraged that "all the big capitalist powers are

---

* Hemingway, not long before the war, had theorized that "civil war is the best war for a writer, the most complete" (*The Green Hills of Africa,* 1935).

taking a hand to support General Franco through an intervention committee which they think it more decent to call a Non-Intervention Committee." He was reacting against hypocrisy; but he was also oversimplifying the war into one "between the two religions of capitalism and communism," and he was clearly against "land owning" and for "labor."[5] Yet, he left the impression that true non-intervention would have satisfied him, whatever then the outcome of the war. For Shaw, a victory for the wrong side in Spain was preferable to a general European war, which the internationalizing of the Civil War seemed to be making inevitable.

Almost every comment Shaw made, both public and private, reflected his continuing ambivalence. When a vicar's eighteen-year-old son was charged with violating English law by agreeing to fight for the Republic, there was a great outcry among intellectuals, but Shaw's reaction was ironic, rather than outraged, in a statement to the *Yorkshire Evening News*:

> Asking an airman to fly to Spain and fight on the Government side was no more seducing him from his allegiance than Mussolini was seducing Italian soldiers from their allegiance to the King of Italy by sending them to Spain to fight for General Franco.
>
> In December last it was perfectly legal for any Englishman to volunteer for the Spanish Civil War on either side.
>
> But as this plea was disallowed, and the Act of 1934 enables the Government to do what it likes to anybody, there is nothing more to be said.
>
> It was passed to terrorise the Communist Party, and it would be nullified if the sentences under it were not exemplary.
>
> All the stuff about Phillips's youth and emotional folly is nonsense. The policies of Lenin and Stalin cannot be dismissed as boyish fancies.
>
> Phillips's tactics were silly, but they were those of the organised group in this country at which the Act was aimed.
>
> A year's interval for reflection will do him more good than harm, and will give him prestige as a Communist when he emerges."[6]

In the third act* of *Geneva*, G.B.S. continued to play the role of interested bystander. There the three dictators defend their

---

* In a later revision, the fourth act (a new act had been inserted).

actions to the International Court, Battler posing as the champion of civilization against Bolshevism, and pioneer of a post-Semitic world; and Bombardone the savior of the world from "the chaos called Liberty and Democracy," self-appointed because those who have the brains and the divine call for the task "are not chosen by the people: they must choose themselves: that is part of their inspiration."[7] Since Flanco is striving to protect his country from the horrors of Communism, he has Bombardone's support as well as Battler's. That support, the commissar reminds the Italian, is more than moral: It included "the help of your guns and soldiers."

Bombardone's ready answer is, "I cannot prevent honest men from joining in a crusade, as volunteers, against scoundrels and assassins."

Sir Orpheus Midlander (a composite of the two Chamberlains, Austen, and Neville) is only an interested listener—until the judge comments that he "can of course assure General Flanco of British support. . . ." Rising, Sir Orpheus protests, "Oh no, no, no. I am amazed at such a misunderstanding. The British Empire has maintained the strictest neutrality. It has merely recognized General Flanco as a belligerent." But the General knows the full value of England's non-help to both sides, and when he enters, smartly uniformed and sophisticated, he *"salutes Sir Orpheus with a distinguished consideration that contrasts very significantly with his contemptuous indifference to the two leaders. Sir Orpheus, as before, waves a gracious acknowledgement of the salute."* Later, when Battler accuses Flanco of ingratitude, the General's answer is that he owes his victory in part to the dictators, but equally to "the masterly non-intervention policy" of Sir Orpheus's nation. Besides, says the independent-minded Spaniard, as a man of action he is out of place among "talkers" like Battler and Bombardone:

BBDE: Inconceivable nothingness that you are, do you dare to class me as a talker and not a man of action?

FLANCO: Have you done anything?

BBDE: I have created an empire.

FLANCO: You mean that you have policed a place infested by savages.*
A child could have done it with a modern mechanized army.

BBDE: Your little military successes have gone to your head. Do not
forget that they were won with my troops.

FLANCO: Your troops do fairly well under my command. We have
yet to see them doing anything under yours.

BBDE: Ernest: our valet has gone stark mad.

FLANCO: Mr. Battler may be a useful civilian. I am informed that he
is popular with the lower middle class. But the fate of Europe will
not be decided by your scraps of Socialism.

JUDGE: May I recall you to the business of the court, gentlemen.
General: you are charged with an extraordinary devastation of
your own country and an indiscriminate massacre of its inhabitants.

FLANCO: That is my profession. I am a soldier; and my business is
to devastate the strongholds of the enemies of my country, and
slaughter their inhabitants.

NEWCOMER: Do you call the lawfully constituted democratic government of your country its enemies?

FLANCO: I do, sir. That government is a government of cads. I stand
for a great cause; and I have not talked about it, as these two
adventurers talk: I have fought for it: fought and won.

JUDGE: And what, may we ask, is the great cause?

FLANCO: I stand simply for government by gentlemen against government by cads. I stand for the religion of gentlemen against the
irreligion of cads. For me there are only two classes, gentlemen
and cads: only two faiths: Catholics and heretics. The horrible
vulgarity called democracy has given political power to the cads
and the heretics. I am determined that the world shall not be ruled
by cads nor its children brought up as heretics. I maintain that
all spare money should be devoted to the breeding of gentlemen.
In that I have the great body of public opinion behind me. Take a
plebiscite of the whole civilized world; and not a vote will be cast
against me. The natural men, the farmers and peasants, will support me to a man, and to a woman. Even the peasants whom you
have crowded into your towns and demoralized by street life and
trade unionism will know in their souls that I am the salvation of
the world.

BBDE: A Saviour, no less! Eh?

* Ethiopia.

FLANCO: Do not be profane. I am a Catholic officer and gentleman, with the beliefs, traditions, and duties of my class and my faith. I could not sit idly reading and talking whilst the civilization established by that faith and that order was being destroyed by the mob. Nobody else would do anything but read seditious pamphlets and talk, talk, talk. It was necessary to fight, fight, fight to restore order in the world. I undertook that responsibility and here I am. Everybody understands my position: nobody understands the pamphlets, the three volumes of Karl Marx, the theories of the idealists, the ranting of the demagogues: in short, the caddishness of the cads. Do I make myself clear?

BBDE: Am I a cad? Is Ernest [Battler] here a cad?

FLANCO: You had better not force me to be personal.

BBDE: Come! Face the question. Are we cads or gentlemen? Out with it.

FLANCO: You are certainly not gentlemen. You are freaks.

BATTLER: Freaks!

BBDE: What is a freak?

JUDGE: An organism so extraordinary as to defy classification.

BBDE: Good. I accept that.

BATTLER: So do I. I claim it.

The talkathon ends with a Shavian *deus ex machina*—a telephoned message that the earth's orbit has altered, and that humanity is likely to be frozen out of existence. The news causes each character to react according to his real nature, rather than his public image, and Flanco calmly reflects, "I await the decision of the Church. Until that is delivered the story has no authority.

SIR O: May I suggest that you use all your influence at Rome to obtain an immediate decision from the Church against this story.

FLANCO: You shock me. The Church cannot be influenced. It knows the truth as God knows it, and will instruct us accordingly. Anyone who questions its decision will be shot. My business is to see to that. After absolution, of course. Good morning. [*He goes out*].

WIDOW: He at least has something to offer to men about to die.

COMMISSAR: Dope.

JUDGE: Why not, if they die comforted?

BATTLER: Men must learn to die undeluded.

BBDE: Flanco is dead; but he does not know it. History would have kicked him out were not History now on its deathbed.

BEGONIA: I must say I thought the General a perfect gentleman. . . .

When the play was first performed in London late in 1938, the war in Spain was still going on, and interest in the Shavian stage caricatures of men still busy making the news drew audiences to 237 performances. For the theater program, Shaw wrote, "The critics are sure to complain that I have not solved all the burning political problems of the present and future in it, and restored peace to Europe and Asia. They always do. I am flattered by the implied attribution to me of Omniscience and Omnipotence; but I am also infuriated by the unreasonableness of the demand. I am neither Omniscient nor Omnipotent; and the utmost I or any other playwright can do is to extract comedy and tragedy from the existing situation and wait to see what will become of it." He was still refusing to commit himself, or do anything in behalf of either side. It was almost as if he were saying that, at eighty-two, he was above the battle. Besides, no one had listened. As he had said a few years earlier in a public lecture, he had been addressing assemblies for a half-century, and "So far as I can make out, those speeches have not produced any effect whatever. In the course of them I have solved practically all the pressing questions of our time; but . . . they go on being propounded as insoluble just as if I had never existed. . . ."[8]

Later, after the Second World War had broken out, and Franco was aiding Hitler (in a minimal fashion), Shaw's old friend H. G. Wells called the General a "murderous little Christian gentleman." But, in the late thirties, Wells saw his old utopian visions constantly frustrated, often by his own country's confusion of cross-purposes, and came to the "plague upon both your houses" opinion about Spain. People were too foolish, he felt, to avoid another world war. In 1933, in his novel *The Shape of Things to Come*, he had predicted the increasing collapse of the boundaries separating military and civilian life, with semi-military organizations of uniformed civilians taking the lead; and a general European war breaking out in January, 1940, over Poland. Bombers, tanks, poison gas, and long-range, remote-control "air torpedoes" would change the face of war, and strike terror among civilian populations, forcing them to live under-ground. Earlier, he had already predicted an atom bomb, manu-factured from uranium. Now he felt that it was too late for the writer to do anything but watch and wait.

Two weeks before the war in Spain began, Wells published an essay in *Collier's*, "The Next War," in which he described himself as having turned into an onlooker upon the world's strug-gles, unable to identify strongly enough with any position to take action. He was discouraged by the irrationality of the world's leaders, and saw the world liberal community headed for conflict with "nationalist patriotism." Only the repudiation of nationalism in favor of a world community could bring peace, he felt, but it was likely to be a futile hope. Within a few weeks, he saw his prediction of conflict breaking out along liberal-nationalist lines come true, but his natural sympathies with the "new liberal Re-public" died rapidly when he saw the cross-purposes of parties and ideologies tearing the Spanish Republic apart. "The interven-tion of Italy and Germany is on traditional nationalist lines," he noted; "it was to be expected and has been greatly facilitated by the stupid confusion in the British mind and will." The real enemy of mankind is not the Fascists but the Ignorant Fool."[9] At a dinner party given by Lady Colefax at Argyll House, Wells talked over the flickering candles with Rebecca West, Harold Nicolson, the Huxleys, and the Berensons. The others wanted to talk about Wallis Simpson and the King—it was October, 1936—but Wells insisted on bringing up Spain. Yet, Nicolson noted afterwards in his diary, "He is so intent on finding something quite different to say about it that he might have been talking of dear little Austria."[10] So Wells, in his fashion, stood aside from the battle.* And, after he and the Berensons had gone, the younger generation had its "sad conversation" about Edward and Mrs. Simpson.

Withdrawn into his work on *Finnegans Wake* almost to the exclusion of everything else, James Joyce secluded himself in his Paris flat and ignored the obsessive interest his fellow writers had in the war in Spain. He permitted himself one public appearance in midsummer, 1937, a meeting of the P.E.N. Club, where he vituperated that the major matter of literary concern to writers should be judicial recognition that a writer could not be deprived of his rights in his own work. The piracies of his *Ulysses* were about the only matter which could turn him from his labors on "Work in Progress." A few days later, Nancy Cunard sent him the *Authors Take Sides* questionnaire on the Spanish War. He telephoned her: "I am James Joyce. I have received your questionnaire." When she inquired whether he intended to answer it, he was indignant.

> No! I won't answer it because it is politics. Now politics are getting into everything. The other night I agreed to let myself be taken to one of the dinners of the P.E.N. Club. The charter of the P.E.N. states that politics shall never be discussed there. But what happens? One person made a speech referring to one angle of politics, someone else brought up a conflicting argument, a third read a paper on more politics. I wanted the P.E.N. to take an interest in the pirating of *Ulysses* in the United States, but this was brushed aside. It was politics all the way.

Instead of answering the Spanish War questionnaire, he told her, he would send her the script of his remarks on literary piracy: "Print that, Miss Cunard."[11] Joyce so cultivated disengagement that he even refused to contribute to a magazine in which a writer had taken an anti-Nazi position, because the review

---

* But he did lend his name to a Dependents Aid Committee formed by the Duchess of Atholl to look after the welfare of families of British volunteers in Spain.

was "politically oriented."[12] He did not want his books to be banned in any country because of their author's supposed or apparent political bias.

One writer often accused of not remaining above the battle was W. B. Yeats, whose sympathies had long been with aristocrat and peasant, and who appeared to support General Eoin O'Duffy, leader of a semi-Fascist Irish organization known as the Blue Shirts. Yeats himself wore a blue shirt during the thirties, possibly more for aesthetic than political reasons; yet he must have realized its connotation. And, while Yeats, the most prestigious resident Irish man of letters, affected his blue shirt, O'Duffy was gathering the only really volunteer group to do battle on the Franco side, a Church-blessed battalion of seven hundred Blue Shirts and Irish unemployed who marched to a song by Yeats and had their first taste of battle at the Jarama in February, 1937. It was a wry taste, for the Irish made field contact with a group of Spanish Nationalists from the Canary Islands, and were fired on, losing four dead, and more wounded. Eventually, they were better integrated into Franco's war effort, once finding themselves in the possibly unique position of providing—at the request of Nazi General von Thoma—infantry protection for a German tank advance. By May, the surviving Irishmen had gone home, O'Duffy having contracted only for a six months' engagement— just enough, he hoped, to acquire some headlines at home and enhance his political fortunes as a rival to de Valera. "The Irish who fought for Franco," Brendan Behan quipped afterwards, "appeared to achieve the remarkable military feat of coming home with more men than they went out with."[13]

By the time O'Duffy had gone to Spain, Yeats had become disenchanted, but the Yeatsian marching songs had already been written for the volunteers, such lines as:

What's equality?—Muck in the yard:
Historic Nations grow
From above to below.[14]

Another Yeatsian lyric to march by had a clearly Fascist refrain:

> *Down the fanatic, down the clown*
> *Down, down, hammer them down,*
> *Down to the tune of O'Donnell Abu,*
> *When nations are empty up there at the top,*
> *When order has weakened and faction is strong,*
> *Time for us all, boys, to hit on a tune, boys,*
> *Take to the roads and go marching along.*[15]

One Irish poet ridiculed O'Duffy's pretensions in "Off to Salamanca," a mock ballad:

> *My name is Owen O'Duffy,*
>   *And I'm rather vain and huffy,*
> *The side of every Bolshie I'm a thorn in.*
>   *But before the break of day,*
> *I'll be marching right away,*
>   *For I'm off to Salamanca in the morning.*
>
> CHORUS
> *With the gold supplied by Vickers,*
> *I can buy blue shirt and knickers,*
> *Let the Barcelona Bolshies take a warning,*
> *For I lately took the notion,*
> *To cross the briny ocean*
> *And I start for Salamanca in the morning.*

Somhairle Macalastair's jingling rhymes[16] were an effective counterblast to Yeats's intellectualized verses, but Yeats himself had already disowned them, rewriting them in the hope of making them unsingable. Still, the older versions would not go away by themselves.

Yeats had met O'Duffy only once, and hoped at first that he would mature out of shallow demagoguery into an effective Rightist leader, but by August, 1935, eleven months before war in Spain, he had had enough of the General, although continuing —privately—to espouse benevolent despotism by an educated aristocracy. Afterwards, he refused to take a stand against totalitarianism, but refused also to support it. "Don't try to make a politician of me," he insisted. "Communist, Fascist, nationalist, clerical, anti-clerical are all responsible according to the number of their victims. . . . I am not callous, every nerve trembles with horror at what is happening in Europe. . . ."[17]

Almost every week, Yeats had a visit from Captain Dermot Macmanus, a former Irish revolutionary officer and the one who had introduced him to O'Duffy. "We constantly discuss the war in Spain," he wrote Ethel Mannin. "The last time I met him I suddenly remembered that I did not know on which side were his sympathies and he did not know on which side mine were, except that neither of us wanted to see General O'Duffy back in Ireland with enhanced fame helping 'the Catholic front.' I don't know on which side a single friend of mine is, probably none of us are on any side. I am an old Fenian and I think the old Fenian in me would rejoice if a Fascist nation or government controlled Spain, because that would weaken the British empire. . . . But this is mere instinct."[18]

Publicly, he controlled his instincts. In a poem he insisted,

I never bade you go
To Moscow or to Rome[19]

and in another he was cynical about the efficacy of revolutions ("The Great Day"):

Hurrah for revolution and more cannon-shot!
A beggar upon horseback lashes a beggar on foot.
Hurrah for revolution and cannon come again!
The beggars have changed places, but the lash goes on.

And a verse-editorial, "Politics," was a wry reflection upon a line of Thomas Mann's which he attached as epigraph—*"In our time the destiny of man presents its meaning in political terms"*:

How can I, that girl standing there,
My attention fix
On Roman or on Russian
Or on Spanish politics?
Yet here's a travelled man that knows
What he talks about,
And there's a politician

That has read and thought,
And maybe what they say is true
Of war and war's alarms,
But O that I were young again
And held her in my arms![20]

Yeats remained on the sidelines until his death, in January, 1939, before the war in Spain had ended and a larger war begun; but his earlier reputation as a supporter of Francoist O'Duffy, rather than his disaffection, lived on.

Other Olympians stood aside—surprisingly, in some cases. Crotchety Ezra Pound even neglected his usual anti-Semitism in replying to *Left Review*. He was too preoccupied with his analysis of money-power in the world, and called the query "an escape mechanism for young fools who are too cowardly to think; too lazy to investigate the nature of money, its mode of issue, the control of such issue by the Banque de France and the stank of England. You are all had. Spain is an emotional luxury to a gang of sap-headed dilettantes."[21] Apparently, he found no evidence of usury in Spain, and, though he was basking in the hospitality of Mussolini's Italy, from whence so many miscalled "volunteers" had come to support Franco, he had little more to say. If the Civil War in Spain at least tapped a humanitarian vein in most people, it was something to which Pound was insensitive. It was, he told William Carlos Williams (a pro-Loyalist), of "no more importance than the draining of some mosquito swamp in deepest Africa."[22] And, just after the end of the Civil War, when Pound arrived in New York on the liner *Rex* and was interviewed by newsmen, he was asked whether he intended to see a certain other American writer not long back from Europe. "Hemingway is a good guy," he observed, "but I don't suppose we'd want to meet him personally. Spain."[23]

T. S. Eliot proved a Rightist disappointment, too. As early as the beginning of the thirties, he had praised Sir Oswald Mosley and British Fascism,[24] and might have been expected to announce support for "Christian" Spain. Instead, he wrote curtly, "I still feel convinced that at least a few men of letters should remain isolated,* and take no part in these collective activities."[25]

The *Right Review* complained further that "in England the Left is allowed to create the impression that the poets and the writers, with all the *mana*, are on their side, while good right wing poets like Roy Campbell are neglected." Worst of all, the reason had been traced to the alleged defection of a Rightist stalwart: "Left Wing literary slime is encouraged by a firm of which one of our official *Royalists* (T. S. Eliot) is a director. . . how much further can decadence go?"[26] For a poet then, the Faber imprint had great cachet value, and Faber had been publishing Auden, Spender, Barker, and others, its policy clearly that literary excellence was the criterion for publication. The *Right Review* worried about it in a confused frenzy of anti-Semitism and pro-Fascism. "The power of literature is immense," it argued. "Poets are the creators . . . of human consciousness." For knowledge and wisdom it warned, one had to stay away from the Scriptures: "Let us not forget that the Bible was largely written by the ancestors of the Ogpu*. . . . These people have always known how to use literature (largely nobler stuff ignobly garbled) for their crooked purposes." At the crucial time of the "moral" and "heraldic" war in Spain, T. S. Eliot's apparent withdrawal became cause for outrage among Rightist extremists.

Eliot's flirtation with Fascism had become less and less perceptible over the years, as he came around to the conclusion that the writer ought not use his influence "in an irrelevant way"— in attempting to exert influence in fields in which he was inexpert.

* An Irishman who wanted no part of either side was Sean O'Faolain, who commented, "Don't be a lot of saps. If X and Y want to cut one another's throats over Z, why on earth must people who do not believe in the ideas propounded by either X, Y, or Z have 'to choose between them'? If you want to know, I do think Fascism is lousy. So is your Communism, only more so. . . . For the love of Mike cut loose from this fixation that every artist no longer can have the guts to be what every artist worth his salt has always been—*an individualist* . . ." (To the editors of *Left Review*, printed in *Authors Take Sides*).
* Soviet secret police. Also GPU, and later, NKVD.

It was "the intrusion of amateurs" where nothing useful could be achieved. It was the old question of élitism: whether the political views of a famous poet were of more importance than those of an obscure, but no less affected, human being in a less public occupation. In a publicity-conscious world, where an outspoken statement by a T. S. Eliot would get headline space in the newspapers, while a passionate outcry from an unknown writer might not even make the "Letters to the Editor" columns, Eliot worried that it was "misusing his fame"—whatever the good will which inspired the misuse. "For example," Eliot recalled years later, "during the Spanish Civil War, I felt the less foreign interference there was on one side or the other the better it was. That point of view now seems rather out of date. So many fictions have been given currency. One's duty as a writer is essentially to protect writers in other countries, men like [Tibor] Déry or Pasternak. The writer has a responsibility to express his views on injustices to other writers—as such." Even that was a giant step forward from the Eliot of 1937, but events since the war in Spain had taught the poet still more: "Of course, the writer has other responsibilities *qua* human being, not purely as a writer. It is not good enough for a writer simply to sign letters drawn up by someone else. This is a cheap way out. But there are occasions when a writer should accept any opportunity to express his views."[27] One of those occasions had been the war in Spain, and Eliot's contemporaries sometimes expressed their views about it with rifle as well as with pen; but, in 1937, many of the Olympian voices were confused or still. The writer was an artist, but he was also a human being; and he could speak only with one voice. It was a lesson Eliot learned only after Spain: "An ineffective protest is certainly better than silence. The writer . . . has the responsibility of any decent citizen of another occupation. Acts of tyranny invite the protest of anyone." Perhaps another poet best expressed that feeling withheld from Eliot at the time of Spain:

Tell them in England, if they ask
What brought us to these wars,

To this plateau beneath the night's
Grave manifold of stars—

It was not fraud or foolishness,
Glory, revenge, or pay:
We came because our open eyes
Could see no other way.[28]

6

THE OTHER SIDE OF THE CAUSE

Lies! Let the Leftwing Muse on carrion prey
To glut her sleek poltroons, the vulture's kin.
My only pickings were a ranker's pay,
With chevrons on my sleeve, and on my skin.
          Roy Campbell
          "WARS BRING GOOD TIMES FOR POETS"

BURLY, QUARRELSOME ROY CAMPBELL, the most distinguished—
and almost the only—poet (in English) espousing the Falangist
cause, was, in 1936 and 1937, in the ironic position of having to
compose his Fascist verse-version of the war from "Bolshevik
Binstead." It was his sarcastic name for the farm owned by his
Communist father-in-law, where the poet and his wife were staying, after having fled from Toledo. South African-born, he had
lived in Spain since 1928, staying away from politics while
farming, fishing, and horse-breaking to make enough of a living
to enable him to write poetry. He had always disliked the mostly
left-wing poets of Oxford and Bloomsbury—or, at least from
the time he failed the entrance examinations to Oxford—and
regularly derided their drawing-room knowledge of life as opposed
to his own. An adopted son of the Spanish soil, he saw that way
of life threatened with extinction by the February, 1936 elections,
which returned the country uneasily to Republican control. It
was the first step, he was sure, toward a Communist Spain, and
he began publicly denouncing the Left.

The last straw for the sombrero-crowned Campbell, who usually considered himself more Spanish in temper than most Spaniards, was the imminent betrayal of feudal Spain by Communists, Anarchists, and Jews, the latter whom he decided had deformed Christian civilization through their agents, Marx, Freud, and Einstein. The proof came during the June, 1936 chaos, when extremists of both Left and Right were busy with campaigns of arson, assassination, and pillage. Campbell himself was arrested by two Assault Guards a few miles from his home and brutally beaten across the face with a rifle butt. He absorbed the punishment "contemptuously," knowing that if he resisted it would cost him his life, and that he stood a better chance of survival if his behavior were "stylish." Hands manacled and face bleeding, he was marched at rifle-point into Toledo, maintaining all the while his "swagger," and savoring the "glory" of his crowd-collecting entrance through the Main Gate of Visagru. At the police station he was released with apologies, but the chief of police warned him that even though he was a foreigner, his life would be worth nothing if he provoked suspicion.

Campbell saw anti-clerical demonstrations grow worse, from beatings to church burnings, and was convinced (rightly enough) that the Republican Government could not control the extremism. No coward, he refused to leave Spain. Instead, as a final gesture of defiance, he and his wife converted to Catholicism.[1] It was still a few weeks before the Civil War was to begin, but he had already begun his personal war, "stepping into the front ranks of the Regular Army of Christ." By early August, two weeks after the war began, he was less a soldier in that army than a refugee, en route to an England he had seldom thought of as home. He had barely escaped with his life. On the refugee boat he met Robert Graves, who was later surprised to read about how Campbell had carried his "flowering rifle" in the forefront of General Franco's crusade.

Although a contributor to the rightist journal *Spain* at war's end described the poet as one who "fought in Franco's forces from the day of the Relief [of Toledo],"[2] and Campbell once called himself, in a letter from the "Madrid front" a "Catholic soldier of Spain,"[3] he was actually (and briefly) only a war correspondent for a journal not usually thought of as employing war correspondents, the Catholic *Tablet* (London). What else he did in Spain is puzzling, since, in a subsequent lecture at the Madrid *Ateneo* he confessed that the authorities had discouraged him from volunteering, "since they had enough rifles and not enough pens."[4] Nevertheless, he drew a remarkable picture of active participation in the war in his long narrative poems included in *Flowering Rifle* (1939), through explanatory and "autobiographical" footnotes as well as the verses themselves.*

According to Campbell, he took prisoners, including—at San Mateo—Britishers of the International Brigade. The Englishmen were "far too scared" to surrender to the Spaniards who had sent Campbell to interpret for them, and wanted to give up *"en bloc, to Italians,"* or continue fighting, worried because "they knew what they deserved" from Franco's troops.[5] He portrayed himself, too, as a heroic messenger for the Nationalists, surreptitiously making his way into enemy territory late in the war to take messages to the besieged soldiers in the Hermitage of Santa María de la Cabeza, "which held out for nine months in the middle of Red Territory."[6] Since the poet dated this adventure as 1939, and added that the bastion finally had been reduced by the "16th battalion of the French International Tank Brigade"—although all International units were withdrawn by the end of 1938— the story raises some doubts.† In a poem submitted to the *Right Review* toward the end of the war (again "as a Cath-

* "He has been accused of being . . . a fascist. He was never a fascist. But, a deeply religious man, he fought against the Reds in Spain. . . . I have never known a more vitalising companion, nor one who had stranger adventures. These were sometimes so extraordinary that people who did not know him well could not, at first, believe they had happened. And yet they invariably had . . ." (Edith Sitwell, in *Taken Care Of* [New York, 1965], p. 195).

† Santa María de la Cabeza actually fell on May 1, 1937, to the XIIIth International Brigade, commanded by a German (Zeisser).

olic soldier of Spain," and from "the Madrid front"), he dreamed "of singing to the Reds/ A Jota that would turn their heads/ Were this machine-gun a guitar."[7] In more spectacular active service, he participated—he claimed—in a cavalry charge in which Spaniards and Moors counterattacked tank-led Loyalist infantry, disabling four Russian-manned tanks and forcing the other sixteen to flee.[8] A versatile warrior in print, he served in the trenches as well, "fighting the valiant Asturian miners"— exceptions to his dispraise of Loyalist fighting qualities[9]—and even was wounded in the ranks, according to a violent quatrain:

> *"Wars Bring Good Times for Poets"*
> (Headline in a Daily Paper)

> *Lies! Let the Leftwing Muse on carrion prey*
> *To glut her sleek poltroons, the vulture's kin.*
> *My only pickings were a ranker's pay,*
> *With chevrons on my sleeve, and on my skin.*[10]

Campbell's most dramatic moment in the Nationalist lines came—according to him—when

> *Cooped in a trench, it was my chance to study,*
> *My neighbour for a day or two, a bloody*
> *Unburied arm, left lying in the snow. . . .*

It was, naturally, a Communist arm, with a symbolically clenched fist. The owner—if he were alive—were better off without "the rebel arm," the poet thought; he was set free "with still one arm to beg its way, reclaimed. . . ."[11] The war, or "Great Popular Uprising," as Campbell renamed it, was remarkable, too, for the way the poet had previsioned it. He had prophesied, he claimed, "the British International Brigade and its surrender at San Mateo, long before the Spanish War, in a vision: and . . . actually dedicated his prisoners to his wife in a poem printed before the war!"[12] There had been three hundred British prisoners taken at San Mateo in 1938, and the alleged prophecy had appeared in the dedicatory poem to

Mithraic Emblems, where a vaguely defined surrender is
described:

> But when the bullets whistle
> Up goes the white flag, and down comes the Thistle. . . .

And the captives of the poem are part of a "legion of the lost"
—thus, by extension, men of the benighted Internationals. Pleased
with his prescience, Campbell snickered in *Flowering Rifle* that
he not only *foretold* it—he had *willed* it: "The sword was fathered
by the Pen," and the captives "hog-tied with iambic twine," for
his verse had "drilled them with my pen before my gun. . . ."

Through the jogging rhythms and obsessive anti-Semitism
of Campbell's war poetry appeared the most preposterous rewriting of the history of the conflict. For some reason, it required
rewriting history farther back in time than even Soviet encyclo-
pedias cared about (According to the Campbellian chronicles the
Spanish Armada was the real victor in 1588, not Elizabeth's
England). Through the pervasive scurrility and spite in the dis-
connected portions of verse which make up *Flowering Rifle* one
learns that the destruction of Guernica was a Red hoax, that
General Quiepo de Llano's voice was "like a sunbeam,"* that
the murdered Garcia Lorca was a literary lightweight and a
"coward," that the Nationalists were often so short in arms that
they had to use great stores of weapons providentially captured
from the enemy, that "Red" volunteers outnumbered Franco's
foreign troops four to one, that sexual license was widespread in
the Republican areas (Barcelona being worse than Sodom), while
there was nothing but sanctity and bliss in the Nationalist sectors.

Campbell's vitriol was directed as much against English
writers who had taken up the Loyalist cause—he had been be-
laboring them for years—as against the "Red Republic." Not
only had he "Grown wiser in the company of mules/ Than they
with learned pedantries of fools." They were "red Bloomsbury,"
bought with "foreign cash" to propagandize for a "dead"

---

* His obscene tirades on the Nationalist radio embarrassed even his own side.

Democracy propped up only as a front for the "butchers of the
Soviet":

> As now in England the Triumphant Lie
> Is mesmerizing multitudes to die
> By radio, by newspaper, and worse,
> In literature, in painting, and in verse,
> Where modern Southeys, to the mode who clown,
> For going Red, can bum the Laureate crown:
> While unbought men, who think and understand . . .
> Like criminals are shunned throughout the land—
> As for myself I glory in my crime—
> Of English poets first in all my time
> To sock the bleary monster in my rhyme. . . .[13]

Not only did he disagree with everything his contemporaries
thought: he disagreed, too, on how that thought should be expressed, seeing his Popean heroic couplets as a symbol of rebellion
against Left-inspired license of every sort:

> Free verse and prose are slippers for the dons
> Unfit to clang this marching age of bronze. . . .
> The couplet is a verbal pair of hands
> With a two-handed punch, more clean and deft
> Than his one-armed and butterfisted Left.[14]

There was a Campbellite in England whose praises of the
poet were almost as extreme as the poet's own. It was Count
Potocki de Montalk, Polish émigré editor and publisher of the
self-styled *Right Review*. Not as dull as Douglas Jerrold's Rightist
English Review had been, it pretended to be a literary magazine,
and published the Count's own crackpot outpourings, and poetry
and prose from D. S. Savage, Roy Campbell, and others, as well
as woodcut illustrations, in a crude hand-set, hand-printed curiosity
of literary journalism. The Count was proud of his having been
noticed by Hugh Gordon Porteus in *The Criterion*, and reprinted
the paragraph:

> *The Right Review* is a very different kettle of fish altogether.
> It is not so well printed as *The Left Review*, and it does not draw on
> the same range of established writers, but it is in other respects a

far more interesting production. It appears to be produced rather as a gesture of defiance than anything else: defiance of Catholics, Communists, Jews, Legal Administration, anti-Monarchists and Mr. Rickword. It has the rare negative quality of not being boring at any point. Its Editor, Count Potocki de Montalk, is a persecuted poet and Pretender to the Polish throne. On the face of it, one would say that the pose and the policy are so absurd and so impracticable that the Count might be a paid puppet of the Left. But his ideas are not all so foolish as they look, and his incidental criticisms are pungent and salutary, expressed with wit and vigour. Here is another lonely figure born out of the eighteenth century, to whose spirit he belongs, fighting singlehanded against enormous odds. Merely as a curiosity it should be seen. . . .[15]

His magazine was needed, the Count rationalized, because "In England there is a noticeable reaction to the Right among intelligent people: but there is a lack of literature to voice this feeling. Right writers are undoubtedly boycotted by the self-constituted intelligentsia, who are, as we have said before, the worst enemies of the human race. A writer who values his bread and butter must not 'go Right.' " It was his way of recognizing the fact of literary history that there have been few widely read Rightist writers. The Count would redress the balance. On the next page were two pro-Franco poems by Roy Campbell, that other spirit out of the early eighteenth century.

Not reluctant to name names in his verse, Roy Campbell, with his flowering rifle, shot down a platoon of English writers whose mistakes included being on the wrong side in Spain. Herbert Read and Aldous Huxley had "tender hearts that bleed," while Auden and Spender were harmless mediocrities, and Ralph Bates's "false experience of the land must yield/ To mine both in the letters as the field." Hemingway's *Spanish Earth* film script was singled out for a special rebuttal, Campbell claiming that the film perpetrated a fraud, that the Republic had to "beg for foreign corn," while "on our side the harvest has been rolled,/ Brave as a lion with its mane of gold." Hemingway, Robert Graves suggested, was a kind of Campbellian rival in the poet's mind, for both were

English-speaking outsiders in Spain, and were bullfighters, big-game hunters, and soldiers as well as writers, "though Hemingway imitates the voice of the people and Campbell the voice of the aristocrat." Both thought "very well of themselves as he-men; both despise intellectuals as sissies." Further, Graves wrote, both men "had a romantic love-affair with Spain during the Civil War. Yet not with the same Spain. . . ." In one poem on the subject Campbell even denies that Hemingway's Spanish earth is Spanish:

> *The scum of Europe into it was poured. . . .*
> *And by Brunete you may see in stacks*
> *Dead bodies climbing on each other's backs*
> *To make a huge paella of the plains. . . .*[16]

Flowering Rifle is not the best poem in English inspired by the war in Spain, but it is the longest. Amid its rubbish, it must be said, are satirical and descriptive gems, including Campbell's brilliant explanation and defense of the heroic couplet; and here and there the excitement and pageantry on the surface of the war rise to the surface of his verse in vivid, powerful images. In the dunghill of *Flowering Rifle*, exuberant, combative lines, of which Byron or Pope might have been proud, occasionally do burst into bloom, triggered by the battlefield Campbell's beloved Spain had become. His poem had ended with a sort of prophecy beyond the more fastidious Catholicism of an Alexander Pope, the final tableau disclosing the Blessed Virgin smiling upon her triumphant Fascists. But the arrogance was another prophecy. When the war ended, General Franco received a telegram from the new Pope Pius XII: "Lifting up our heart to God, we give sincere thanks with your Excellency for Spain's Catholic victory."[17] Campbell might have claimed that his magic had worked.

Toward the end of the war, an elderly English writer who liked to think of himself as a poet and historian, but who was more a prose stylist and religious controversialist, came to Spain to visit the battlefields and gain an audience with General Franco. He was Hilaire Belloc, who had already called the General "the man who has saved us all." For Belloc, the religious factor was conclusive: The fate of Christendom—and especially of Roman Catholicism—was in the hands of the Spanish Nationalists. The journey over the bad Spanish roads, lengthened by at least one vehicle breakdown, was exhausting for Belloc, but he was exhilarated by the sight of so many soldiers who were doing holy battle against the anti-clerical Republic. He found the Franco headquarters at Pétrola in impressively good taste—a castle of brown-pink stone, with a broad courtyard. Once it had belonged to the Duke of Villahermosa, and it was there that Cervantes once imagined Don Quixote staying. Franco had just concluded a long cabinet meeting, and was tired; but he gave the elderly author of *The Path to Rome* (1902) ten minutes of his time. When it was all over, the General bade his guest goodbye with "Come and see me again when it is all over."[18] It was Belloc's last pilgrimage.

A two-generation veteran of the literary wars, Belloc was one of the best-known of the few outspokenly Rightist authors writing in English. On both sides of the Atlantic, support for Franco came primarily from Roman Catholic writers, who usually turned to journalism, rather than the "creative" side of authorship, to propagate their views that—to use Belloc's words—"patriotism, the traditions of an independent peasantry and more important than either, religion," required a victory for the rebellion. Rightist journalism itself was often as "creative," or more so, than the opposing propaganda which came from Moscow. Francis Yeats-Brown, for example, the author of *Lives of a Bengal Lancer*, imaginatively described how the Soviet GPU in Spain used metronomes to hypnotize and torture priests, drove prisoners mad by confronting them with "cubist designs," questioned captives under bright lights (already by then a common totalitarian practice), and dosed them with castor oil until they wallowed miserably in their own excrement.[19] Yeats-Brown had been one of the men *English Review* editor Jerrold had considered when helping Franco's emissaries plot the flying of the General out of near-exile in the Canaries to take over the rebellion.

Jerrold himself left few journalistic inventions untried in his own books and articles, which set out to prove that the Franco cause was beyond reproach. Like Belloc, he had had a chance to talk to the great man ("that in itself is a privilege"), and discovered that Franco was "a thousand times more important" than a great man—"a supremely good man, a hero possibly; *possibly a saint.*" The lines appeared in a chapter of *Georgian Adventure* (1937) appropriately titled "The Last Crusade." Elsewhere in his writings, one learned that the Franco regime was utopian in the last degree: "If the national government errs, it errs on the side of informality, of clemency and casualness to friend and foe." Jerrold's war, as he saw it, was a strange one. There had been no rebellion: only a preventive reaction to a Communist plot to take over Spain. There were no sizeable quantities of Nazi or Italian arms or troops in Spain ("only volunteers"), and the destruction of Guernica had been a "Red" frame-up. There were no atrocities on the Nationalist side, and prisoners were given "a fair and public trial." Further, the Englishmen taken prisoner "much preferred their Spanish captors to their late comrades. . . ." The war Jerrold described was an amazing and heartwarming phenomenon, and he went to Spain to see it for himself. "The first thing I saw in Spain," he reported, "were the ruins of the main street of Irún dynamited by [Red] hooligans in the name of progress. There was only one house standing, and it was used as the office of the military governor, who had organized a reception for us. But my eye rested, not on the welcome prepared for us, but on the governor's desk bare of any ornament except for a crucifix, and so, facing the crucified Christ, I drank to the Spanish resurrection."

There were some people in uniform, Jerrold conceded, but it was primarily "a civilians' war":

> As I motored through the whole length and breadth of Nationalist Spain in March, 1937—from San Sebastian to Vittoria, Burgos, Salamanca, Seville, Málaga, Algeciras, Xeres and Toledo to the western suburbs of Madrid—I saw everywhere sights that tugged at my

heart-strings. For this was England again, the England of my youth. In all the open spaces men were drilling—boys and fathers of families and the inevitable drill instructors, and young officers who needed drilling as badly as their own men. And in the lines before Madrid the same memories came to life. The same humour, the same courage, the same queer, heroic and untidy characters, and there, piled against the firing steps, the same rifles with a cork or a piece of yesterday's newspapers stuck in the muzzle.

With Yeats-Brown, Jerrold went as far as the line, even hearing the ping of a spent sniper's bullet as it struck a tree they had just passed. "That was grand," said Y-B. "That was bloody silly," said Royal Navy veteran Jerrold, and ducked into a communication trench. He had not come to Spain to be killed, or merely "to recapture old memories," but "to get the wherewithal to kill new and foul lies. Aha! say the wiseacres, you didn't go with an open mind!"[20] Jerrold's mind was no more open when he left Spain than when he arrived.

Equally frank about his bias was minor Catholic novelist Arnold Lunn, who went to Spain, then prefaced his book about it: "My political prejudices are easy to define. I accept Christian tradition in favour of the economy of the farm, the village and the small town, and against the megapolitan civilisation of the giant cities. . . , and I regard Communism as the final form of the servile state. . . ." The jury, he hoped, "will make allowances for my bias in favour of Nationalist Spain."[21] To make his point convincing beyond reasonable doubt, Lunn suggested to the wavering that "Russia is not the only country in which interesting experiments are being made. Germany has something to teach us. . . ."[22] It was a note struck by a number of English and American devotees of the Nationalist cause. Florence Farmborough, for example, an Englishwoman formerly resident in Valencia, and authoress of *Life and People in National Spain*,* pointed out that "Chancellor

* Its dedication page: "I dedicate these pages with pride and humility to Generalissimo Franco, the great Spanish soldier and patriot, whose faith, nobility and courage have made him and his brave armies invincible in the Crusade against the Common Foe of Civilisation."

Hitler declares that Generalissimo Franco represents Civilised Europe against the savage hordes of Communism."[23] Miss Farmborough steadfastly remained in Spain when the war began, moving to Fascist-held Salamanca where she broadcast propaganda on Sunday evenings to English-speaking countries, "an honour rivalled in magnitude by the happiness which I experienced in being able to give a description of National Spain and of her great leader. . . ."[24] Among her radio talks were pious biographies of Nationalist generals (beginning in hierarchical order with the Generalissimo), inspirational messages about "The Youth of National Spain," "The Woman's Work in National Spain," and "Aspirations of National Spain." Winding up the series with a flourish, she concluded with an educational session on the "Poison-Pen Campaign Within the British Press," which she analyzed as having been influenced "by business magnates of British or Jewish nationality, chiefly the latter, whose lucrative business may have gone awry in the Mediterranean, or in other strategic points . . . by reason of Franco's noble and determined stand against the International Communist."[25]

Another woman writer who lived in Spain at the time the war began was the minor American novelist Helen Nicholson (Baroness de Zglinitzki), who in *Death in the Morning* (1937) wrote what Arnold Lunn called "a beautiful and moving account of life in Granada during the first two months of the war." According to Miss Nicholson, the choice in the conflict lay between "Franco's army in overalls, fighting in the snow of the Guadarramas," which had shown "how far an intrepid spirit can triumph, even over the might and machine-guns of Russia," and "the Madrid Government, composed of Anarchists, jailbirds and Russians, [who] were determined to exterminate every man of brains and outstanding ability in Spain. . . ." In her novel *The Painted Bed*, also about the war, the climax comes when a Republican air raid causes destruction and death, but also brings a vision of Christ upon the cross. The fact that Miss Nicholson was one of the most significant novelists writing in the English language to write "creatively" from the Franco side is indicative of how unevenly the Civil War split intellectual activists in England and America.

To publicize the imbalance in that split, Nancy Cunard had conducted her poll of English writers to find out which side in Spain they backed. The question, somewhat loaded, asked: "Are you for, or against, the legal Government and the People of Republican Spain? Are you for, or against, Franco and Fascism? For it is impossible any longer to take no side. Writers and Poets, we wish to print your answers. We wish the world to know what you, writers and poets, who are amongst the most sensitive instruments of a nation, feel." In July, 1937, the results were published as *Authors Take Sides on the Spanish War*.* Since most of the better-known professional writers in England did reply, including some normally reticent ones, the poll gave a reasonably fair picture of feeling on the issue of Spain. Only five were firmly on Franco's side, while sixteen issued responses which could be construed as neutral or noncommittal. The remaining hundred committed themselves, in varying degrees of passion and at a variety of lengths, to the cause of the Loyalists, Samuel Beckett offering the briefest reply: "¡UPTHEREPUBLIC!"

When returns had begun to come in, Miss Cunard had typed and classified them. By June, she had amassed enough replies to try to interest a London publisher, but none she applied to were interested. But Randall Swingler, who had just taken over as editor of *Left Review*, liked the idea, and as a last resort, she

* The difference in the response since Spain can be seen by comparing the reaction of writers to the Spanish War and the *Authors Take Sides on Vietnam* volume published in London in September, 1967.

Although the very fact of publication contradicted its text, it carefully disavowed any special role for the writer other than his place in the "cross-section of the intellectual community," and many of the 259 contributors explicitly disclaimed any natural right to be heard, either individually or collectively. As the *Times Literary Supplement* (London, September 21, 1967) observed, "It is clearer than ever that there has been a very widespread retreat indeed from the sort of generous and poetical involvement which led some writers to take sides *in* the Spanish War as well as *on* it."

turned over her material to him. Swingler collected a few more
pro-Loyalist opinions, plus a disappointing statement from
Bernard Shaw, and added a list of prominent sponsors. Taking
whatever credit there was for the pamphlet, *Left Review* published
it at sixpence, and inspired the preparation of a similar survey
(*Writers Take Sides*) in the United States.*

Of the five English writers in Miss Cunard's book who took
up the other side of the cause, only three have names which meant
anything to literature after 1937. Succinctly, one answered, "Mr.
Arthur Machen presents his compliments and begs to inform that
he is, and always has been, entirely for General Franco." Edmund
Blunden suggested that "it was necessary that somebody like
Franco should arise—and although England may not profit by
his victory I think Spain will. The ideas of Germany, Italy, etc.,
in your document do not square with those I have formed *upon
the whole* of the recent history of those countries. . . ." Evelyn
Waugh, who complained early the next year when the *New
Statesman* allegedly misused the word Fascist by identifying
gangster tendencies with "Fascist mentality,"[26] was the best-known
Francophile:

> I know Spain only as a tourist and a reader of the newspapers.
> I am no more impressed by the "legality" of the Valencia Govern-
> ment than are the English Communists by the legality of the Crown,
> Lords and Commons. I believe it was a bad Government, rapidly
> deteriorating. If I were a Spaniard I should be fighting for General
> Franco. As an Englishman I am not in the predicament of choosing

---

* Meanwhile, Miss Cunard went about furthering the cause in other ways, sometimes
from the South of France, sometimes from London, even from Spain itself. She
edited and published six numbers of *Les Poètes du Monde Défendant le Peuple
Espagnol*, which contained pro-Loyalist poems by Tristan Tzara, Langston Hughes,
Rafael Alberti, W. H. Auden, Nicolás Guillén, Randall Swingler, Pablo Neruda and
others. She composed her own poems about the war, and had them published in
New Statesman, *Voice of Spain*, *Life and Letters To-day*, and *Left Review*. In the
last days of the Republic she wrote "lucid and vivid accounts" of what was going on
in Spain for the *Manchester Guardian*, and afterwards publicized the plight of Spanish refugees in southern France to try to get world-wide help for them. In a period
of collective action, she had remained independent (Hugh Ford, *A Poet's War*,
p. 279n).

between two evils. I am not a Fascist nor shall I become one unless it were the only alternative to Marxism. It is mischievous to suggest that such a choice is imminent.

On a journalistic trip to Mexico while the war in Spain was going on, Waugh found that war "very much more real" to Mexicans "than any other piece of contemporary history." (Not only was Mexico involved in social revolution and church-state warfare, it was the only nation other than Russia actively helping Republican Spain.) In the vestibule of a public library he found a picture titled "Spain," a depiction of a woman in travail among the bombs, "painted with Indian ferocity; a really frightful picture." The other side of the *Causa* was represented by a taxi driver's Franco flag on the front of his car, and—more significantly to Waugh in contrast to the picture in the library—"a sweet, heady cocktail on sale in the smart bars called a 'Franco.' Even a partisan of Franco like myself, could see something ironical in these two different modes of expressing sympathy."[27]

Nearly a generation later, Waugh made one of his rare visits to Spain—to write a travel piece for a magazine. Time and events had mellowed him, but a view of Franco's monumental *Valley of the Fallen* brought forth his observation that the "great memorial" was "not to victory, but to pacification. . . . While Picasso, in exile, draws doves of peace for the Russians, Franco has kept the peace. Whatever the inconveniences and frustrations of his rule, he has enforced twenty-five years of recovery and consolidation. . . ."[28] Waugh had not changed his mind. But Waugh's persona, Gilbert Pinfold (in the thinly veiled autobiographical novel of 1957, *The Ordeal of Gilbert Pinfold*), is obsessed by a sense of political guilt, so obsessed that in the middle of one of his hallucinations he is impelled to make a truculent apologia to a fellow passenger on the *Caliban*. "I had every sympathy with Franco during the Civil War," he confesses, but "I never had the smallest sympathy with Hitler." And, although Pinfold-Waugh admits that he "once had hopes of Mussolini," he insists that he "was never connected with Mosley." It was as far as Waugh could retreat from the extreme rightist position to which his pre-war romantic toryism had led him.

In May, 1938, the results of a poll similar to the one conducted by *Left Review* were published by the League of American Writers as *Writers Take Sides*. A Communist-sponsored group, but—like the Brigades—not wholly Communist in membership, it nevertheless managed to elicit replies from a wide spectrum of American authors, from Maxwell Anderson to William Carlos Williams. And, again, only a handful of writers announced for the other side of the cause, one of them—E. E. Cummings—doing so by returning the letter unanswered and without comment in an envelope addressed to Donald Ogden Stewart, League of "American" "Writers."

For vehemence, Right or Left, elderly novelist Gertrude Atherton was unmatched this side of Roy Campbell. There was little to choose between Communism and Fascism, she wrote, but the latter had at least the dubious virtue of being "frankly cynical and selfish," not pretending to be democratic. Communism, she thought was "theoretically . . . a finer ideology, but it is the more reprehensible, because whenever it has attained to power it has debased the ideal and enslaved the victims." She professed "no love for Franco," but hoped that "he will mop up the Communists, and send home, with tail between legs, all those gullible Americans who enlisted to save 'Spanish democracy.' Then we can leave Franco to the tender mercies of Destiny. . . . Of course, you will not publish this answer. . . ."

By far the most controversial writer in England to espouse Franco's cause was the novelist-painter Wyndham Lewis, who restricted his civil war pronouncements (but for a novel which appeared in May, 1937) to polemics and painting, in the latter case "The Siege of Barcelona" (later retitled "The Surrender of Barcelona"), now in the Tate Gallery. His tirades quickly earned him a title bestowed by fellow Francophile Roy Campbell, who wrote him—when worried about Lewis's health—"Intellectually, you are Moscardó to the whole of Europe; and we cannot afford to lose you." (Campbell had been busy—at "Bolshevik Binstead" —writing poetry extolling General José Moscardó, the successful defender of the Alcazar at Toledo.) "I gloried in the title of Moscardó," Lewis answered. "You may rely on me to behave on all occasions in a manner in no way inferior to that of the 'Eagle of Castille.'—Pay no more attention to bulletins about my health than you would to the Madrid radio reports of Francoist reverses."[29]

Lewis's major contribution to the Franco cause was his novel *The Revenge for Love*, satirizing, often with great gusto, sham Communists and committed Communists among a London literary and artistic set. Most of Lewis's Bloomsburyites are parlor pinks, whose every feeling is bogus (the novel was originally to be titled *False Bottoms*); but one, Percy Hardcaster, is an inadvertent but authentic gun-running revolutionary hero who loses a leg in Spain, and ends the novel as he begins it, in a Spanish jail. Still, he had not intended to be "a *front-fighter* or anything of that nature, but rather a careerist of the propaganda section: wielding the pen, not the pistol." Back home the hero is exhibited before

an impressive grouping of salon-Reds—of Oxford and Cambridge 'pinks'; a subdued socialist-leaguer; the usual Marxist don; the pimpled son of a Privy Councillor. . . . And there were three sturdy 'independents' ('friends of Soviet Russia') from the headquarter-staff of the Book Racket. The roster contained other fish and fowl and more or less good red herrings. And Percy's protruding artificial limb pointed pointedly at one and all, and his eyes looked over the top of it steadily but not unkindly at the lot of them. But it was a cowed group round Percy—this man-of-action almost frightened them. A veteran of the *Ten Days that Shook the World* would have had less effect than this *grand blessé* of a month's standing. He was a *workman*—that, too, was calculated to provoke almost a panic, in the uninitiated; to whom a communist *workman* was distinctly an alarming notion. They soon got used to this, however. After all he had written pamphlets (and a Red playlet) which Collett's Bomb-Shop carried as a stock-in-trade: this made him more human—almost a 'Leftie' P.E.N. man. . . .[30]

Satirizing Loyalist atrocity stories, Lewis has Percy admit that some of the tales, at least, are propaganda—that hospital nuns did not rub salt into the wounds of the enemy wounded, nor did they refuse bedpans to the needy. They were strictly "Spanish Front" stories, he tells a credulous girl. (" 'That's atrocity propaganada—a most important branch of our work,' he said, swelling very slightly with importance.") It was a more satisfying occupation for a Leftist writer working for the Cause in Spain than "arming its malcontents with Czechoslovakian machine-guns," the novelist suggested. Still, his Percy Hardcaster says, half-believing it, "It's better to have a Cause to live for, than have nothing to live for, after all! Even 'a cause' is better than nothing." It was a hopeless, unrealistic cause for a writer, Lewis ridiculed, for "There had been only fifteen years of communism, but more than twice that number of centuries of fascist authorship. Even when the earth had all turned to Marx, there would still be this ominous shadow on the earth—that is, its time set up against its space—fascist to the marrow, controlled by Athenian and Roman aristocrats. The super-earth, of this dark immortality of *books!* A book was a blackshirted enemy."

Lewis fully intended that his books, at least, would be blackshirted enemies of Republican (therefore, "red") institutions. Like Roy Campbell, he contributed to the *British Union Quarterly* (formerly the *Fascist Quarterly*), having such companions in its table of contents as Mussolini, Goebbels, and Oswald Mosley, and he elaborated his findings about Spain as *Count Your Dead: They Are Alive!*, published in April, 1937, a month before his novel. In it he battled "the Spain of Moses Rosenberg" (Marcel Rosenberg was the Soviet ambassador to Madrid during the civil war), drawing a touching picture of a gallant, ungunned Franco fighting for the heroic peasantry, noble aristocracy, and humble Church against the rich, corrupt, Rosenberg-controlled Republic. The odds against Franco were overwhelming, Lewis diagnosed, making it necessary for the altruistic Germans to help restore law and order, and prevent atrocities the British and French were sponsoring. The cure, to prevent the war in Spain from mushrooming into a larger war, he argued, was to permit those countries opposing "Jewish" communism, particularly Hitler's Germany, to rearm. As late as 1950, five years after the close of the war forced upon Europe by a rearmed Germany, Lewis still saw his 1937 polemic as "a first-rate peace pamphlet."[31] And that war had become "the European civil war, which had begun in Spain. . . ."[32]

Critics have called Wyndham Lewis a great writer; and a few have even labeled *The Revenge for Love* not only as Lewis's finest novel but one of the century's great satires. The evaluation may be a confusion of excess with success. Lewis for many of his creative years suffered from a defective humanity—so defective that it irreparably marred much of his art. "Reality is in the artist, the image only in life," he once wrote (in *Blast*), "and he should only approach so near as is necessary for a good view." Lewis may have approached too closely. "We—the human kind— . . . consist of a group of idiots," his fictional spokesman said in a later novel. "In addition to this degraded caricature of man, there are perhaps a few dozen—perhaps a few hundred men of intelligence. This more intelligent, this more sensitive handful, they are all we need to consider." For the thin column of writers supporting that other side of the *Causa*, this sensitive handful were all marching with Franco.

7

THINGS UNSIMPLE
"Hemingstein" at War

*If you are a writer and, now that you have
seen it, you want to get some of it down
before it should cauterize itself away, you
must renounce the luxury of . . . simplicity.
. . . I would like to hope that, in writing
from now on about this war, I will be able
to do it as cleanly and as truly as Luis Quintanilla draws and etches. . . .*
Hemingway,
Preface to ALL THE BRAVE *(New York, 1939)*
a collection of Quintanilla's
war drawings.

" 'Paper bleeds little,' " *Robert Jordan quoted
the proverb.*
"But it is very useful," Pilar said. "Es muy
útil."
Hemingway,
FOR WHOM THE BELL TOLLS
(New York, 1940).

IN HIS ROOM at the Hotel Florida, within range of the German
batteries on Monte Garabitas, the nearest sector of the Madrid
front, Professor Hemingstein was holding a briefing over the

usual abominable breakfast. Fascist shells often pockmarked the Gran Via and the buildings along it, but the Professor offered a comforting analysis of the situation. He had a large map spread out on the table, and, looking out over his steel-rimmed glasses and bushy mustache, he explained to an audience of correspondents, politicians, and officers that it was ballistically impossible for shells to hit the Florida. "He could talk in a very military way and make it all sound very convincing," Claud Cockburn recalled. "Everyone present was convinced and happy." Then there was "a whistling incoming roar like a subway train,"[1] and a shell—the first to reach the hotel—crashed into the room above. Shards of ceiling plaster obliterated the map of the front.

While they all picked the plaster out of their hair, their unhumiliated host blandly picked up the interrupted threads of his lecture, looking slowly round the table at the whitened faces. "How do you like it now, gentlemen?" he asked; and "by some astonishing trick of manner conveyed the impression that this episode had actually, in an obscure way, confirmed instead of upset his theory—that his theory had been right when he expounded it and this only demonstrated that the time had come to have a new one."[2]

The burly, confident Hemingway—"Hemingstein" to the troops he visited, notebook in hand, enormous flask of whisky on his hip—was somewhat of an expert on military matters, having been wounded in Italy in 1918, and having written a book called *A Farewell to Arms.* The most famous living American writer, his presence was an inspiriting force to the Loyalist cause. He knew it, and performed accordingly.* Once, visiting the Americans of the Abraham Lincoln Brigade, he played his role of war

* "Everyone was very happy to have Mr. Hemingway there, partly because he was obviously a fine man to have around when there was war and trouble, and partly because to have so famous an author there, writing on behalf of the Republic, made people feel less alone in the world—in a sense, which was no fault of Mr. Hemingway, it helped to foster the illusion that sooner or later the 'world conscience' would be aroused, 'the common people' in Britain and France would force their Governments to end non-intervention, and the war would be won" (Cockburn, *In Time of Trouble,* p. 258).

correspondent for the North American Newspaper Alliance but in reality was busy being Ernest Hemingway. He was liberal with his whisky, he was lavish with precious Lucky Strikes and Chesterfields, he asked his reporter's questions "like a big kid, and you liked him. . . 'What then? What happened then? And what did *you* do? And what did *he* say? And *then* what did you do?' " The Government was giving ground all over its dwindling remnants of Spain, and *New York Times* correspondent Herbert Matthews, accompanying Hemingway, was publicly pessimistic. Not Hemingway. Sure the enemy would get to the sea, and cut Republican Spain in two, but it was nothing to worry about: "It had been foreseen; it would be taken care of; methods had already been worked out for communication between Catalonia and the rest of Spain; by ship, by plane, everything would be all right." Besides, Hemingway had heard that President Roosevelt had made an unofficial offer to ship two hundred warplanes to France, if France would deliver two hundred of its planes to Spain. "The war will enter a new phase now; the Government's resistance will redouble; the people of Spain and Catalonia were fighting mad; the political organizations and trade-unions were rounding up replacements; the people were anxious to put a stop to Franco's drive to the sea; the people wanted to counter-attack."[3]

It was a piece of fiction from a practiced fictioneer. Hemingway knew, and the Lincolns knew, after the disaster at the Ebro, that they had been reduced from five hundred soldiers to a hundred and twenty dirty, ragged, hungry, lice-ridden men, nearly without shelter in the cold downpours which alternated with a throbbing sun. They knew, too, that the entire XVth Brigade had only thirteen hundred effectives left, and that supplies would become increasingly meager. But Hemingway personified that part of the world outside Spain on which the Republic's hopes for survival were so groundlessly based, and his courage under fire was as calm—and as consciously foolhardy—as his regenerative optimism. Only when it was all over could he admit it. The war was already lost long before he got there, he thought later—lost when the Nationalists took Irún, cutting off the Basques from the rest of Republican Spain, in the late summer of 1936. "But in a war you can never admit, even to yourself, that it is lost. Because when you will admit it is lost you are beaten. The one who being beaten refuses to admit it and fights on the longest wins in all finish fights; unless of course he is killed, starved out, deprived of weapons or betrayed. All of these things happened to the Spanish people."[4] In Spain, then, Hemingway was living out the philosophy which had always been the motive force of his fiction.

A complex of motives drew Hemingway to Spain. A country he knew and loved was in agony. Its government represented anti-Fascism. An island of resistance to encroaching dictatorship, it stood almost alone. And the experience of war—the re-experience of the tension and the danger and the glory—drew the writer who knew he could never make a personal farewell to arms. Intense as this commitment grew through the early months of the war, it remained an undoctrinaire one, as Jordan explained to Fernando in Hemingway's still unformulated next novel:

"Then you are Communist?"

"No, I am an anti-fascist."

In January, 1937, Hemingway became chairman of a committee formed to send an ambulance unit to Republican Spain, under the auspices of the American Friends of Spanish Democracy, and announced that he would go to Spain shortly himself. The sponsoring organization was, at the least, pink; but there was no political spectrum to medical aid, and Hemingway did not think of himself as a political person. He had already raised $40,000 on personal notes for medical supplies and ambulances for the Republic. From the distance of an ocean, he had done all he could do, and it was time to order his own kitbag from Abercrombie & Fitch.

On February 27, having finished his Florida Keys novel, *To Have and Have Not*, Hemingway sailed from New York on the

French liner *Paris*. To help pay off the notes, he had contracted to report the war in Spain—from the Government side—for the North American Newspaper Alliance. John Wheeler, a Hemingway friend and the executive vice-president of NANA, had suggested the assignment, and, at the opulent rate of about one dollar a word—and with $40,000 in new debts—covering the war for NANA was difficult to resist. (Wheeler protected his news agency from bankruptcy by specifying that no matter how much copy Hemingway filed he was to receive a maximum of $1000 in any working week.) The novelist's assignment, according to the promotional material NANA sent to subscriber newspapers, was to get "both from the bombed towns and bombed trenches the human side of the war, not just an account of the game being played by general staffs with pins and a map."⁵

Although Hemingway had been a successful newspaperman for more years than he had been writing novels, his trip had the outward appearance of a junket, for it was difficult to take seriously an author-correspondent accompanied by the famous Brooklyn matador, Sidney Franklin—especially when Franklin told the press at the dock that he had no interest in Spanish politics and was going to Spain only to fight bulls. Hemingway justified the presence of his friend by describing him as an aide who would "tag along and help Ernie get into trouble and out of it and fight bulls in whichever arena we happen to pass."⁶ But the bullfighter from Brooklyn was denied an American visa to enter Spain on the reasonable grounds that he was not a *bona fide* correspondent. From Paris on March 12 Hemingway cabled his annoyance to NANA: "Jack Dempsey turned newsman overnight, so why not Franklin?"⁷ In a dispatch to NANA published from Toulouse under a March 16 dateline, Hemingway put his rage in better perspective: "On the day on which the American State Department, following its policy of strictest neutrality, refused Sidney Franklin permission to accompany me to Spain as a war correspondent, fearing he might engage in bull-fighting, 12,000 Italian troops were landed at Málaga and Cádiz."

When the State Department remained adamant (one of its better moments in the 1930's, perhaps), Hemingway arranged to have Franklin smuggled over the border, one of the bullfighter's initial assignments being to corner "all the Johnnie Walker in Madrid."[8] It was not a series of gestures to be expected from an engaged writer, and Loyalist-minded American newspaper readers may have wondered whether he was the same Hemingway who had been so outspokenly and idealistically Republican in sentiment the month before. One dispatch from the *Paris* before he had left New York had even quoted him as answering a question about how he expected to react under fire—"when the eggs start scrambling all around," Hemingway colorfully rephrased it— "We're going to take along a bottle of Scotch and drink plenty. We've got it figured out we'll see twice as many shells and not get scared half so much."[9]

Some who wondered how much of the high jinks was façade and whether there was any serious commitment to a cause behind the trip might have pondered something more pragmatic than idealistic in remarks Hemingway had published a year before, in *Green Hills of Africa* (1935)—"about what a great advantage an experience of war was to a writer. It was," Hemingway went on, "one of the major subjects and certainly one of the hardest to write truly of and those writers who had not seen it were always very jealous and tried to make it seem unimportant, or abnormal, or a disease as a subject, while, really, it was just something quite irreplaceable that they had missed." But, perhaps a line later in the same paragraph, he hinted at a restoration in balance: "Writers are forged in injustice as a sword is forged."

Josephine Herbst, who knew Hemingway in Madrid, and had known him well for years before that, thought that he "had answered a definite call when he came to Spain. He wanted to be *the* war writer of his age and he knew it and went toward it. War gave answers that could not be found in that paradise valley of Wyoming where he had fished or even in the waters of Key West when the tarpon struck. What was the deepest reality *there* was in an extreme form *here,* and to get it he had to be in it and he knew it."[10] But few of Hemingway's impulses arose from unmixed motives, and his commitment to the cause of Spain was no less for the junketing atmosphere which surrounded it, and his innermost needs as a writer which the cause satisfied.

Without his Sancho Panza, Hemingway flew into Spain from Toulouse on March 16, 1937. He had arrived in Europe at one of the many low points in the war for the Republic. Some of its best shock troops had been slaughtered at the Jarama, and repeated defeats and retreats suggested that Hemingway would arrive barely in time to witness the end. Franco was again in the suburbs of Madrid, and had already announced his intentions of attending Mass within a week in the Madrid cathedral. The Spanish capital was in the grip of a tightening rebel pincers, and was struggling desperately to keep it from snapping shut north and east of the city, at Guadalajara. Behind Madrid, the enemy controlled the Casa de Campo and all the western approaches, and the shattered buildings of University City were again changing hands, floor by floor and room by room.

At the Alicante airfield, he found everyone celebrating the rare phenomenon of a Loyalist victory—the Fascists had been turned back between Guadalajara and Brihuega. To rush to the battlefield he acquired a car and driver and headed for Madrid, passing through Valencia at five in the morning of the twenty-second. In the gloom before sunrise, there were two hundred men waiting for the recruiting station to open.

Hemingway knew what to expect in Madrid from his old friend Luis Quintanilla, the painter, with whom he had talked in France two weeks before. Quintanilla, then on foreign missions for the Government, had been in the early fighting, even helping to lead the attack on the rebel-held Montaña Barracks. Hemingway wanted to know how Luis's studio was, and whether the pictures were safe.

"Oh, it's all gone," he said, matter-of-factly, explaining that a bomb had gutted the entire building.

"And the big frescoes in University City and the Casa del Pueblo?"

"Finished. All smashed."

"What about the monument to Pablo Iglesias?"

"Destroyed," he said. "No, Ernesto, let's not talk about it. When a man loses all his life's work, everything that he has done in all his working life, it is much better not to talk about it."[11]

The greatest victory the Loyalists were to achieve had taken place while Hemingway was in Paris arranging for his and Franklin's entry into Spain. But there was still the aftermath to see, and Hemingway went out to the Guadalajara front, where, in rain and flurries of snow, the dead still lay where they had fallen. Between the eighth and the fourteenth of March, Loyalist units (including the XIth and XIIth Internationals) had met and contained a Nationalist offensive directed at the northeast approaches to Madrid. Mussolini had committed more than half of the striking force—thirty thousand of his "volunteers" (some of whom, and their families as well, thought they were going to easy garrison duty in conquered Ethiopia). By the time Hemingway arrived, the Fascist advance had turned sour, bogged down by sleet and rain, then turned into retreat by a broad Loyalist counterattack. There had been a three-day lull, while both sides regrouped in the mud. Then, on the eighteenth, after fierce fighting, the Italians were routed, retreating down the Guadalajara road in the opposite direction from Madrid so rapidly that Government troops at first could not maintain fighting contact. Again, as with earlier battles at the Jarama River and the Corunna Road, an attempt to encircle Madrid and isolate it from the rest of Loyalist Spain had been thwarted.

The exhilaration of the victors descended upon Hemingway. A man whose reputation as a writer gave him the world's ear, he had arrived just in time to influence—they hoped—the course of world opinion toward Italian intervention and the Loyalist cause. Although Government casualties had been nearly as heavy as Italian losses, it was clear to Hemingway that what he saw was the aftermath of a major enemy defeat and withdrawal. Along the roads, he reported, "were piled abandoned machine guns, anti-aircraft guns, light mortars, shells, and boxes of machine-gun ammunition, and stranded trucks, light tanks and tractors were stalled by the side of the tree-lined route. Over the battlefield on the heights above Brihuega were scattered letters and papers, haversacks, entrenching tools and everywhere the dead."[12] Up and down the trails through the red hills and plateaus north of Guadalajara, and along the narrow banks of the River Henares, Hemingway went on a guided tour of the carnage. Then, from his hotel room in Madrid, while listening to shells "exploding with a great whoom," he composed an enthusiastic dispatch which declared, "I have been studying the battle for four days, going over the ground with the commanders who directed it and the officers who fought in it. I have been checking the positions and following the tank trails and I can state flatly that Brihuega will take its place in military history with the other decisive battles of the world." Perhaps it would have—had the side which claimed the field also won the war.

The twenty-eighth was the first warm spring day, and Loyalist soldiers savored the quiet and the sun, sprawling with their shirts off and—in the least romantic side of war—"seam-picking" their clothes. Taking Hemingway in tow was Gustav Regler of the Thaelmann Battalion, a German (and then Communist) novelist. The American, he knew, had written *A Farewell to Arms* about the Italian retreat at Caporetto in 1917, and despised the Italians as fighters who ran away from a fight. At the muddy trenches by the battered Arganda bridge, on the Madrid-Valencia road, Hemingway found himself steered by Regler to a battalion in the process of regrouping after the battle. It was at the lower end of the Fascist pincer around Madrid, and in sight of the enemy lines, but an officer was helping to clean a machine gun, and other men were helping a wounded officer onto a motorcycle, to be taken for medical aid and returned as fast as possible, so that the unit would not be left without its commander. Hemingway was surprised to hear all of them speaking in Italian. The wounded man was Randolfo Pacciardi, non-Communist commander of the Garabaldi Battalion of Internationals.

When Hemingway wrote his next dispatch he included references not to the plucky Garibaldis (as the Government's stress was on the Spanish resistance to Italian "invaders") but to the enemy "Italian dead which burial squads have not yet reached. The tank tracks lead to where they died, not as cowards, but defending skilfully constructed . . . positions where the tanks found them and where they still lie."

With Regler's Thaelmanns Hemingway met Werner Heilbrun, the chief surgeon of the XIIth International Brigade (which included the Garibaldis as well).* The day before, when he heard that Hemingway was coming, Heilbrun had remarked, "He could have earned much more fame and dollars on the other side."[13] Hemingway was equally impressed by the idealism and courage of the Germans, all anti-Nazi, many of them Communists—"and they marched like the Reichswehr. They also sang songs that would break your heart and the last of them died on the Muela of Teruel. . . ." The Battalion was, he confessed, "where my heart was."[14] The German Internationals adopted him, from Brigade general on down. Quickly, to them, he became *Hemingstein.*

The General called Lukacz was actually the Hungarian writer Mata Zalka, author of *Doberdo.* Barely forty, he had already lived several lives under several names, fighting under his own for Austria in the First World War, becoming a Russian prisoner of war (and later a Red Army officer), and turning up as "Kemeny," a hero on loan in the Greco-Turkish battle for Smyrna in 1922. It was a brigade of writers. Among others, the Thaelmann Battalion

---

* The Thaelmann Battalion was later transferred to the XIth Brigade, which created some confusion in references to them. Hemingway used the two numbers interchangeably.

itself was commanded by Ludwig Renn (Arnold Vieth von Gols-
senau), author of the celebrated pacifist novel *Krieg*. Elated that
Hemingway had agreed to dine at the officers' mess, Lukacz sent
a messenger to the nearest village inviting all the young women to
come because he was expecting a great writer there as his guest.
Twenty turned up, and all were elaborately introduced to Hemingway. All stayed to help serve, and although the meal "was of
the plainest kind," according to Gustav Regler, "they all wore
their best clothes and served it as if it were a royal banquet. One
of them, Paquita, fixed a high comb in her raven-blue hair and
danced a tango after the tables had been pushed aside, and everything was human dignity and beauty, and the cries of *Olé!* were
tomorrow's music and Hemingway was no longer a guest but the
homecoming brother of everyone in the room."[15] It was no wonder
that Hemingway could recall with such affection those days after
the Guadalajara victory. "I think I can truly say for all those
I knew as well as one man can know another, that the period of
fighting when we thought that the Republic could win . . . was the
happiest period of our lives. We were truly happy then for when
people died it seemed as though their death was justified and
unimportant. For they died for something that they believed in
and that was going to happen."[16]

One day, Hemingway brought Joris Ivens with him to the
Brigade. The Dutch director-cameraman was making a pro-Loyalist
documentary film for which Hemingway was to write the commentary, the project having been financed by "Contemporary Historians," a group sponsored by Lillian Hellman, John Dos Passos,
Hemingway, and Archibald MacLeish. Wandering between the
Garibaldis and the Thaelmanns, with stops among the Spaniards,
Hemingway did more than simply collect material for his NANA
dispatches and assist Ivens and John Ferno with their filming.
Some of his activities were clearly irregular—but, then, so was
his position. On his third day there, Regler found him prone in
the mud beside a young Spanish soldier whom he was teaching
how to use a rifle against "the *caprones,* the Fascists." In his

Basque beret and lumberman's jacket he was everywhere in the zone east of Madrid, his pockets filled—against sudden hunger pangs—with raw Spanish onions, and his large, flat, silver flask of whisky at the ready—but usually empty by four in the afternoon. "Professor Hemingstein with his six-quart whiskey flask," Vincent Sheean once identified him.*

It was Werner Heilbrun who supplied him with gasoline and food at the Brigade hospital, and who often, in the early days, bedded him down at the old-castle-turned-hospital at Moraleja when it was too late to go back to Madrid at night. He even furnished Ivens's film team with transport to some of the attacks, and "a big part of the film that I remember," Hemingway later observed, was "the slanting smile, the cap cocked on the side, the slow, comic Berlin Jewish drawl of Heilbrun."[17] He remembered, too, running with the cameras and "taking cover in the folds of the terrain on the bare hills," and the thirst which came not from the ever-present dust in hair, eyes, and lungs, "but the real dry-mouth that only battle brings." It was part of what he described in narrating the film as "the ultimate loneliness of what is known as contact. Where each man knows there is only himself and five other men, and before him all the great unknown." It was "the moment when six men go forward into death to walk across a stretch of land and by their presence on it prove—this earth is ours. Six men were five. Then four were three, but these three stayed, dug in and held the ground. Along with all the other fours and threes and twos that started out as sixes. . . ."[18] This was the retaking of the Arganda bridge, which took the Valencia road over the Jarama River.

* Quoted in Edwin Rolfe, *The Lincoln Battalion.* Elsewhere Sheean wrote, "This flask, a battered silver contraption of great cubic capacity, . . . had a long career in the owner's service. It had developed a certain flexibility with the passage of years, and when rhythmically pressed between the thumb and forefinger it emitted a tom-tom noise like the drums that accompany a Moorish dancing girl. I saw it . . . under a variety of conditions in Spain, and always with pleasure. The old flask must have been a welcome sight to many beside myself, for it was as inexhaustible as its owner, and as generous" (Vincent Sheean, *Not Peace But a Sword* [New York, 1939], p. 237).

One of the French battalions had been scattered and nearly wiped out in the end-of-March counterattack, and stragglers from it were wandering through the streets of Arganda, looking for wine cellars to break into—"they had much grief to drown," as Regler compassionately put it. Their looting forays were an embarrassing breach of discipline, and André Marty correctly ordered their arrest "to sweat themselves sober," adding that if any resisted they should be shot as an example to the others. On their way to meet leaders of the ragged group, Regler told Hemingway, who was accompanying him, of his last encounter with Marty-directed discipline. Two Anarchist volunteers had lost their heads in an engagement near the Escorial, west of Madrid, imagined enemies everywhere, and tried to stampede their unit into running away. As a brigade commissar, Regler had them taken into custody and brought to him, where he realized that their problem was nervous exhaustion rather than cowardice. To Marty, he reported that he had decided to send the pair to a sanatorium. Quickly, Marty responded. He knew a suitable place, near Alcalá de Henares.* There, Regler had just discovered, Marty had had the Anarchists shot by a Russian execution squad which had already liquidated hundreds of others the paranoiac Marty found to be spies, traitors, cowards or "international criminal elements."

"Swine!" was Hemingway's only comment, as he spat on the ground.

The gesture won over the bitter Regler, who confided to Hemingway "inside stories of operations and crises . . . , feeling certain that he knew what it was all about. I gave him secret material relating to the Party, which he respected, because it was fighting more actively than any other body, although he despised its Martys. He used my material later in *For Whom the Bell Tolls*, . . . brutal interpolations in a work of romantic fiction. . . . He

---

* Not so coincidentally, it seems, Alcalá de Henares was the site of a Soviet-manned airbase, from which snub-nosed Russian Chato pursuit planes flew in defense of Madrid.

depicted the spy disease, that Russian syphilis, in all its shameful, murderously stupid workings. . . ."[19]

At the Arganda town hall, Hemingway offered the demoralized Frenchmen his flask, and asked them about the battle, listening with unfeigned sympathy. They answered without hesitation, while he stood with his flask ready beside each speaker in turn, saying nothing but snorting now and then to show he understood. "The knives of the Moors seemed to flash again, and the survivors raised their faces to the square-figured man in the shapeless jersey and absurd cap. *'C'est défendu, n'est ce pas?'* they asked, and he nodded and gripped their shoulders reassuringly and repeated with an almost childish gravity, *'C'est défendu.'* " When the confrontation was all over, the Frenchmen invited Hemingway to go back with them to the Arganda bridge, to see that they were going back into the line freely and willingly. Surreptitiously winking at Regler, he asked if the request was in order, understanding that whether it was or not, it was the only way both morale and discipline could be restored. Although some in the straggling formation were rifleless, they went off in the direction of the dangerous road they called *l'avenue de la Mort,* Hemingway—who had offered to march at the head of the column —following in the rear. Even to those who had never heard of him before, or to whom his reputation beyond Spain meant nothing, he "had the calming effect of a buffalo straying shaggily over the tundra, knowing its water-holes and its pastures."[20]*

Through the April fighting around Madrid Hemingway was in every sector of the front, from the Casa de Campo and University City in the west to Morata de Tajuña in the east. He was locating material for dispatches to New York. And he was following behind the infantry to film the tanks "as they moved like ships up the steep hills and deployed into action," while—in his descrip-

---

* Cf. Vincent Sheean on a later incident: "I was, to tell the truth, not very alarmed . . . in spite of the definite, instantaneous danger. I suppose this was because Hemingway was pulling us out of it. I had the kind of confidence in Hemingway that a Southern Negro has in the plantation owner ('It's all right, the cap'n's here ain't he?')" (*Not Peace But a Sword,* p. 337).

tion—shells overhead "were sounding like aerial trains" and bombs "like clutches of eggs" made craters in "great towering black flowerings of death." His hotel room at the Florida was barely less exposed than the front line, in one sector only seventeen blocks away. Like others in Madrid, he lived amid the shelling and the random bombs, coming down in his robe and slippers to help into the hotel for aid a woman punctured by a shell fragment, watching a policeman cover a headless trunk, eating what passed for breakfast after passing a charwoman scrubbing blood off the corridor floor. The smaller rooms in the back, the side away from the shelling, were expensive. After a shell hit the sidewalk in front of the hotel, Hemingway moved to a spacious corner room on the exposed side. It cost less than a dollar a day, and after all, no shell (up to then) had actually *hit* the Florida.

At an American hospital on the Valencia road he visited Robert J. Raven, a wounded American who had asked to see him. Behind the wide bandage where there once had been a face, there were no eyes, but only a "yellow scabby area" that "looked like some hill that had been fought over in muddy weather and then baked in the sun." There were no lips, "but he talked pretty well without them and had a pleasant voice." A former social worker from Pittsburgh, he wanted to be a writer, and he and Hemingway talked about books.

"They tell me Dos Passos and Sinclair Lewis are coming over, too."

"Yes," said Hemingway. "And when they come I'll bring them up to see you."

"Gee, that'll be great," he said. "You don't know what that'll mean to me."

"I'll bring them."*[21]

In Madrid that April, Hemingway met another of the many

---

* Raven, who afterwards became the hero of numerous Spanish Aid rallies in the U.S., was—ironically—not wounded by the enemy but by an inept comrade. A Canadian soldier had pulled the pin on a grenade and handed it to him; and before the horrified Raven could heave it into the enemy lines it exploded.

writers who had committed their persons as well as their pens to the cause of the Republic, André Malraux. The author of *Man's Fate* was flying for the Loyalists, somehow managing to bring his aerial coffin back safely each time. Half-seriously, they agreed to divide the war between them: Malraux would take everything up to the Italian defeat at Guadalajara—the part of the war that was already history—and Hemingway would take everything which came afterwards. For Malraux it was no jest, and he turned out copy so fast (too fast, Hemingway later commented to Malcolm Cowley) that his novel *L'Espoir*, afterwards translated as *Man's Hope*, was in print by December of the same year.[22] Hemingway was already planning to do a novel with a Spanish War setting. Eventually he fulfilled his half of the bargain—*his* novel would begin in May, 1937.

After Sidney Franklin had been successfully slipped across the frontier, the matador became the manager of Hemingway's Madrid headquarters, buying the food, cooking the breakfasts, typing articles, scrounging for gas and vehicles, employing one inefficient chauffeur after another, and covering Madrid gossip "like a human dictaphone."* For a while, Hemingway had a "suite" of two rooms on the fourth floor of the Florida, one for Franklin. There was an elevator, but the writer and the matador climbed the stairs: to save electricity, the elevator didn't run. In Hemingway's room was a tall wardrobe generally too crowded to permit it to be used for clothes. Instead, it housed coffee, whisky, ham, bacon, eggs, and marmalade—one of the finest private hoards in Madrid. While Hemingway was film-making he had two cars

---

* Franklin stayed seven months. With no bulls to fight, and few to eat (the matador complained about the quality of the steaks in Madrid), Franklin left not caring "one way or another" who would win the war. Hemingway managed afterward without his services, and even—according to one story—felled a pair of bulls. There were some fighting bulls in the hills surrounding the Lincolns' transport base at Fuencarral, near Madrid. As a result of the war, they had become wild and unapproachable, and several of the drivers, with Hemingway along, went out "on safari." They bagged two bulls, which supplemented rations at the base, but could not have provided steaks of pre-war quality.

assigned for his use, a source of some ill feeling among the irregular and free-lance writers who had none. To them it was no consolation that it was difficult to get a reliable chauffeur—one of Sidney Franklin's major assignments for Hemingway. One driver he acquired was Tomas, four feet eleven inches high and seething with patriotic sentiments and the effects of Hemingway's Scotch whisky. "Long live Madrid, the Capital of my Soul!" he once exclaimed, through a gap of missing teeth, when, returning, they sighted the city "rising like a great white fortress across the plain."

"And of my heart," Hemingway added (". . . having a couple myself. It was a long ride").

Hemingway's love for Madrid was reinforced each time he caught sight of the city again, whether he had been away for the day at a nearby encampment, or had been gone for weeks or months. It even came through the terse cabelese in which many of his dispatches were sent to NANA for extension and translation:

> There were poppy petals in the newdug trench blown from the grassy fields whipped flat by the wind from the snowcapped mountains stop across pinewoods of the old royal hunting lodge rose the white skyline of Madrid stop forty yards away a fiat light machine-gun tapped in sharp deadliness and the bullets passed with the quick cracking sound that makes recruits think theyre explosives stop we sheltered our heads behind the upthrown dirt.[23]

The day after Hemingway had returned to Madrid with the gap-toothed Tomas, they went out again to the Guadalajara sector and were stalled on a muddy road near Brihuega, behind seven lumbering Loyalist tanks. Three planes found the targets, raising geysers of mud around them, hitting nothing but the hillside. The next day, Tomas could not get the car to start, and, the day following, any close call thereafter was the same. Hemingway finally sent a note to the Press Department asking for someone a little more brave. The next driver absconded with forty litres of gasoline—and the car—and was arrested on the road to Valencia. The third, an Anarchist boy named David, was as brave as he was reliable, and had only one defect—he couldn't drive a car. But his vocabularly (it "changed my whole conception of profanity") was so attractively foul that Hemingway and Franklin kept him on to listen to, and briefly solved the transportation problem by driving David.

Two chauffeurs later, Hemingway acquired Hipolito, who *could* drive, wore "an automatic pistol so big it came half way down his leg," and had fought at the taking of the Montaña barracks. During the nineteen-day continuous shelling of Madrid at the end of April, when the main streets were turned into "a glass-strewn, brick-dust powdered, smoking shambles," Hipolito drove around the craters and the rubble. At one point their car was the only active vehicle in Madrid, and it almost lost that distinction during one bombardment, when Hipolito had put the car in a side street and then joined Hemingway for lunch.

> We were still eating when Hipolito finished and went up to the car. There was some more shelling sounding, in the hotel basement, like muffled blasting, and when we finished the lunch of bean soup, paper thin sliced sausage and an orange, and went upstairs, the streets were full of smoke and clouds of dust. There was new smashed cement work all over the sidewalk. I looked around the corner for the car. There was rubble scattered all down that street from a new shell that had just hit overhead. I saw the car. It was covered with dust and rubble.
>
> "My God," I said, "they've got Hipolito."
>
> He was lying with his head back in the driver's seat. I went up to him feeling very badly. I had got very fond of Hipolito.
>
> "I thought you were dead," I said. He woke up and wiped a yawn on the back of his hand.
>
> "*Que va hombre,*" he said. "I am always accustomed to sleep after lunch if I have time."
>
> "We are going to Chicote's bar," I said.
>
> "Have they got good coffee there?"
>
> "Excellent."
>
> "Come on," he said. "Let's go."
>
> I tried to give him some money when I left Madrid.
>
> "I don't want anything from you," he said.

"No," I said. "Take it. Go on. Buy something for the family."

"No," he said. "Listen, we had a good time, didn't we?"

You can bet on Franco, or Mussolini, or Hitler, if you want. But my money goes on Hipolito.

On the eighteenth of May, Hemingway returned to New York on the *Normandie,* and found himself in the turnabout position of reporter being interviewed by the press. Publicly, he was certain that Madrid would not be captured, and that the Republic was gaining strength. "The reason why Franco is out of luck," Hemingway told them confidently, "is that Madrid lies in this big plateau, with all the defensive forces grouped together and fighting from the inside like a boxer; they can make Franco lead every time anywhere along his tremendous front. . . . And each time they are there, waiting for him." Also, he thought, "the coming European war" had been delayed by Republican survival.

Back home, Hemingway applied himself to preparing *To Have and Have Not* for the printer, and appeared to break the continuity of isolation of his heroes in a post-Spain revision of the ending. The revelation of outcast Harry Morgan, dying in his launch, became one which the author had recently received: " 'No matter how a man alone ain't got no bloody f---ing chance.'

"He shut his eyes. It had taken him a long time to get it out and it had taken him all his life to learn it."

The theme was much the same in his commentary for Ivens's film, *The Spanish Earth,* which he revised for the edited version, and then took to the White House on July 8 for an advance private showing to President and Mrs. Roosevelt. There had been a public preview of two sequences from the film a month before at a standing-room-only and turn-away crowd at Carnegie Hall on the evening of Friday, June 4, the opening session of the militant Second American Writers' Congress. Archibald MacLeish was in the chair, and Joris Ivens introduced the scenes from the film, after which Hemingway delivered the first—and the last—public address of his life.

Before the meeting, Walter Duranty of the *New York Times,*

Hemingway, John Gunther, and F. Scott Fitzgerald had dinner together. Hemingway was nervous, and confessed that he had no last line for his speech. "You should know," Duranty told him, "that the last line of a speech is the most important." But Duranty's own remarks were less than memorable, and when he stormed up to a point that needed emphasis he shouted, "See!"[24] Afterwards, *Time* (June 21) pictured Hemingway, bespectacled, mustached, and heavy-set, above a caption reading *"Walter Duranty: He pounded with his cane"*; and the leaner, older Duranty was shown with the line *"Writer Hemingway: No one becomes accustomed to murder."*

"A writer's problem," Hemingway said, "does not change. He himself changes, but his problem remains the same. It is always to write truly and having found what is true, to project it in such a way that it becomes a part of the experience of the person who reads it." One thing he thought he had learned, watching "some new friends and some of long standing . . . live and fight and die," was that there were "worse things than war. Cowardice is worse, treachery is worse, and simple selfishness is worse." He left little ground for optimism for the writer in his time:

> . . . It is very dangerous to write the truth in war and the truth is also very dangerous to come by. I do not know which American writers have gone out to seek it. . . . and when a man goes to seek the truth in war he may find death instead. But if twelve go and only two come back, the truth will be the truth and not the garbled hearsay that we pass as history. Whether the truth is worth some risk to come by, the writers must decide themselves. Certainly it is not more comfortable to spend their time disputing learnedly on points of doctrine. And there will always be new schisms and new fallings off and marvelous exotic doctrines and romantic lost leaders, for those who do not want to work at what they profess to believe in, but only to discuss and maintain positions, skillfully chosen positions with no risk involved in holdings them. Positions to be held by the typewriter and consolidated with the fountain pen. But there is now, and there will be from now on for a long time, war for any writer to go to who wants to study it.[25]

Collections taken at subsequent showings benefited the Loyalist cause, but Hemingway did not remain in the U.S. for them.
By the middle of August, he was off on the *Champlain*, and, by
September, was back in Spain, this time on the Aragon front, with
the Americans of the XVth Brigade. There was no longer any
desire to report from the bastions of the decimated Thaelmanns.
"When we've won," Werner Heilbrun had told Regler in a rare
moment of optimism, "I shall accept Hemingway's invitation to
Key West. He has told me about his boat, and about landing
two-hundred-pound fish. I've never done any fishing, but perhaps
one can just lie on deck and watch the fins cutting through the
water, and then turn over on the other side and see the bottom
and the coral growing."[26] They had been sitting high above the
medieval walls of Huesca, in the surrounding hills, grown gray
with the late dusk of mid-June. Huesca never fell, but in the
attempt and its aftermath Lukacz was cut down by a shell and
Heilbrun died in a strafing attack by an enemy plane. "I think
I cried when I heard Lukacz was dead," Hemingway thought. "I
don't remember. . . . Everyone else who had been killed was re-
placeable. Werner was most irreplaceable of all; but he was killed
just afterward. . . . There is no man alive today who has not cried
at a war if he was at it long enough. Sometimes it is after a battle,
sometimes it is when someone that you love is killed. . . ."[27]

Meanwhile, in the U.S., *To Have and Have Not* had been
published. It was dull, complained Sinclair Lewis—and Spain
was at least partly to blame. "Please, Ernest!" he appealed in his
short-lived "Book Week" column in *Newsweek.* "You could have
been the greatest novelist in America if you could have come to
know just one man who wasn't restricted to boozing and wom-
anizing. Perhaps you still can be. Please quit saving Spain and
start saving Ernest Hemingway."[28]

When Hemingway caught up to the Americans of the XVth
Brigade, they were resting under a grove of Aragonese olive trees,
by a small stream, recuperating from the storming of a fortified
Nationalist town sixty miles south of Huesca. Since he had last

seen them, in the spring, they had "become soldiers. The romantics
have pulled out, the cowards have gone home. . . ." At heavy cost,
they had just taken Belchite, which had been surrounded for
months. It had been a three-day battle fought at the kind of close
quarters seen earlier in University City, going "from house to
house, from room to room, breaking walls with pick-axes, bombing their way forward as they were shot at from street corners,
windows, rooftops and holes and walls by the retreating Fascists."
When it came to courage, Hemingway recognized only its quality,
and not the flag under which it was demonstrated, describing how
American and Spanish troops effected a juncture which cut off
the last four hundred Nationalists of the town garrison inside the
cathedral. "These men," he wrote, "fought desperately and bravely
and a Fascist officer worked a machine-gun from the tower until
a shell crumpled the masonry of the spire on him and the gun."
Finally, there had been a final rush at the cathedral square, and
"after some fighting of the sort you never know whether to classify
as hysterical or the ultimate in bravery," what was left of the
garrison surrendered.

Leader of the final assault had been Robert Merriman,
brigade chief of staff, whom Hemingway identified as "a former
California University professor." Actually, Merriman had been
an economics instructor at Berkeley, working on his doctorate in
economics there, after undergraduate study at Nevada. There was
probably something of the six-foot-two major in the Robert Jordan
of Hemingway's next novel—a volunteer who has left his university in the West (Montana), where he had been a teacher, to
take up the cause of Spanish freedom.

Through the early autumn Hemingway and Matthews bounced
about the hills of Aragon in an open truck, visiting front-line
observation posts by day, drawing back at night to sleep in the
rear of the truck, cooking the food they had brought from Valencia
over open fires in village houses. It was "a fine life," he thought,
"but the donkeys wake too early and make too much fuss about
it and the chickens do not know how to leave sleeping correspond-

ents alone." At the end of September, he went back to Madrid to listen to the shelling, scrounge for some non-Spanish Scotch whisky—and write a play. The local drinks with alcoholic content he found unsuitable "for internal use," and employed one pseudo-English concoction called "Milords Écosses Whisky" as an after-shave lotion: "It smarts a little but feels very hygienic. I believe it would be a possible cure for athlete's foot, but one must be very careful not to spill it on one's clothes because it eats wool."

The play was finished by the middle of November. Set mainly in the Hotel Florida, where most of it was written, it was *The Fifth Column,** about a daydreamed extension of the author, a correspondent named Philip Rawlings, an attractive heel who files no dispatches home and is busy with a mistress. But even she does not know how involved he is with the cause, as a counter-spy for the International Brigades. Rawlings' choice is between the old life (the girl's real name, Hemingway notes, "might also have been Nostalgia") and staying on in Madrid. He chooses war ("I've signed up for the duration").

Written "by popular demand" of the foreign correspondents who used the Florida as headquarters,[29] it showed that Hemingway had retained his ear for dialogue; but it suffered, too, from its made-to-order origins, and bogged down in concocted melodrama. There was probably a good play to be developed out of the hot observation post called the Florida, but no one ever wrote it. Like much of the writing done in the white heat of events it described, *The Fifth Column* remained more artifact than art. Hemingway's own apologia for the work appeared in the preface to the published play: "While I was writing this play, the Hotel Florida . . . was struck by more than thirty high explosive shells. So if it is not a good play perhaps that is what is the matter with it."

---

* The phrase, often associated with Hemingway because of the play, originated in a radio speech by Fascist General Mola, who boasted that his four armed columns attacking Madrid would be assisted by a "fifth column" of Franco agents and sympathizers within the city.

The next month, with the International Brigades inactive (having earned a rest in reserve), Hemingway travelled to the southern tip of the Aragon front, where the drab, walled Nationalist city of Teruel was under seige. The attack had begun in zero weather, soon made worse by intermittent blizzards and "a wind that made living a torture." It was, for internal political reasons, an all-Spanish counteroffensive—at first—beginning with the capture of the ridge to the west of the town known as the *Muela de Teruel*—the tooth of Teruel. "Across a country cold as a steel engraving" Hemingway watched the battle, drove all night through the snow in order to file his story in Madrid, then drove all night again in the "Siberian weather conditions" to get back to the Teruel sector—"with two frozen fingers and eight hours nonconsecutive sleep in the last seventy-two."

Toward the "great yellow mass of the Mansueto, the natural, battleship-shaped fortress" which defended Teruel, he advanced with the infantry under heavy machine gun and rifle fire. The view of the battle "was splendid," but the soldier lying next to him was having trouble with his rifle, which jammed after every shot. Hemingway showed him how to pound the bolt open with a rock. As the weather cleared, he moved forward with the troops, over the Mansueto and up the last slopes to the town. "In the pleasant autumn-feeling dusk" Hemingway (looking like "Wallace Beery three years back") and Matthews ("like Savonarola") then took the road downhill into Teruel with an infantry unit. "It was a peaceful feeling night and all the noises seemed incongruous. Then in the road was a dead officer who had led a company in the final assault. . . . we lifted him, still limp and warm, to the side of the road, and left him with his serious waxen face where the tanks would not bother him now, or anything else, and went on into the town. . . . We had never received the surrender of a town before. . . ."

Hemingway's dispatch was dated December 21, 1937. Barely a week later, Franco's counterattack began, not soon enough to relieve the town (in which resistance actually continued until

January 8), but soon enough to encircle it and put the captors under seige. In desperation, then, the Internationals were called in, but the Army of Africa and the army of Il Duce recaptured the city in February, in the last two days taking seven thousand Loyalist prisoners and a hoard of munitions, weapons, and vehicles. There were fifteen thousand other Republican casualties, including trapped Canadian, American, and German Internationals who had been desperately awaiting reinforcements which never came. These were the "foreign Reds" whom Franco's publicists had reported arriving in overwhelming numbers, a story intended to justify the continued German and Italian military presence. After the battle, Franco reported to Germany that he had found "very few" foreigners among the 14,500 captives taken. This fact, he suggested, had to be kept "strictly confidential." The "foreign Reds" Franco had hoped to display in great quantities as prisoners had apparently fought to their deaths.[30]

By the time the Teruel siege had boomeranged on the Loyalists, Hemingway had gone home—to attempt to get his Madrid play* into production.[31] Still, he insisted—with less force than before—that the Republic could yet win the war—"if the Italians don't send any more troops." The Hemingway who had "accepted" the premature surrender of Teruel had little else now to provide any excuse for optimism.

At Key West, Hemingway chafed and brooded. When he decided that he wanted to be back in Spain, he tried to sail secretly on the *Ile de France*, having his name kept off the list of passengers, loading no baggage and boarding the ship hatless and without overcoat. The stratagem failed: he was too public a personality not to be noticed. By the time he disembarked at Le Havre, the military situation had grown worse, the Loyalists still reeling back after the Teruel disaster. An old hand now, he knew what to

---

* In New York, John Gassner, then play reader for the Theatre Guild, had, to his surprise, received a copy of *The Fifth Column* from the hands of a uniformed Spanish army officer—who brought it over from Spain for Hemingway apparently as an adjunct to the official business which brought him to the U.S.

order in France to take over the Pyrenees—a stock of food, plenty of whisky, some large cans of gasoline, and quantities of what was more useful than money, American cigarettes. (His Spanish Government customs pass permitted it all to enter Spain without examination.)

When the eight-fifteen moved out of the station in Paris en route to the border town of Perpignan, Hemingway turned from a scrutiny of the crowded platform, now receding, to Vincent Sheean. "Are you *muy emocionado?*" he inquired. When Sheean said no, Hemingway explained the lack of feeling as old age. Nearby was a thin young man with horn-rimmed glasses and brown tweed coat, and Hemingway introduced him to Sheean. It was Jim Lardner, Ring's son, on his way to try to make himself useful in Spain while on his vacation time from the Paris edition of the *Herald Tribune.* "One of you has to decide," Hemingway joked, "which is the *chef de bureau,* since you're both from the *Herald Tribune.*" Adjourning to Sheean's compartment, the three writers—veteran, comer, and fledgling—gossiped over "copious draughts" from the capacious Hemingway flask. "I don't know why you're going to Spain, anyhow," Hemingway said to Sheean, thinking of the fact that Barcelona was again in danger of falling. "You can't get a story there. The only story you could get would be to get killed, and that'll do you no good: I'll write that."

"Not half as good a story as if you get killed," Sheean said, "and I'll write that." Lardner thought it was one of the most hilarious exchanges he had ever heard, and threw himself back on his seat and roared.[32]

It was dark when they arrived in Barcelona, but not dark enough to hide the damage done ten days earlier by three days of Italian air raids, the most concentrated bombing of a large city since aircraft had been used in war. An enraged Hemingway began adding editorial-like polemics in a new pictorial, *Ken,* to his newspaper contributions. He had the massive Italian intervention uppermost in his mind, warning *Ken*'s readers that unless an Italian defeat in Spain made Hitler lose confidence in his potential ally, "You will have to fight tougher people than the Italians, and don't let anybody ever tell you you won't."[33] Hemingway had arrived in Catalonia in time for the Republican withdrawal from Lérida and Gandesa, on April 3. In Gandesa, one hundred forty British and Americans of the XVth Brigade had been taken prisoner, after a courageous rear-guard action which had held up the enemy advance long enough for the main body of Republican troops to regroup. Some who got through to their own lines had to swim the cold, fast flowing Ebro River naked, and then find their way past crowds of bedraggled refugees who clotted the roads to the east.

Three of those who made it to the other side of the Ebro were without clothes but for a hat which one of them, in the excitement, forgot to remove. Between riverbank and the road stretched a field of cockleburrs. They wavered, but there was no choice other than to cross it, barefoot. When they reached the road they lay down alongside it, exhausted, and no longer caring whether friend or enemy came by first. What happened was normally only the substance of daydreams—a new Matford roadster came along and stopped by them, and Hemingway and Matthews jumped out. They hugged the dumbfounded Americans, then shook hands, while Hemingway, "speaking in explosions," filled in the naked men—one (John Gates) dressed still only in a damp cap—on the rapidly worsening military situation. Then, turning toward the Ebro, Hemingway shook his hairy fist in the direction of the enemy. "You Fascist bastards!" he cried. "You haven't won yet. We'll show you."[34]*

The town next in the way of the enemy was Tortosa, and

---

* Gates's story differs from Hemingway's laconic dispatch, which only reported that "John Gates, Joseph Hecht and George Watts, had swum the Ebro River opposite Miravet. When we saw them at noon they were barefoot and had just been given clothes. They had been naked since they had crossed the river at daylight. . . ." Edwin Rolfe (in *The Lincoln Battalion*) quoted Gates in 1939 as saying that *four* men (he added Lewis Gayle) had made it across the Ebro. "Naked and shivering," Rolfe added, "they made for the road and stopped a truck, from which they salvaged bits of clothes—a shirt, a coat and two pairs of ragged trousers. They were dressed in these odds and ends when they reached the remnants of the brigade."

Hemingway, staying dangerously close to the very fluid front, reported optimistically that it could be defended. But the defenders were desperately tired, ill-supplied, and disheartened, making inevitable Franco's march to the sea, to cut what was left of the Republic from Barcelona—and what remained of Catalonia. It was heartbreaking for Hemingway to see positions almost naturally impregnable given up so easily, and, in discouragement, he wrote that the Nationalists were advancing north to the French border and eastward to the sea "in a country where positions could be held by determined graduates of any good girls' finishing school."

Soon Hemingway had to retreat in the direction of Barcelona, only one ridge between him and the enemy. German bombers had already made all the major crossings of the Ebro impossible; but Hemingway and his driver found a small bridge which was being repaired with planks. Along an acrid-smelling road, pitted with bomb craters, they threaded the car, only to find a mule cart on the bridge approach. "You cannot go there!" a guard shouted at the farmer leading the cart, heavily laden with grain, cooking pots, household goods, and a jug of wine. "But the mule had no reverse and the bridge was blocked. So I pushed on the wheels, the peasant hauled on the mule's head and the cart rode slowly forward followed by the car. . . ." On the Ebro delta, near the sea, "the artillery were still only warming up like baseball pitchers lobbing them over in the bull pen."

One of the refugees he had caught up with before the Tortosa withdrawal was another old man, this one without mule or cart. He had been the last one to leave his town before the Fascists arrived, having stayed behind to take care of his two goats, one cat, and four pair of pigeons. Now he was sitting by the side of the road, too tired to go on.

> "And you have no family?" I asked, watching the far end of the bridge where a few last carts were hurrying down the slope of the bank.
> "No," he said, "only the animals. . . . The cat, of course, will

be all right. A cat can look out for itself, but I cannot think what will become of the others."

"What politics have you?" I asked.

"I am without politics," he said. "I am seventy-six years old. I have come twelve kilometers now and I think I can go no further."

"This is not a good place to stop," I said. "If you can make it, there are trucks up the road where it forks for Tortosa."

"I will wait a while," he said, "and then I will go. Where do the trucks go?"

"Towards Barcelona," I told him.

"I know no one in that direction," he said, "but thank you very much. Thank you again very much."

.   .   .

There was nothing to do about him. It was Easter Sunday and the Fascists were advancing toward the Ebro. It was a gray overcast day with a low ceiling so their planes were not up. That and the fact that cats know how to look after themselves was all the good luck that old man would ever have."[35]

At first only a cabled dispatch from Barcelona, the vignette—when Hemingway recognized it as a contemporary parable—was reclassified as a short story and added to the canon (while four later, longer tales of Spain he published as short stories were never considered by their author as worthy of permanence). He might have similarly translated his dispatch about the farmer and his mule cart. Probably *he*, too, knew no one in the direction of Barcelona, but the difference was one of awareness—he had not yet experienced the desolateness of recognizing the fact. Or that a cat—but not a man—can look out for itself. Both were central experiences of an age of war and unreason.

The first of the short stories designated as such was "The Denunciation" (*Esquire*, November 1, 1938). It concerned a Fascist former customer of "Chicote's Bar" in Madrid who is recognized by one of the old waiters and—with reluctance—denounced to the *Seguridad*. A lightweight piece, it is most memorable for Hemingway's consistent and unideological willingness to see virtues he admired in people who fought against the *Causa*. "Most of Chicote's old customers are on Franco's side," the story pointed out; "but some of them are on the Government side. Because it was a cheerful place, and because really cheerful people are usually the bravest, and the bravest get killed quickest, a big part of Chicote's old customers are now dead." The second, "The Butterfly and the Tank" (*Esquire*, December, 1938), was set again in the same café, and told of the pitiful, meaningless shooting of an over-gay civilian who had annoyed the patrons by spraying an elderly waiter with perfume from a flit-gun he had bought for a wedding joke. In a city under seige, where everyone displayed ill-concealed strain, the forced gaiety was as much the product of the seige as it was Chicote's alcohol. It was, said the manager, a result of the man's gaiety coming "in contact with the seriousness of the war like a butterfly. . . . Like a butterfly and a tank."

The body lay like a dead sparrow, waiting for the man's wife to claim it. "And I sat there . . . and looked out of the sandbagged window and thought of the wife kneeling there and saying, 'Pedro. *Pedro*, who has done this to thee, Pedro?' And I thought that the police would never be able to tell her that even if they had the name of the man who pulled the trigger."

The story, like the others, was based closely upon an incident in a real bar in the Gran Via between the Puerta del Sol and Cibeles, the only place which had real Scotch whiskey left. Even the minor characters were photographically drawn from witnesses to the incident, poet Langston Hughes discovered, and the incident itself little embellished:

> What led up to the shooting that afternoon was that a ragged little Spaniard of middle age had wandered drunkenly into the de luxe bar filled with foreigners, top-echelon army men and government officials. In his hands he had, of all things, a flit gun. With alcoholic good humor the little man began to spray people with flit. Some Spaniard at the bar objected to this. When the man kept on, an argument developed. The little drunk called the other man a few bad names. Spanish cursing is vile indeed. We have nothing like it in English. The Spaniard at the bar drew a pistol and shot the little

drunk dead. From this real-life episode Hemingway fashioned a fictional story.[36]

All that Hemingway had inserted was a motivation for the flit-gun's purchase.

The last of the *Esquire* stories, "Night Before Battle" (February, 1939), was the first in conception, drawn from an incident which had occurred while Hemingway was helping film *The Spanish Earth*, early in 1937, when the Nationalists were stopped at the Casa de Campo and University City. It was a story he could not have released earlier, while there was still hope for the Republic, and while a semblance of Popular Front unity permitted the world to think that all the political shades of the left had made common cause. Its hero is Al, an American volunteer— and a Communist—who serves with the tanks defending Madrid. The villain: war, in the form of the weak government of Premier Largo Caballero, unequipped to make military decisions, yet often determining strategy.

In Chicote's, Al confides to the narrator that he expects to be killed in the next morning's poorly conceived attack. "I don't mind dying a bit," he says. "Dying is just a lot of crap. Only it's wasteful. The attack is wrong and it's wasteful. . . ." Now that he "can handle tanks good," and is able to train new tankers, his experience will go down the drain. Offered various consolations for the evening, including a girl from Ceuta ("No, I'm going to see plenty of Moors tomorrow without having to fool with them tonight."), he snaps out of his depression with "And don't give me any pep talk either because we've got a political commissar and I know what I'm fighting for and I'm not worried. But I'd like things to be efficient and used as intelligently as possible."

The old waiter, whose twenty-year-old son is with a Loyalist machine gun company, asks how things are in his son's sector, and Al's response is, "What party are you, Comrade?"

"I am of no party," the waiter says. "But my boy is a Communist."

After some vaguely optimistic talk in communiqué-jargon,

Al adds that the waiter need not worry about his son ("It's fine up there"). "God bless you," the waiter says as they leave the café. "God guard you and keep you."

"Jees," Al says outside in the dark street, "he's kind of confused politically, isn't he?"

Later, with bar hours over, a mob congregates in the narrator's hotel room (much as in Hemingway's at the Florida): camp-following females, the camera crew, correspondents, a couple of mercenary pilots (flying for the Government at a thousand dollars a month), and Al (there to take a bath). "What kind of money do they make?" one of the pilots asks, looking toward Al.

"They get ten pesetas a day," I said. "Now he gets a lieutenant's pay."

"Spanish lieutenant?"

"Yes."

"I guess he's nuts all right. Or has he got politics?"

"He's got politics."

"Oh, well," he said. "That explains it. . . ."

The long story, crowded with people and small talk, conveys as much of the atmosphere of a segment of besieged Madrid as anything which has appeared in print; and in Al, the politically committed volunteer, about to die uselessly in a foredoomed attack, Hemingway had symbolized the futility of a Cause. He may not have produced "literature" in the documentary "Night Before Battle," but he had written a chapter of the history of his time.*

While in England the references to Italy and Germany were being removed from *The Spanish Earth*, so as not to offend the *Duce* and the *Fuehrer*, a Spanish-language version of the film had its premiere in Barcelona on April 25, 1938—a showing inter-

* There were also two other stories, published in *Cosmopolitan*, the first of them "Nobody Ever Dies" (March, 1939). The second was "Under the Ridge" (October, 1939), which tentatively made a few points Hemingway was also underlining in his novel-in-progress, but again failed to make the canon of collected stories, the fate of the *Esquire* pieces.[37]

rupted for forty minutes by an air raid alarm. In the audience was Hemingway, who was applauded for five minutes when someone discovered him there and pointed him out. He was still trying to report the war from a now divided Spain, which meant going from Catalonia to the Valencia-controlled area—Murcia, Alicante, and Castellón—by air, skirting the Franco-held coast. It was also the only way to get from Barcelona to Madrid, where he had not been since the previous December, before communications had been cut.

Valencia always seemed to Hemingway to be half a world apart from embattled Madrid and turbulent Barcelona. The countryside was lush and the city relatively unscarred by bombers. The transplanted Republican capital, it was the home of Government offices and the Press Bureau, and even had—as a result of these—a social life far more normal than in Madrid. As late as May, 1938, when Spain was fragmented and reeling, he found "six varieties of hors d'oeuvres, excellent meat stew, and unlimited oranges," and cafés as well-stocked as the restaurants. It was at the Press Office in Valencia that Stephen Spender had once met Hemingway, and concluded at first sight that he did not belie the impression of his appearance suggested by his novels. But Spender wondered how an author "whose art concealed under its apparent huskiness a deliberation and delicacy like Turgenev" could reveal outwardly so little of this inner sensibility. One afternoon a glimpse of the "esthetic Hemingway" Spender suspected appeared when the pair were walking through the streets of Valencia. Making conversation, Spender observed that the bookshops in the city had nothing but Spanish and a little French literature, and since he had no books with him he was thinking of acquiring a copy of Stendhal's *La Chartreuse de Parme*, which he had never read. Hemingway commented "that he thought the account at the beginning of the hero, Fabrice, wandering lost in the middle of the Battle of Waterloo, with which La Chartreuse opens is perhaps the best, though the most apparently casual, description of war in literature. For war is often really like that,

a boy lost in the middle of an action, not knowing which side
will win, hardly knowing that a battle is going on. He warmed to
the theme of Stendhal, and soon I realized that he had that kind
of literary sensibility which the professional critic . . . nearly always lacks." Looking for an opening to continue the conversation
Spender mentioned the battle scenes in Shakespeare. Switching
personae, Hemingway suddenly reacted with annoyance: "Why
do you talk to me about Shakespeare? Don't you realize I don't
read books?"[38] For the rest of the walk, he was a Hemingway
character, talking about boxing, confiding that he had come to
Spain to see if he would lose his nerve under fire, suggesting that
Spender was "too squeamish." By then they had reached a
taverna on the shore. Inside were some gypsy players. Seizing a
guitar, Hemingway began singing Spanish songs.

The somewhat unreal atmosphere of Valencia suggested that
things might not be as bad as they really were, and Hemingway
looked hard for reasons for optimism in the steadily deteriorating
military situation. Paradoxically, he found it in the inherent
separatist tendencies among Spanish regions: "Madrid now has a
war of its own and is proud of it. Extremadura and Andalucía
have their war and do not have to worry about Catalonia. . . .
Catalonia is fighting on her own now and considers she has something worth fighting for. It's a strange country all right, and
history has proved that when you divide it is when it becomes
most dangerous. United, there has always been sectional jealousy.
Once divided, comes the pride of province, of section, of city and
of district. Napoleon found this out to his defeat and two other
Dictators are discovering it today." It was whistling in the dark,
but he was right—almost right—in concluding from the solidarity
of Madrid that there was "a year of war clearly to be seen ahead
where European diplomats are trying to say it will be over in a
month."

On the last day of May, Hemingway landed back in New
York, telling newspapermen that he "wanted to write some short
stories and a novel," and admitting that he was "a little jaded

with active reporting on the war front," but that he might go back "if things get warm over there." On September 1, he was off again for a last look. It was almost over.

Again, the Loyalist troops were preparing to fall back across the Ebro—the last swing of the seesaw in that sector. This time it was a more orderly withdrawal than the previous spring. The last day the Fifth Army stood on the lower banks of the river was November 5. With Hans Kahle, who had commanded the XIth Brigade, and Henry Buckley of the London *Daily Telegraph*, Hemingway drove south from Barcelona to cover what they did not yet know would be a withdrawal. With the bridge at Mora la Nueva destroyed, there was no way to cross—until Kahle located a flat-bottomed scow and four oarsmen, whom Hemingway paid in cigarettes. The currents were strong and unpredictable, for the Fascists upstream at Comorasa had opened the floodgates. The visit to the line was brief: a climb up the river bluffs, a look at the destroyed town and at the trucks and tanks moving up the riverbank to the lone, jammed bridge at Garcia. There was a house curiously cut in two with some of its second-floor furniture still in the unscathed half—a table with two chairs set precisely on either side of it. "That shows just what you've got to do when a bombing starts," Hemingway said. "Just sit down at the table. Easy."[39]*

A strong hint from Lister, the commanding general, started the correspondents retreating back to Barcelona. To avoid the congested Garcia bridge they went back to the river to look for a boat. This time there were more newsmen, but only a single boat and two undernourished boatmen. The river—and even the

---

* "At a regimental command post, close to the German lines in the Second World War, [John] Groth and Hemingway were eating dinner with some officers one night. Suddenly the German 88's began to break their way in. To a man, everyone hit the floor in the accepted fashion, and groped for helmets. Or so Groth thought. But when the candles were lit, he was stunned with what he saw, for there was Hemingway still at the table—bareheaded, his back to the firing, still eating his dinner, alone" (Philip Young, *Ernest Hemingway* [University Park, Pa., 1966], p. 171).

Compare also to the Orwell episode (Chapter 3) of the bomb-bisected house in his novel *Coming up for Air*.

other side—was already under artillery fire, and, although the boatmen pulled as hard as they could, their overloaded boat kept twisting in the dangerous rapids towards the jagged wreck of the Mora bridge. Hemingway grabbed an oar and dug at the water. Fortunately, he was on the right side, and the boat veered away from the ruined bridge,[40] and toward the newly readjusted frontier of the Spanish Republic. It was probably his last visit to the line.

Hemingway was again on his way home from Spain when English critic Cyril Connolly published *Enemies of Promise*, in which he wondered whether Hemingway, whose style suffered "from the limitations of realism," could write a great novel about the war in Spain. "It is a style in which the body talks rather than the mind, one admirable for rendering emotions; love, fear, joy of battle, despair, sexual appetite, but impoverished for intellectual purposes." Hemingway, Connolly thought, was "fortunate in possessing a physique which is at home in the world of boxing, bull-fighting and big game shooting, fields closed to most writers . . . ; he is supreme in the domain of violence and his opportunity will be to write the great book (and there have been no signs of one so far) about the Spanish war."[41]

In the first months of 1939, the last strongholds of Republican resistance were surrendering. At about the same time, Hemingway began his novel, intending to put into it not "just the civil war" but "everything I had learned about Spain for 18 years."[42] Behind a pile of blank manuscript paper, in a location removed from the life of action, the Hemingway persona could not compete so powerfully with Hemingway the artist. When Madrid fell, on March 31, ending the war, he was less than twenty thousand words into the novel. Writing and revising it took him nearly eighteen months, during which time he discarded one title and found another, and wrote his editor at Scribner's, Maxwell Perkins, that while under arms he was loyal to his side, but once a war was over he was a writer—not a Catholic writer or a Party writer

or any other prefixed writer.[43] He was harking back to the con-
trolling concept of his lone public speech—that a writer had to
write as truly as he could. His first title had been *The Undiscovered
Country* (a reference to death, from *Hamlet*), but it was dropped
in favor of *For Whom the Bell Tolls*, from a John Donne devotion:
It became the novel's epigraph:

> No man is an *Iland*, intire of it selfe; every man is a peece of
> the *Continent*, a part of the *maine*; if a *Clod* be washed away by the
> *Sea*, *Europe* is the lesse, as well as if a *Promontorie* were, as well as
> if a *Mannor* of thy *friends* or of *thine owne* were; any mans *death*
> diminishes *me*, because I am involved in *Mankinde*; And therefore
> never send to know for whom the *bell* tolls; It tolls for *thee*.

The piece of the continent washed away was Spain, and
nearly a million men died in the war that had torn it apart. The
world had been grossly diminished. Worst of all, as Hemingway
wrote in the preface to Regler's novel, the loss of Spain had been
accomplished through betrayal, which took not only the form of
Fascist intervention, but of tragically shortsighted aloofness of
the Western democracies and equally tragic foreshortened intervention of Russia, supporting only what it approved, and only
as long as it was useful to Communism. To put those complexities
in the novel would be to satisfy no party.

To focus upon the general predicament of the Spanish people,
Hemingway chose not one of the International Brigades he knew,
or one of the Army units he travelled with, but a group of Republican guerrillas representing many sectors of Spain and the moral
and political spectrum, and operating in nominally Fascist country, the forests of the Sierra de Guadarrama, sixty miles northwest
of besieged Madrid. The time: the sixty-eight-hour period between
Saturday afternoon and Tuesday noon of the last week of May,
1937. To the guerrilla unit comes Robert Jordan, a former
American teacher of Spanish at a Western university, his mission
to blow up a strategically located bridge near Segovia. The destruction of the bridge is to be timed with the beginning of a
Loyalist offensive, but whether it will take place on time—or at

all—is complicated by Government disunity, and Communist cross-purposes and ingrained suspicion. The guerrillas, all of peasant stock, are willing to cooperate in Jordan's mission—all except Pablo, who is surly, untrustworthy, and narrow in outlook; but the strong-willed Pilar, earth-mother and wife of Pablo, dominates the group. With them is the refugee girl, Maria, whose brief idyll with Jordan Pilar sponsors and oversees. (The daughter of a Republican village mayor who with his wife has been murdered by the Fascists, she had been abducted and raped by them as well.) Jordan is sure that the attack will not succeed; still, he obeys his orders. The bridge is destroyed but he is badly wounded in the withdrawal which follows, and left to die. Without bitterness he tells Maria, in Donne-like terms, to go on to Madrid ("But I go with thee. As long as there is one of us there is both of us.")* Alone, he tries to convince himself, "If we win here we will win everywhere." And his life ebbs without bitterness, in a war his side is doomed to lose. At the close, a sympathetically drawn Lieutenant Berrendo, a sensitive and devout Fascist cavalry officer, rides through the woods unaware that in a few paces he will loom in the sights of the dying Jordan's submachine gun. The bell will toll for both of them.

Hemingway's ironic balance is not restricted to the final paragraph—it is sustained through the novel. Pilar describes the massacre of the leading (thus presumably Fascist) citizens of a town near Ávila by Pablo and his mob, and we learn of equivalent Nationalist brutality—seventy-two hours later when the Fascists retook the town. And Hemingway's incidents never arise out of Loyalist atrocity propaganda, but are soundly parallel with the facts, even when the facts may cause some revulsion from the

---

* Despite the attempts of critics to "inflate Maria into a symbol of almost everything," according to John M. Muste, "she is such a pallid figure . . . that she hardly seems human at all. Jordan calls her his 'rabbit,' a term which would have been highly insulting to any Spanish woman." (Arturo Barea points out that in colloquial Spanish the word for *rabbit* is also the word for the female genitalia.) "Instead [of a new kind of heroine] we have one more erotic daydream, entirely too much like Catherine Barkley" (J. M. Muste, *Say That We Saw Spain Die*, pp. 116-17).

Loyalist cause. Thus the description of how the enraged proletariat of a small *pueblo* first beat all the male members of the
middle class with heavy flails and then fling them over a cliff is
close to what happened in the Andalusian town of Ronda.* We
see this duality throughout *For Whom the Bell Tolls.* Nowhere is
there the facile simplicity of uncomplicated idealism, for Hemingway can separate the cause from its followers, and from those
who seek to take advantage of it, this best illustrated in Jordan's
contrast between the idealistic communism and the practical communism of Madrid.

One was not visible to everyone, but was available in the
hotel headquarters of the Russians who had armed Spain—as far
as they went—on their own terms, directing much of the resistance
to the rebels. There one encountered "the cold, practical, hard-
headed, cynical ruthlessness of the Comintern mind, completely
unsentimental and in no way deceived by the propaganda which it
daily originated and disseminated."[44]

The other was symbolized by the headquarters of the International Brigades,† where "you felt that you were taking part
in a crusade. That was the only word for it although it was a
word that had been so worn and abused that it no longer gave
its true meaning. You felt, in spite of all bureaucracy and in-

---

* A. E. Hotchner records that when he asked Hemingway in 1954 (in Madrid) how
much of *For Whom the Bell Tolls* came from actual events, Hemingway's answer
was, "Not as much as you may think. There was the bridge that was blown, and I
had seen that. The blowing of the train as described in the book was also a true
event. And I used to slip through the enemy lines into Segovia, where I learned a
lot about Fascist activity which I carried back to our command. But the people and
events were invented out of my total knowledge, feeling and hopes. When Pilar remembers back to what happened in their village when the Fascists came, that's
Ronda, and the details of the town are exact" (*Papa Hemingway*, p. 131). Although
Hemingway's services had been to the losing—and still outlawed—side in the Civil
War, he had no difficulty revisiting Spain in the 1950's, and even revisited the mountain top in the Escorials where Pablo's band had hid out, and picnicked by the once-
blown bridge. "Nothing's changed," he told Hotchner. "Just as it was. They put it
back together after the war, reassembling all the stones that had fallen into the
river bed after we blew it" (p. 142).
† Established and directed, if not entirely manned, we must remember, by Communists ranging from idealist to pragmatist.

efficiency and party strife something that was like the feeling you expected to have and did not have when you made your first communion. . . . It gave you a part in something that you could believe in wholly and completely and in which you felt an absolute brotherhood with the others who were engaged in it. It was something that you had never known before but that you had experienced now and you gave such importance to it and the reasons for it that your own death seemed of complete unimportance; only a thing to be avoided because it would interfere with the performance of your duty. But the best thing was that there was something you could do about this feeling and this necessity too. You could fight."[45] But after six months' exposure, if the fighting were hard and desperate, and the bureaucracy and political rivalries blatant, the purity of feeling became polluted. All that was left—if one were strong enough and free-spirited enough to have anything left—is reflected in Jordan's hilltop soliloquy:

> You're not a real Marxist and you know it. You believe in Liberty, Equality and Fraternity. You believe in Life, Liberty and the Pursuit of Happiness. Don't ever kid yourself with too much dialectics. They are for some but not for you. You have to know them in order not to be a sucker. You have to put many things in abeyance to win a war. If this war is lost all of those things are lost.
>
> But afterwards you can discard what you do not believe in. There is plenty you do not believe in and plenty that you do believe in.[46]

Neither Jordan nor Hemingway believed in the inspired propaganda of the Marxist *La Pasionaria,* in the attractive cynicism Mikhail Koltzov (Karkov in the novel), or in the organizing idealism of André Marty, and some of the bitter denunciations of the novel came from some of the American veterans of the Internationals who admitted, as Alvah Bessie did, that Hemingway was "unequivocably on the side of the Spanish people" but insisted, too, that he had betrayed the anti-Fascist cause.* To Bessie, the attack on Marty was unforgivably vicious. The organizing genius of the Brigades had been fictionalized into a "criminal imbecile," and that Hemingway connected Communism with "the incompetence, the red tape, and the outright treachery that strangled Spain," was something Bessie not only resented, but prophetically feared. Writing in *New Masses,* he predicted, ominously, "I am afraid he will live to see every living and dead representative of the Abraham Lincoln Battalion attacked and slandered because of the great authority that attaches to Hemingway's name and his known connection with Spain."[47]

Major Milton Wolff, the last commander of the Lincolns, and an officer who swam the Ebro with the remnants of his battalion, then reorganized it, and led it back against the enemy, was outraged, too, and told Hemingway so in a bitter letter. "So I was just a rooter in Spain," Hemingway countered. "O.K. Did it ever occur to you that there were 595,000 some troops in the Spanish army beside the 15th Brigade and that the entire action of my book took place and was over before you personally had ever been in the line . . . ?" But Hemingway refused to let the accusation drop there. What, he wanted to know, "given what experience I have and what talents I may possess[,] what would you like me to have done to aid the cause of the Spanish Republic that I did not do?"[48] The letter was signed "Hemingstein."

Hemingway had once said that all good books were alike in that they were more true than if they had really happened. Because of the controversies *For Whom the Bell Tolls* aroused, and its topical subject matter, it was difficult to see at the time that the novel was conceived on an epical scale and relentlessly carried to a tragic conclusion fully in accord with its internal nature.

* The writer of the "other" famous novel of the war, André Malraux, was equally disappointed at Soviet duplicity. Never a Communist, he nevertheless had worked closely with Communists aiding the Spanish Republic; but when the Nazi-Soviet pact was signed on August 23, 1939, he told Louis Fischer in Paris, "We are back at zero" (Fischer, *Men and Politics*).

Not only Hemingway's grandest attempt in the novel form, it is one of the best (although not the most perfect) of his books. To Malcolm Cowley, it is the "one great and often underestimated novel about the Spanish civil war, . . . a soundly constructed and extremely complicated work in which politics plays an essential but not major part." Noting that it was begun when the war was all but over, and completed after the larger war Hemingway had predicted would follow a failure in Spain had begun, Cowley added, "I suspect that if it had been finished two years earlier, it might have ended as another optimistic tragedy, like *The Grapes of Wrath*. But Hemingway was writing in a despondent period. He knew that the Spanish Republic was already doomed when Jordan set out on his mission behind the Fascist lines."[49] The reasons for it were as complex and as disillusioning as the sacrifices of the Jordans were courageous and futile, and Hemingway felt compelled to do what his hero did not live to accomplish, and could not have accomplished as well. "He would write a book when he got through with this," Robert Jordan had thought to himself. "But only about the things he knew, truly, and about what he knew. But I will have to be a much better writer than I am now to handle them, he thought. The things he had come to know in this war were not so simple."[50]

8

THE AMERICAN "INTERNATIONALS"

*It is very difficult to write the truth in war
and the truth is also very dangerous to come
by. I do not know just which American
writers have gone out to seek it. I know many
men of the Lincoln Battalion. But they are not
writers. They are letter writers.*

   Hemingway,
   in a speech, "THE WRITER AND WAR,"
   delivered June 4, 1937.

IT TOOK SEVERAL MONTHS to form an American battalion. Even
before recruiting began, Americans went to Spain on their own
to join units already in action, in some cases because the Loyalist
plight seemed to them too desperate to wait for formalities, in
others because the volunteers were from futureless make-work
depression projects, or unemployed altogether. "I don't know
when the Spanish war started," one memoir confessed. "Everyone
started to talk about it at once. First it was going to be a short war.
Everybody was going to get the hell knocked out of them for
standing up against democracy. I don't know about that. I don't
know how it started. What I do know—I was out of a job and
sick of the whole rotten business. All of a sudden they began
having big pep meetings, sometimes in the parks, on Union Square
and so forth, and throwing up posters and trying to pull money
out of you to send over there. They didn't ask for men at first. You
had to give money and get over there and win the war goddamn

fast. I believed myself that we had to do it before they got over here and beat hell out of us."

So James Caldwell left, on a third class ticket, with "about 7 or 8 fellows, maybe 10," for Le Havre. By train and truck the group crossed France, stopping for a drunken layover in Paris. From Hendaye they crossed the border into Spain, and were soon in desultory training in Madrid. It was early in November of 1936, and there wasn't much time for training, even for volunteers like Caldwell, whose weapons experience had been limited to Coney Island shooting galleries and vague memories of boyhood rabbit hunting. It hardly mattered at first, when activity was limited to motley drill in a deserted public square, hours of being aimlessly ferried about in trucks, and trying to keep warm and dry. Finally, a young American officer attached to the bedraggled group "told us to get up and line up. He gave cartridges to everybody who didn't have any. He had two men distribute the guns. He broke the news to us that there was going to be a battle."

"He said that when you started going you couldn't stop because when you stopped you were as good as dead. He said the only way to win a war was to start and keep going. He was a college boy."

The ground was muddy and their feet "like clods." When they went into action against a background of hammering artillery, Caldwell had no idea how frightened he was "till suddenly I noticed it. Because suddenly my whole face and body was broken out in sweat and my hands holding my gun were trembling like a leaf. Nobody seemed to want to talk. I didn't talk. I was too scared. I began to wonder where in the hell I was and what we were doing. Because I wasn't doing anything and I couldn't see anybody else doing anything." Afterwards there was rifle fire, and "men shouting in Spanish. . . . I don't know any Spanish. . . . But I knew they were shouting in Spanish. I kept running at a dogtrot with my rifle cross my thighs in front of me like this. I didn't even feel like shooting it. Besides I couldn't see anything to shoot at."

They withdrew by truck, which was better than by foot. Back in the dim, barnlike garrison in Madrid, Caldwell was offered soup from a large black kettle. Afterwards, he went to sleep in a corner of the room, sitting up. It had been his first action.

The next promised to be better, for tanks were being brought up to the University City front. It was to be a counteroffensive. But when the tanks came to cover the advance, "One of them wouldn't start. There weren't any more than eight or nine tanks. With the one that wouldn't start that made seven." It was clearly not going to be a good day, especially since "At the top of the hill there was the whole damned Italian army. Sitting back was the artillery. There were tanks. There were machine guns. They turned the whole God damned works on us. . . . I still hear em puffin and blowing about the Italians at Guadalajara. But boy when the People's Front came tearing [back] down that hill it was the rottenest, meanest, lousiest defeat I've ever seen. . . ."

The Italians neglected to follow up the rout, and again the omnipresent trucks took the Internationals away. "There must have been 500 wounded. There may have been 10,000 for all I know. After your first battle you don't care about that anymore. I would like to get a chance to tell those little crawling bastards in the U.S. who seem to think that hot air is the main constituent of war against fascism . . . . You don't fight a war with 500 or 500,000 fat little American boys and 100,000,000 lungs full of good old hot American air. You fight a war with good generals and with good artillery behind to break em up in front and with good tanks to swing em around. The spirit and all the rest of it is all very fine. But a machine gun is a machine gun. . . ."

The war ended for Caldwell in University City, where buildings and even classrooms changed hands so often that there was no front. "It's a funny thing to be fighting in a city because you don't know what you are fighting or who. We were shooting at the building across the street because they were shooting at us." There wasn't much to eat, but the tobacco shortage seemed more important—that and the cold. "We slept in our big coats. There was only one thing in the world I wanted and that was a cigarette. You'll find that is what suffering means in a war. Towards the beginning of a war you want a cigarette. You keep on wanting that cigarette until the war is over or you are killed. . . ."

He slept in a classroom. "One of the men in our room was dead when I woke up. He had been killed after I had gone to sleep. I had never spoken to him and didn't feel sorry that he was dead. . . . You hear a lot of God damn sobbing and wailing about the men who get killed in a war. But if you have been in a war and seen them killed you are not sorry."

Running across the square just before dawn to occupy a building supposedly "flushed by the [artillery] barrage except for a few snipers," Caldwell completed his contribution to the Cause. "You have probably noticed already that I am wounded. The way I walk. . . . That is because when I was running across the square something hit me and I fell down. . . ." For a while he lay in the damp, cold building to which he was first carried, because when they tried to get him out, ". . . it was no use. Because the fighting was going on in every doorway. . . ."

"I stayed alive I guess because it's very hard for a man to die. . . . Even when he has had his tail shot off and has nothing more to live for. . . . The next thing I remember was after they had operated on me in a little garrison hospital. They had removed the part of my belly that you get to care the most about. . . .

"I don't know why I didn't die. Death is the best thing. The only thing that war can give a man. . . .

"You do not fight a war with a bunch of little nuts howling their silly brains out back in America.

"You do not fight a war by reading the Communist handbook.

"You do not fight a war by raising your fist in a cellar in Brooklyn.

"You do not fight a war by applauding 'The Spanish Earth' in Cincinnati.

"You do not fight a war by printing pamphlets.

"You do not fight a war by saying any God damn thing on earth.

"A war is fought with generals.

"A war is fought with maneuvers.

"A war is won with good generals.

"A war is won with clever maneuvers.

"You have got to learn that it does not matter who is right. Because in a war there is no right. There is no use in people getting shot in a war for something that is right. Because in a war nothing is right. . . .

"You asked me to tell you what happened to me in Spain. . . . Other people were there longer and could tell you more. . . ."

While Caldwell was recovering in the charity ward of a New York hospital, his friend Spivak, who had taken him to his first meeting, came to see him. "He was very enthused and pleased. He ran saliva all over me because I had been in Spain for the glory of the Italian machine-gunners. . . . He said that the people would fight on forever because they were united and free. He said that Franco would not march into Madrid until the last God damn man was dead. I told him more about the war. He said they were holding a pep-meeting tonight and were sending more money over. He said the People of the world were aroused. He said never in his lifetime had he been so stirred."

Several weeks later, Caldwell, again walking the streets unemployed, met Spivak for the second time since Spain. Spivak was still enthusiastic. "He said that the Communist Party was having a big rally in Madison Square Garden the next week. He said they wanted me especially to come. They came and got me in a car. There were many people there. They were helping to fight the war in Spain. They were grinding Franco's machine gunners into the dust. . . . There were many of the dark thin girls you always see. There were many of the fat greasy men in glasses you always see. . . . We sat in a special section reserved especially for us. . . . They cheered us because they don't know what war is. They cheered us because they don't want to know. . . . They cheered us because the war they were fighting was not the war in Spain.

"The war in Spain was fought with guns. . . .

"You probably know what's the matter with me. I'm the fair-haired boy who did it. When you read about Guadalajara—thank

me. I'm the boy who did it. When you read about the Alcazar—
kiss me. They were my nuts. I gave them to you. I gave them to
you for the glory of the Communist handbook. They were my
present to the people of America. They should be hung on the
Statue of Liberty. . . ."[1]

When *Defense in University City* appeared, in the closing
days of the war in Spain, Simon and Schuster, Inc. wrote to
Caldwell "urging him to extend his account of his experiences . . .
into a full length book" which they were eager to publish. *Writer's
Digest* reprinted it in full, advertising it on the cover as "A Writer
at the Front." Ezra Pound reviewed it on the front page of the
Meridiano di Roma. It was, up to then, perhaps the most intriguing
first-person account of the war in Spain by an American volunteer,
and registered the profound disillusion of those who had poured
themselves into the Cause only to discover that Spain had become
a pawn of the great European powers. There was only one thing
wrong: It was fiction.

"James Caldwell" was really a twenty-year-old Cincinnati
writer, Robert J. C. Lowry, who with his artist friend James Flora
was producing a series of odd-sized (5½" x 14"), strikingly
designed pamphlets collectively titled *The Little Man.* Lowry had
written the tale—actually dictated it—in a single long nighttime
session with his friend Flora, who scribbled it down while Lowry
talked, "pacing the floor and being James Caldwell, the first-
person hero whom I created out of the heavy flurry of magazine,
motion-picture and newspaper accounts of the Spanish Civil War
and the defense of University City. . . ." The factual background
came mainly from picture stories in *Life,* and newsreels, and the
author later confessed that some of the people and incidents were
"direct reflections of photographed incidents." All in all, Lowry's
sanguinary imagination was too vivid—or perhaps he dictated
too loudly—for he remembered "that my nighttime spoken account
of James Caldwell's war adventures was too much for the lady

from who I had rented that furnished room. The next morning she asked me to leave, which I did."[2]

Lowry had never met any of the writer veterans of the war, nor had he been to Spain; he was not a soldier himself until 1942, and later he saw combat in Italy. Like Stephen Crane's *The Red Badge of Courage*, written by a young man who had never witnessed a battle, "James Caldwell's" saga had the surface impression of being the real thing, and communicated a sense of emotional honesty. Yet any careful reader with some military knowledge could have picked its facts and its logic apart, had he not been disarmed by the seeming innocence and raw candor of a young man whom the Cause—whatever it was—had victimized. Lowry had done more than read *Life* and watch "The March of Time" at his neighborhood theater. He had apparently remembered as well that Hemingway's Jake Barnes, war veteran hero of *The Sun Also Rises*, had lost another "part of my belly that you get to care the most about." And he had learned something about how to write Hemingwayish dialogue. It had more of the "feel" of what war was really like than most of the true accounts —quite a stylish accomplishment, however contradictory it was to the idealism most of the American Internationals not only took to Spain with them, but—if they survived—brought back home.

There were volunteers, and there were some sheep misled to the slaughter. The latter were few, but their defections were a well-publicized embarrassment. For many Americans, going to Spain was a carefully weighed decision. Novelist Alvah Bessie went, he thought, because "the historical events of Spain had coincided with a long-felt compulsion to complete the destruction of the training I had received all through my youth. There were two major reasons for my being there; to achieve self-integration, and to lend my individual strength (such as it was) to the fight against our eternal enemy—oppression; and the validity of the second reason was not impaired by the fact that it was a shade weaker than the first. . . ."[3] Like the volunteers from other countries, the Americans were defying the wishes, if not the laws, of their government. In the United States it was the Neutrality Act, bulwark of 1930's isolationism, although there was pettier legislation dubiously applicable, and dating back almost to the first session of the first Congress. For a while, various publications ranging the spectrum of the Left printed advertisements soliciting funds to send volunteers to Spain, *The Nation* in a full-page advertisement of the "Friends of the Debs Column" asking for funds to help equip and send Americans in aid of the Loyalists. But, early in 1937, on the advice of its lawyers, the magazine discontinued publishing such advertisements, declaring in its pages nonetheless that *"The Nation* hopes that United States law will not be applied against American volunteers to Spain as it has been so loosely interpreted in the past. We have ourselves used foreign volunteers. If we stop our volunteers from Spain it will only help fascism."

Almost the only way a prospective American volunteer could make good on his desire to go to Spain was to involve himself somehow in the secret and conspiratorial processes through which the Communist apparatus funnelled men to the International Brigades.* Other than attempting to get there equally illegally on one's own, there was almost no other way, whether one's politics were radical or liberal, or even if one had no political views at all. A few made it on their own; most volunteers had to accept the only means available. A writer might make his way over on the strength of press credentials: It was easier to get to Spain to write than to fight.

For the committed Communists among the Americans (perhaps forty percent of the total), a young former City College student declared the motive for volunteering in appropriately Marxist jargon: "The real test of every Spain volunteer—to prove how strong is the tie between his idealistic romanticism and

---

* This means is described graphically and bitterly in John Dos Passos's novel *The Adventures of a Young Man.*

dialectical materialism. . . ." The writer was Wilfred Mendelson, who had been in the line then about two weeks. He had just read— in the field—Arthur Koestler's *Spanish Testament* (with its "Dialogue with Death"), and was especially impressed, he wrote his sister, by the lines, "A man may and does know he is going to die. But he can never *believe* it." Thirteen days later he was dead, near the Ebro.[4]

Reasons for committing one's self to the Cause, and the extent of the commitment, were almost as varied as the volunteers. Evan Shipman, whom Hemingway called "one of my oldest friends, a fine poet and good prose writer," originally went to Spain—via France—in order to drive an ambulance on the Loyalist side. The son of an editor of the old *Life*, Shipman always hoped some day to inherit enough money to start his own magazine. His preparation was unpromising. He was dropped out of Groton for low grades, and expelled from the Salisbury School for staying out all night. After the First World War, he went to Europe and mixed with the American expatriates, drank, wrote poetry for the little magazines, drank, and came home again a decade later. Hemingway had once brought him to Gertrude Stein in Paris and announced that his friend would buy Ford Madox Ford's *transatlantic review* when he came of age. No, predicted André Masson, Shipman would support a surrealist magazine. Josette Gris disagreed, forecasting that young Shipman would buy a house in the country. "As a matter of fact," Gertrude Stein remembered later, "when he came of age nobody who had known him then seemed to know what he did do with his inheritance."[5] Shipman loved trotters, and, when back in New York got a job on the racing sheet the *Morning Telegraph* as trotting-horse columnist. In 1935, he published a book of short stories about trotting-horse people, *Free for All*. But when Hemingway arranged the purchase of some ambulances for the Loyalists, the nonpolitical Shipman decided that he had to drive one of them.

Tall and lean, with an old-fashioned cavalryman's mustache that made him look like a pre-1914 British officer, he looked nothing like a potential ambulance driver to the State Department, which in the interests of American neutrality refused to validate his passport for Spain. Shipman—with a cover job as a correspondent in Paris—went anyway, and, toward the end of April, 1937, had reached Toulouse, intending to take the heavily traveled smuggler's route over the Pyrenees along with a group of volunteers for the International Brigades. It was one time when the alternative route—via fishing smack—should have been employed, for the *gendarmerie* caught up with Shipman's group even before their bus had left the city en route to a frontier point. All of them were committed to jail in Toulouse.

Stewing behind bars, the usually unmilitant Shipman worked up so much indignation that he changed his mind about what he would do when he got to Spain. Instead of driving one of Hemingway's ambulances, he vowed from his cell, he would enlist in the Brigades and shoot Fascists. After twenty-six days, Shipman's group was released, and received word to reassemble in Marseilles. There they were met by Brigade agents and taken to the waterfront. At the dock was an attractive vessel, the *Ciudad de Barcelona,* but, to their disappointment, they were hustled instead aboard several dirty little boats, which pulled out almost immediately, hugged the coast all the way into Spanish waters, and spilled them out safely the next evening. (A few days later the big ship left with a cargo of three hundred recruits for the Internationals, some fifty of them Americans, and eighty airplane engines. Halfway across, the *Ciudad de Barcelona* was torpedoed by an Italian submarine. Fifty-two volunteers went down with the ship, trapped below decks.)

In a short time (training rarely lasted a month), Shipman was at the front, fighting in the costly battle of Brunete, an action so fierce that the American George Washington Battalion, in its first action, was almost a total casualty. (The few "Washingtons" left had to merge with the survivors of the Abraham Lincoln Battalion in order to reconstruct an effective fighting force.) At Brunete, Shipman fought with reckless courage, not with the

Americans but with a Franco-Belgian battalion to which he had been attached as an interpreter and runner. On the last day of the battle, in a stand the battalion made—against orders—which prevented a rout, he was badly wounded.

When Hemingway saw him again, it was months later. Shipman was convalescing, and was "ragged, limping and profoundly cheerful."

"Tell me about when you were wounded," Hemingway asked him after they had settled down to a drink.

"Why, Hem, it was absolutely nothing. It was nothing at all. I never felt a thing."

"What do you mean, you didn't feel a thing?" (Hemingway knew that a machine gun bullet had passed completely through Shipman's thigh.)

"Why, it was really nothing. You see I was unconscious at the time."

"Yes."

"You see the planes had just caught us in the open and bombed us and I was unconscious at the time. So I didn't feel a thing when they came down and machine gunned us. Really, Hem, it was almost like having an anaesthetic beforehand."

He paused and turned his drink around in his hand. "Hem," he said finally, "I can never thank you enough for having brought me over here. . . . I want you to know that being in Spain is the happiest time I have ever had in my life. Please believe me, Hem. You really must believe me absolutely."[6]

Through the efforts of friends, Shipman was invalided back to the States, and took up the old life. When a bigger war intervened, he went off again to serve. But Spain limited him, as it did the war service of some other former volunteers in Spain, their premature activism rendering them suspect. Shipman—unable to become an officer—rose to regimental sergeant-major in a tank outfit, a position high enough to enable him to read confidential warnings sent to the regimental brass to look out for Shipman, the suspected Red.

Afterwards it was back to the trotting column, now become famous enough to cause some desultory talk of collecting his columns for a book. He still wrote poems, but few were published, and he seemed not to care in his last years. He was, to the end, as Malcolm Cowley[7] (who was as fond of him as was Hemingway) put it, "Gentleman, soldier, poet, judge of horseflesh and wine, no judge of women or success."

Unlike Shipman, most of the nearly four thousand Americans who volunteered to fight in Spain did not find it the happiest time of their lives, except at an emotionally or intellectually fulfilling moment. Few of them wrote memorably about the experience of war—but then half of the American volunteers never came back— a fact that caused one veteran to reminisce, wryly, "I was a company commander. But that's only because if you lived long enough, you were bound to end up one." The writer who threw up his work to take his chance in an area where he was clearly an amateur had not necessarily been unsuccessful when brandishing a typewriter. One of them, biographer (then a journalist) Louis Fischer, may have been the first American to volunteer for the Internationals, enlisting two days after the beginning of the siege of Madrid. "I am as proud of that as I am of anything I have done in my life," he declared later. "A nation was bleeding. Machine guns were being mounted on the ivory tower. It was not enough to write. . . . I wanted to do something. Friends said my articles were a contribution to the cause. But I wished to contribute work as well as words." He went to André Marty, who asked him what he thought he could do. Fischer said he could organize. "We need a quartermaster," Marty said, and Fischer thereupon became a major, or *commandante*, and quartermaster of the International Brigade. It was still a very informal organization, and Fischer took no pay and swore no allegiances. For uniform he wore a corduroy jacket which buttoned up to the neck, long corduroy pantaloons with patch pockets, and heavy army boots. Because he went hatless, Marty complained.

At the start Fischer continued to live in the Grand Hotel, where he had stayed as a correspondent, but at seven in the morning Marty, or Lucien Vidal, his chief of staff, would telephone and bark, "Where are you? The staff is meeting." Reluctantly, Fischer moved to a room in a house on the edge of Brigade headquarters at Albacete. Until he enlisted he had been sending weekly articles to *The Nation.* These stopped. He had informed no one of his volunteering, and it was assumed in the U.S. that he was lost in the chaos of the Nationalist advance on Madrid.

The Brigade Quartermaster's job was more than to find ways to feed the volunteers at the Albacete base, often as many as three thousand. He had to clothe the new arrivals as well as feed them, maintain the barracks, and supply the troops with arms. Each task he inherited was a nightmare of disorganization and supply shortages, made worse by the wholesale losses of equipment characteristic of an army in retreat. A battalion at the front would send emissaries to Albacete to ask for replacement of cooking utensils, clothing, and bedding lost in battle. Usually, Fischer had nothing to give them—which caused one battalion commander to threaten to send armed men to forcibly acquire what he needed, or arrest Fischer if he could not. Begging everywhere, he found his best source of supply in the unlikeliest place, sitting beside a kerosene stove in a cold room, a woolen blanket over his legs and thick scarf around his neck. It was Martínez Barrio, then Vice-President of the Republic and President of Parliament. Huddled by his stove, he would receive officers and civilians on the business of the Republic, or in his additional capacity as civil governor of Albacete. "I must have four hundred pairs of socks tomorrow," Fischer would appeal. "Four hundred Frenchmen and Poles are arriving in the morning."

Sometimes Fischer and the Vice-President would trade. The Brigades had, for example, five thousand pairs of army shoes sent from abroad by various groups friendly to the Republic. On rare occasions, supply trains would get through from France, the material forwarded by the French Communist Party: uniforms, blankets, woolen sweaters and hats, underwear, canned food, and field kitchen equipment. Supplies of this kind were let through intermittently by the timid French government, depending on the vagaries of internal French politics, negative pressure from the appeasement-minded British Foreign Office,* and the chances of the Republic's survival. Once, as Fischer's quartermaster crew opened one bale from France, out came a baby's rompers, and Fischer thought that the comrades to the north had gone crazy. Then came a silk blouse, and he was sure. But then came the barrel of a machine gun, and, after that, several dozen revolvers. Marty guarded the smuggled arms zealously, for the supply of weapons available to the Brigade had a somewhat antique cast. Major Fischer's armory was an old church, where he placed, under heavy guard, several hundred rifles, each catalogued. Some, Fischer remembered, were marked "Oviedo, 1896." He remembered that because that was the year he was born.

The personality of Marty loomed over the Albacete camp. Once Fischer told him that a French Communist deputy named Dutilleul was addressing members of the Brigade. "What?" he yelled. "Who gave him permission? I am the only one who makes speeches here." He called an orderly and had Dutilleul brought to him. "Marty," Fischer learned, "wanted to be the only boulder on the beach."[8]

Although Fischer's work as Brigade Quartermaster took most of his time, he knew many people in high places in Spain because of his journalistic work, and took a day off each week to visit Madrid or Valencia, and proffer advice to Republican officials (including President Largo Caballero) or chat with foreign correspondents. Before long he was unable to resist resuming communications with *The Nation*. In Madrid he had seen a German

* Stanley Baldwin, the British Prime Minister, told former Cabinet Secretary Thomas Jones on June 27, 1936, "I told [Foreign Secretary] Eden yesterday that on no account, French or other, must he bring us in to fight on the side of the Russians" (Jones, *A Diary with Letters* [London, 1954], p. 231). It remained British policy on Spain.

air raid on defenseless civilians, and cabled an article describing the bombing. "From outside comes no help," he wrote. "Where is the world which answered the call of Belgium? Where is the humanitarian heart of the millions who go to church and pray to God, or of the millions who call themselves idealists yet go about their business signing letters, having manicures, seeing cinemas, while a city of culture and beauty is ground into dust?"

Fischer's organization supplied Brigade cantonments within a thirty-mile radius of Albacete; the system of having regional subordinates handle much of the work seemed to be successful. But one assistant, a Pole named Wolf, suddenly disappeared. A query to Marty was greeted by a fierce answer that he knew nothing, but Fischer soon found out that Wolf had been forced from his room at gunpoint one night by three Polish comrades. He had been accused of "Trotskyism." Incidents multiplied, and Fischer (a Soviet partisan, rather than a Party member) told Marty, "Listen, you are not a dictator nor am I a child." Still, Marty thought that was the appropriate relationship.

Fischer's long journalistic experience in Russia (his family, in fact, was still in Moscow) gave him entrée to the Soviet army officers guiding the Republican effort,* and he sometimes dined with them at the Grand Hotel in Albacete, or visited them at the front. Reprimands from Marty for neglect of duty followed, and, finally, after returning from a trip to Valencia, Marty called Fischer into his office. "I talked to some of your friends in Valencia," he said, with an air of warmth and cordiality. "They feel it is such a pity for you to waste your time with kitchen problems and clothing distribution when you could be doing far more important things."

In forty-eight hours, Fischer had turned over his responsi-

---

* A substantial part of the Republic's officer corps, particularly in the highest ranks, defected to the Nationalists—or were involved in the insurrection from the start. The Republic started to defend itself while desperately short in generalship. The Soviet offer to fill the leadership gap was hardly altruistic: it was an ideal opportunity for the Red Army to give its officers experience in the field, while directing part of the war as it desired.

bilities to a successor. Afterwards he visited his family, observing an increasingly purge-haunted Moscow; then he went on to the United States to lecture for Spanish Relief. The first American to volunteer, he was the first to be separated from active duty.

Spain, Fischer later wrote, postponed his "Kronstadt," his equivalent of the Russian sailors' revolt so ruthlessly suppressed in the early days of the Soviet nation. In Spain, he saw "no more tireless workers, valiant fighters, and devoted partisans" than the Russians who had been sent to bolster the Republican war effort: "They seemed to pour into the Spanish struggle the pent-up revolutionary passion which no longer found application in Russia." In Russia, meanwhile, the Stalin regime, he already knew, was busy "burying its brains." What he did not yet know was that many of the most dedicated Russians working in Spain were being executed or exiled on their return home. Rather than permit them to contribute their new knowledge and experience to Russia, Stalin had ordered them eliminated, considering their experience in Spain unhealthy, and likely to result in their re-assimilating into Soviet life only with difficulty.

Keeping his disenchantment to himself (until after the Nazi-Soviet Pact of 1939), Fischer was able to continue to work for the Loyalist, where—considering Communist strength in the Republican camp—a critic of Soviet Russia would have had no welcome. As correspondent again, he limited his anti-Communist activism "to talking to Loyalist Prime Minister [by then] Negrín and a few of his close collaborators about the true horror of Russia. . . ."[9] For Fischer, Spain was not the end of his interest in revolutionary causes. Later he was to write the best biographies of Gandhi and of Lenin to appear in his time.

Most of the writers among the American volunteers—unlike Fischer—were late arrivals. A good index of American involvement was the official organ of the English-speaking battalions of the Internationals, *Volunteer for Liberty*. Theoretically an eight-page weekly, it was first edited by British novelist Ralph Bates, who published the first issue from Madrid on May 24, 1937. Sixty-three issues later, on November 7, 1938, the last issue was published from Barcelona, marking the withdrawal of the International Brigade from Spain. When Bates left for a fund-raising speaking tour of the United States in August, 1937, he turned over the editorship to American poet Edwin Rolfe, the first of three American editors who completed the *Volunteer*'s run. It had first been published on coated stock, but, by September, 1937, when Rolfe took over, it was being printed on whatever paper could be found. The difficulties of publication were nearly insuperable. The Spanish typesetters could read no English, and produced some imaginative copy. Photographers rarely could get fresh film, and had even more problems trying to acquire developing chemicals. Contact with the Brigade was often broken. Mails were delayed or lost; couriers never reached the rear; front-line correspondents (usually soldiers with other duties) were sometimes killed. By the end the *Volunteer* was rarely meeting a deadline or publishing in its accustomed size, and sometimes appeared only as a hortatory broadside leaflet.

Even before the *Volunteer* reached that stage it had become an embarrassing bore to the volunteers. Like most Party sheets, it expended its opportunities on blatant propaganda in Party jargon, and anti-POUMist tirades, and served a slim diet of news. When American novelist Alvah Bessie took Rolfe's job as line correspondent, he realized his limitations, but complained that the *Volunteer*'s stock was sometimes even too stiff for other uses to which discarded newspapers were traditionally put. "The men were fed up with the *Volunteer;* it published too much 'horse-shit' about how-to-win-the-war and we-must-keep-our-morale-up, and our-glorious-XVth-Brigade and our traditions and the machinations of the Fascist powers. The men knew all about that stuff. They wanted to read about themselves, their exploits, human-interest stories. . . , the gripes and gags, the jokes and the guys who really did the stuff. They were the men who should have written the paper; but either they were in action, fighting; or they were in reserve, resting; and they had neither the time, the inclination, nor the talent."[10] Hemingway had already noted, candidly, that he didn't know many men of the Lincoln Battalion, but that those he did know were not writers—only "letter writers." In the fall of 1937 and through 1938 he met many more of the Lincolns, including Bessie; but his earlier remark stood up well.

Bessie, red-eyed and wrinkled right up into his high, balding forehead, looked older than his thirty-three years, and was one of the most professional of the volunteers with writing backgrounds. He had worked for the *Brooklyn Eagle*, done criticism for *New Masses*, and written fiction, even acquiring a Guggenheim Fellowship for creative writing. He had already seen his short stories reprinted in the annual O'Brien anthologies, and had published a lengthy, realistic family chronicle novel, *Dwell in the Wilderness* (1935). When he arrived in France, en route to the border, the Republic still seemed to have a chance. The Loyalists (it was January, 1938) had just retaken Teruel, but by the time Bessie went into the line at five in the morning of March 30 the situation was again gloomy. Until then, he had submitted to air attacks and re-encamped each night with the Lincolns, who for some reason were marching fifteen or twenty kilometers daily, first south, then back north. If it did nothing else, it reduced the new men to a standard of living and a mental attitude comparable to that of the veterans. But there were only about fifteen rifles then left in the entire Battalion.

Early on the morning of the 30th they were marched down toward a road in the hill country behind Teruel (by then lost again to the enemy) where there were stacked cases of unused Russian rifles, still in their factory packing of grease. Since they had no rags with which to clean them into firing condition, the Lincolns tore wide strips off their underwear. Bessie's rifle bore the impress of the Czarist Imperial Eagle. Under the partly obliterated emblem was the only thing new about the weapon— a Soviet hammer-and-sickle stamp.

Days in the line—mostly static trench war and patrol activity

—were followed by the exhilaration of preparing for an offensive. Once they began practicing river-crossing, no one needed to be told where they were going. There was only one difficulty to the operation once it was underway: They had to cross the Ebro twice—once advancing, later in flight. It was Teruel all over again, and the Loyalist had to give up gains at irreparable cost in men, materiel, and morale. The assault would have been daring had the French border above them been open to channel new weapons and supplies, but, with the frontier closed, the offensive was a dangerous drain on what defensive potential the Republic had left. It was to begin just after midnight on the morning of the 25th of July. Not long before, *teniente* Aaron Lopoff, fiction writer for American pulp magazines, and his *sargento-ayudante*, a minor novelist named Alvah Bessie, had visited their Captain, a lanky young man with no literary aspirations. Milton Wolff was busy reading Thomas Mann's *Joseph in Egypt*.

Lopoff was twenty-four. He had started to study aeronautical engineering, dropped out of school for lack of funds, then left home briefly to bum around the country—the "happiest days of his life," he said. Afterwards, he scratched out a living through the Federal Writers Project and by writing for the pulps. In the Ebro offensive, Lopoff commanded a company. In the wretched retreat after the offensive had been contained and counterattacked by Nationalist reinforcements, the whereabouts of Milton Wolff were still unknown; and when the leaderless Battalion was re-assembling across the Ebro, Lopoff became temporary commander of the Lincolns. By then, the only way the Battalion operated at all was through augmenting the Americans who were left with green Spanish replacements, a start toward such integration having been made some months before, even to the point of turning the *Volunteer* into a bilingual paper.

Fighting to hold on, the Loyalists fell back slowly, sometimes gaining time through September by temporarily regaining a knoll or an olive grove. At Hill 481, Lopoff led his men into the attack, revolver in hand. At Hill 666 he was in the trenches, snatching up a rifle exuberantly and shouting, "I haven't fired a rifle in a dog's age." Later that night, at Sierra de Pandols, a Spanish soldier found Bessie and said, *"La pistola del Commandante,"* and thrust an automatic into his hand. It was wet and sticky. Lopoff had been shot in the head while leading his company in an attack, falling in front of the enemy's barbed wire. As he was carried back he asked, "Did the company take the hill? Is the company all right?" They said *yes* to everything, and he said, "That's good."

At a military hospital at La Sabiñosa, to the rear, Lopoff died. Had he recovered, he would have found writing difficult, even for the pulps, for his wound had threatened to cost him his sight before it cost him his life. In the *Volunteer* for October 6, 1938, Bessie wrote what Edwin Rolfe called "a restrained but grief-stricken elegy."[11]

Rolfe was even newer to the line than Bessie, although he had been in Spain longer, for he had first taken on the rear-area task of editing the *Volunteer for Liberty*. The young poet was the second and last professional writer to run the Brigade's publication. When replacements were once being issued rifles, cartridges and hand-grenades, Bessie had met a new man who said his name was Rolfe. "Edwin Rolfe? . . . The poet?"

"The same," said the recruit.

"Christ!" said Bessie incongruously, "You know Carnovsky of the Group Theater, and Phoebe Brand . . . , they told me you were here in Spain; that I should look you up. . . ."

Rolfe, Bessie noted, "was frail; he resembled a bird; he had a fine delicate bone structure and he did not look as though he should be in an army. "I asked him what he was doing here and how he liked it, and he said it was pretty tough at first, but that he liked it fine. He had volunteered to quit the desk job when the call came after the Fascists reached the sea. I do not think I have ever met a gentler guy, a less pugnacious guy, less a soldier. But he had the iron of conviction in him, just the same. He had a tiny automatic pistol someone had given him, . . . though I could not imagine him ever using it. I felt better to have another writer on the spot. . . ." Yet, in Spain up to then, Rolfe's writings were primarily unrealistic exhortations headlined in bold-face in editions of *Volunteer for Liberty*. While the undermanned and outgunned Internationals had been backing toward the sea, Rolfe was miles to the rear issuing such headline slogans as **"Do Not Yield an Inch of Ground to the Enemy!"**; **"Drive Out the Invaders of Spain!"** and **"Now is the Time to Strike Back!"** Sandor Voros, no professional writer but an American Communist leader sent to Spain as a political officer—and later the last editor of the *Volunteer*—reflected wryly, "Ed Rolfe . . . gets hysterical in Barcelona and sends us truckloads of two-page special editions, one after the other, giving us not news nor information, which we crave, but deluging us, *à la Pasionaria*, with shrill feminine screams of exhortation fathered by desperate fear." Still, Voros thought, each headline paradoxically lifted the spirits of the men by causing them to laugh at the incongruity of the propaganda.[12]

Since 1928, Edwin Rolfe had been writing "revolutionary poetry" for *New Masses, Partisan Review,* the *Daily Worker,* the *New Republic*—often such unsubtle lyrics as "Homage to Karl Marx," "Backyards at Beacon" and "Kentucky—1932" (the latter about a miners' strike). Even so, his proletarianism was not sufficiently pure to satisfy Marxist novelist Michael Gold, who observed that Rolfe had been "affected by all the influences of modern bourgeois poetry, T. S. Eliot, Ezra Pound, William Carlos Williams."[13] But Gold remained home while Rolfe took his convictions to Spain.

Both Rolfe and Bessie crossed the Ebro in the July offensive, and stayed on the bridgehead during the months it was rocked by Nationalist counterattacks. There were about 1,400 artillery pieces throwing shells at the Loyalists, who could only muster 120 at top strength. (After Teruel, where the Republicans concentrated 180 pieces, many of which fell into enemy hands, they were never able to collect that many on any sector of the front again.) Gradually the 270 square miles retaken from the enemy melted away, and the remnants of the Loyalist forces were rolled back to the Pyrenees. The six days of advancing had been exhilarating, but thereafter Rolfe's scrappy diary, broken off after a month, showed the strain and the horror. Before the final re-crossing of the Ebro, he had been transferred to Barcelona to again take advantage of his writing background: He would be the *Daily Worker*'s last correspondent in Spain. Retreating across a still sound bridge, Bessie "looked back at the yellow Ebro. . . . It was wide and placid in the brilliant sun; its surface shimmered with a million broken flecks of quiet light. I thought of Aaron."

When Bessie, on *Volunteer* business, visited Rolfe at his Barcelona quarters in the Hotel Majestic, the Lincolns were down to 280 haggard effectives. Aside from the familiar crisscrossed paper strips on the windows, the unscarred Majestic had the appearance of a cosmopolitan oasis, complete to liveried bellhops and—to an infantryman's palate—near-normal supplies of food; and Rolfe, appearing completely citified, wore a civilian suit. (As early as April, 1937 Orwell had been dismayed at what had happened to the libertarian revolution in Catalonia.) Still, for Rolfe, the change from the battlefield, and the cries of *"Socorro!"* and the stench of the unburied dead, had come too late. As Robert Payne, who first printed Rolfe's diary entries from the Ebro period, observed, one of the last of the scattered notes read, " 'Knocked out. Spirit good. No crabbing. Laugh and joke about it.' But he was beyond laughing. The tragedy of Spain haunted him the remaining years of his life."[14]

The experience of Spain never let Rolfe go. In a collection of his last poems, it was evidenced most heartbreakingly in the opening incantation of "Elegia." He could not, he confessed, exorcise the reverberating symbol the Republic's lost capital had remained to him:

Madrid   Madrid   Madrid   Madrid
I call your name endlessly, savor it like a lover.
Ten irretrievable years have exploded like bombs
Since last I saw you, since last I slept

in your arms of tenderness and wounded granite. . . .
I speak to you, Madrid, as lover, husband, son.
Accept this human trinity of passion.
I love you, therefore I am faithful to you
and because to forget you would be to forget
everything I love and value in the world.

It was more confession than poem, as was the nightmare imagery of the longer "City of Anguish," where Rolfe used Madrid as symbol of hope and vehicle for his impressions of the war as his personal dream of horror. But for the lines about "majestic Pasionaria," it was free from pomposity and propaganda, and in one section seemed to catch the tone of the murdered Lorca:

The city weeps. The city wakens, weeping.

And the Madrileños rise from wreckage, emerge
from shattered doorways. . . .
                              But always the wanderer,
the old woman searching, digging among debris.
In the morning light her crazed face is granite.

And the beggar sings among the ruins:

All night, all night
flared in my city the bright
cruel explosion of bombs.
All night, all night
there, where the soil and stone
spilled like brains from the sandbag's bead,
the bodiless head lay staring;
while the anti-aircraft barked,
barked at the droning plane,
and the dogs of war, awakened,
howled at the hidden moon.
And a star fell, omen of ill,
and a man fell, lifeless,
and my wife fell, childless,
and, friendless, my friend.
And I stumbled away from them, crying
from eyeless lids, blinded.

Trees became torches
lighting the avenues
where lovers huddled in horror
who would be lovers no longer.

All night, all night
flared in my city the bright
cruel explosion of hope—
all night
all night . . .[15]

Toward the end of his long poem Rolfe had written that it was

Needless to catalogue heroes. No man
weighted with rifle, digging with nails in earth,
quickens at the name. Hero's a word for
peacetime. . . .

A small catalogue of heroes among the American Internationals, nevertheless, would have to include some names who might have, in more placid times, have contributed more to America's literature than a posthumous hint of potential lost. Rolfe's concluding verses had echoed the image evoked by one of them in a poem, "Written During An Airplane Attack," about troops digging protective trenches, and, when the "shadows come," huddling into the trenches, they "become earth." Then, after the smoke and fire and roar there is silence:

We tear ourselves from the earth,
Become men again.[16]

The writer was Daniel Hutner, once a New York University track star, but killed in action in September, 1937, shot by a sniper in the assault on Belchite.

Another potential writer lost in the Aragon during the fighting for Belchite was a rifleman named Sam Levinger, known for the stories he contributed to the "Battalion Wall." In the days when the unit was in reserve, or otherwise not constantly on the move, the men took a leaf from the Spanish and established temporary "wall newspapers"—*periodicos murals,* the Spanish called them. Glorified bulletin boards, they displayed the drawings, poems and stories of the more talented—or at least more inspired—volunteers. Levinger, an Ohio State student who left college to fight in Spain, contributed some of the stories—until August, 1937. Several of them, Edwin Rolfe thought, revealed "a talent which would surely have been recognized in the United States had he lived."[17] But Levinger, as Murray Kempton later put it, seemed "to have been unable to resist the temptation to run away or throw himself away. He was eight years old the first time he tried to run away; after his family had moved from Wilmington, Delaware, to the Middle West, he tried to sail down the Mississippi on a raft as Huck Finn did and it sank three yards off shore. I confess that I would like to think of the men in Spain as having been carried there by Huck Finn and not by Lenin. . . ."

Levinger's background was far from being an impoverished one. He went to Europe with his family; he junketed to Port Said; he became fascinated by picket lines and strikes. Watching one coal strike while a high school boy, he talked back to the sheriff and was tossed into a Cambridge, Ohio, jail. At Ohio State, he was a Young Socialist who spent as much time encouraging picket lines as he did on campus; and strikers knew him as "the kid who sings." But the biggest picket line of all was the one in Spain, and nine months after Levinger first went into combat, he was in the main square of Belchite, where rebels had holed up in the fortified cathedral. It was an action fought by tired men, of the sort he had written about in a poem:

Comrades, the battle is bloody and the war is long;
Still let us climb the gray hill and charge the guns,
Pressing with lean bayonets toward the slope beyond.
Soon those who are still living will see green grass,
A free bright country shining with a star;
And those who charge the guns will be remembered,
And from red blood white pinnacles will tower.[18]

It was not a very good poem, but Levinger was only twenty, and the first few lines showed that he knew how to communicate the weariness that had not sapped his commitment to Spain. He had no time to learn the graces of versification. As he directed machine gun fire in the storming of the cathedral plaza, he was killed.

Belchite was a costly venture. When it was all over, there were fewer than a hundred unscathed Lincolns left. And replacement troops were thinning out.

So many young soldiers, like Sam Levinger, had wanted to be poets. A similar loss, on the Jarama front in February, 1937, in a battle in which over 300 of the nearly 500 who were involved were killed or wounded, was Joseph Seligman. He was twenty-three. With him was a sonnet:

Not ours to ask why, when we are done,
The little time we spent before the sun
Was bought so dearly, with such wealth of grief,
Such wasted hopes, such sad betrayed belief.

Not ours to ask why you, who had the wealth
To waste a billion stars on empty space,
Could find but one cold world, one dying sun,
For those who might find meaning in your grace.

Not ours to ask why, of endless time
You spent on tearing galaxies apart
You gave but one short day, one bitter day
To those who have your image in their heart.
It is not we shall ask. We shall be dumb,
Back in the nothing that you drew us from.[17]

Late in 1938, *Story* published a long poem about the war in Spain which was so hailed (by Louis Untermeyer, Carl Van Doren and William Rose Benét, among others) that the magazine ventured a separately bound forty-eight page edition at twenty-five cents. It was "Give Us This Day," a series of vaguely connected verse-vignettes in which James Neugass, who had been an ambulance driver with the Internationals, set down his experiences.

He had also produced about a hundred thousand words of prose in rough parallel to it, and a play as well, and the fount seemed endless. But little of the prose reached print—a few pages in *Salud!*, a pro-Loyalist pamphlet. Nothing more was heard of the play, and the star of James Neugass faded as rapidly as it had appeared.

Neugass was then thirty-three. He had been born (in 1905) into a prosperous New Orleans family of bankers and industrialists. His grandfather had been the first president of the New Orleans Stock Exchange, and his father moved north to Wall Street to become a member of Jules Bache and Co. Young Neugass was educated at Phillips Exeter, then went on to study mining engineering at Yale, fine arts at Michigan, Mayan archaeology at Harvard and political science at Balliol College, Oxford, never staying long enough at any of them to earn a degree. When he was twenty-one, he decided that he wanted to be a writer, and since there were no schools for that except experience, he spent seven years in desultory travelling and writing, living in Scandinavia, North Africa, and the Balkans, then settling first in France and then in the Balearics. Funds from home did not make *La Vie Bohème* necessary, and Neugass occupied himself between unsalable translations, poems, and false starts at a novel, and yacht racing, greyhound coursing, and orchid cultivation; and he worked —at intervals—on the Paris *Times*, as a merchant seaman on the Mediterranean, as an art salesman, a private tutor, and movie actor. Meanwhile, he loitered on the outer edges of the Hemingway-Gertrude Stein set, and wrote more poems. The first two were sold —to *Dial* and the *Herald Tribune* "Books" section. The next 448 drew rejection slips.

By 1932, Wall Street was no longer able to support the Neugass method of self-education as a writer, and the poet returned to New York to review books for Malcolm Cowley at the *New Republic*, and Irita Van Doren at the *Herald Tribune*. A more remunerative line of employment turned out to be selling shoes at Gimbel's, a store conveniently owned by a branch of the family.

And Neugass wrote more poems—about four hundred of them—while trying out jobs as rug salesman, cook, social worker, fencing coach, housing inspector, French and German translator, story analyst for MGM, and janitor.[20] When, five years after he had left the Balearics, the islands had become a staging area for Mussolini's troops, Neugass went back, this time to mainland Spain. At Teruel, Segura, Belchite, and the Ebro he served with an American ambulance unit, and in unpunctuated lines strewn with striking images, he wrote about what he saw. A bitter echo of *The Lord's Prayer* gave him his title:

We asked for little: give us this day
our bread gasoline and gunpowder . . .[21]

The olive tree had become almost a cliché for writers about the war in Spain, but Neugass found fresh perspectives:

Deep in the olive trees at sunset
longer than the memory of police chiefs
grow the shadows of headstone olive trees . . .

His admiration for the Internationals had a First World War flavor:

. . . the most ragged
filthy hungry red eyed bastards
that ever went under the name of troops . . .

And his experience as a medic registered in poetry about that side of war which has no equivalent in the Spanish experience other than Captain Tom Wintringham's "Granien."* They "snaked the wounded" down the Segura mountains on men when there were no mules, he wrote; and sometimes they had to extricate them under day-long shellfire beneath "God's hideous sunlight." He "slapped on tourniquets," took down names on medical tags, "pumped the wounded full of morphine," and even wrote their last letters for them. In rear-area hospitals he watched "the single vampire tooth" of a glass syringe[22] draw blood from a newly

* See Chapter 1, "A Battalion of Poets."

killed soldier in order to have blood to transfuse one who might survive; and in the front lines he smoked dry olive leaves when there was nothing else, ate pork fat with wild onions, and unripe olives from "moonlit trees." And he daydreamed of a home that had become unreal:

Those summer girls with dreamy
eyes white and clean as sleep
who slowly walk their big red mouths
Down the quiet streets of a city
heartbreaking summer songs by a lake
where were they? had we forgotten?

The men around him, he knew, had often broken the law or at least violated the terms of their passports—if they had even arrived under legal passports—in order to come to Spain to die, and he was obsessed, as he ended his poem, by the imagery of police searches, fingerprint records and passport photographs:

When in the evening secret service men
lock vaults of cross-indexed finger prints
and the morgues of passport photographs
Where the faces of the Brigades
fade and bleach but do not die
longer than the memory of police chiefs
Grow the shadows of footstone olive trees
deep in battlefield orchards at sunset
thrushes the men had cursed for airplanes
Sleepily find places for the night
secure among the boughs grafted by peace
to the seared and war-torn trunks
Only that the lines shall hold!
nothing else matters there is no
hardship no anguish no other pain . . .

At Híjar, in the Aragon, as the lines were no longer holding, Neugass was wounded, and, in the early fall of 1938, invalided home.

"Give Us This Day," Neugass's Spanish War poem, was his longest—and his last. Hailed at the outset, it was quickly forgotten as the war it celebrated dragged to a close, for by the time it had appeared, late in 1938, Loyalist emotions were nearly spent. Years later, the reprint rights to its thousand lines—for a Chinese anthology of modern American writing—brought him five dollars, bringing his total lifetime receipts from the writing of poetry to $110. Writing was a tough trade.

During and after the Second World War, Neugass worked in factory after factory (some thirty in all), rising to machine shop foreman. And he kept on writing—twelve books in all, including six novels, and translations from Remy de Gourmont, Chirico, Mallarmé, and Lorca. After the torrent of Spanish War writings he now studiously avoided writing of that experience: he may have thought that Cold War passions might get in the way of a sale, and he was having enough difficulty as it was. The thirteenth book was a novel, *Rain of Ashes* (1949), published a few months before (at forty-four) his heart failed as he walked down Christopher Street in New York on a summer evening. *Rain of Ashes* was an autobiographical work set in the overheated Tennessee Williams-like magnolias-and-decay atmosphere of his own young manhood in New Orleans—possibly a last echo of the social guilt which may have been one of the motives which had impelled him to Spain. Even its title, an echo from Edward Arlington Robinson's *Lancelot*, may imply that self-condemnation:

> *God, what a rain of ashes falls on him*
> *Who sees the new and cannot leave the old.*

He had married in 1942, and left two small sons at his death. They "will be discouraged," he had written Harper's, "from becoming writers."

In the *Volunteer for Liberty* of May 25, 1938, was a first-person piece captioned "A New Volunteer Joins the Brigade." Since, by then, volunteers were rare (recruitment had ceased when the Republic, desperate for withdrawal of Italian and German manpower from the enemy side, began talking about counter-withdrawal of the International Brigades) the story had more interest than the usual fare in the *Volunteer:*

> I came to Spain for the first time on April 1, 1938, when the Loyalist army was still retreating through the Aragon. . . . I came on vacation from my paper to find some means of making myself useful in what many outsiders considered a lost cause. From my first day here I knew it was a cause that was not and could not be lost. Two weeks later I resigned my job and joined the International Brigade.

The cause, he continued, was bigger than Spain, for the longer the world delayed in blocking the path of Fascist aggression the more difficult it would be. Then he became personal again:

> It seems rather unnecessary for me to set down my reasons for entering the International Brigade. The cause is so plainly a worthy one that the question which the young men of the world should be putting to themselves is what justification they have for staying out of the struggle. Some of my friends are absolute pacifists and I find it easy to sympathize with their point of view. But the situation today boils down to this: Fascism must be removed from the world for the good of all; the only way fascism can be removed is to fight fascism.

He had come down from Paris on April 1, 1938 in a compartment with Ernest Hemingway and Vincent Sheean, both of whom had known his father, Ring Lardner. Jim Lardner had been working for the Paris edition of the New York *Herald Tribune,* and was using his vacation time to go to Barcelona, although he had secured his own paper's permission to send back some stories, and additional credentials from the *Copenhagen Politiken,* to help him get close to the front. From the line he was certain that the logic of pacifism no longer obtained, and that his usefulness in Spain as a young writer whose one long dispatch to Paris had appeared in mutilated form was less than his usefulness as a man to the dwindling American forces. He had convinced himself by the most thorough research—huddling in a blanket on the chilly floors of unheated Catalan huts and in windswept, scrubby fields, talking all through the night with men who had been in the retreat across the Ebro and were digging in again. In Barcelona, he announced his decision, and Sheean set about trying to change it, suggesting that he work for the Republic in a way better suited to his abilities. He could write, Sheean urged: "It's better than enlisting in the brigades at this late date. Or, in fact, at any date. One more rifle doesn't matter a hell of a lot in the result of a war. You'd be better off doing something else."[23]

Hemingway suggested much the same thing, but Lardner had already decided that one more rifle might very well matter a hell of a lot. Then the Brigade officials refused to consider an enlistment. They had no facilities for training recruits any more, and had no use anyway for poor military material (Lardner was almost helpless without his horn-rimmed glasses). But, when he persisted, the Brigade relented, perhaps figuring on the propaganda value of the famous name, and the chance that he could be kept in a safe rear-area job. At the Majestic in Barcelona, Lardner stopped Hemingway and Sheean on the stairs and went up with them to Hemingway's room, where he said, "I just wanted to tell you that I've got it fixed with the I.B. and I'm going to enlist tomorrow." Again, Hemingway tried to divert Lardner from the Brigades, but when Sheean and Hemingway took him to the first Barcelona showing of Hemingway's *The Spanish Earth* the next day, the film only reinforced his determination to enlist. After the audience dispersed (somewhat late because the film had been stopped in the middle by an air raid alarm), Lardner bought a pair of khaki trousers, a leather windbreaker, and heavy shoes—his "uniform" —and signed up, leaving most of the baggage and provisions he had brought with him from Paris to Sheean.

For two weeks Lardner remained at Badalona, just to the north of Barcelona, at what he first thought was a replacement base. But it was an encampment of *inútiles de guerra*—men returned from the line as unfit for war service for emotional or political reasons. He had been dumped there, it seemed, so that his life would not be needlessly risked while the International

Brigade figured out what to do with him. Early in May he turned up in Sheean's room at the Majestic just after dawn, and demanded a bath and a chance to shave. He was a deserter from the rear, he explained, and he intended to desert to the front if the I.B. authorities refused to send him any other way. It was about the time that John Gates, the political commissar of the Fifteenth Brigade, arrived in Barcelona, and Gates suggested that there was no reason why Lardner could not join the Lincolns, then in reserve at Mora la Nueva, above the Ebro. He could get his training on the job—in fact, there was little chance of his getting any training any other way, for the Internationals' camp to the south had been abandoned. A new recruit (and Lardner was one of the last volunteers) had no other way to learn but on the line.

Just before his 24th birthday, Lardner showed up on foot at Lincoln Battalion headquarters at the village of Darmos, in his new soldier's clothes and with a new rucksack in which he carried a French grammar, a Spanish-English dictionary and a copy of *Red Star over China*. (The book was no political clue. He was not a Communist: only questioningly curious about politics and events.) Wolff was told of Lardner's arrival: "You know who he is, Ring Lardner's son."

"Yeah, I know!" said Wolff, somewhat puzzled. "What do you expect me to do about it?" He put Lardner in Company Three.

In the days before the last Ebro offensive, there was still disappointingly little to do. "Since I joined . . . more than two months ago," he wrote his brother Ring, Jr., on July 13, "we have not been near a trench nor put in a single day's fighting. This in spite of the fact that we are supposed to be shock troops. A lot of planes have passed overhead but none has condescended to notice our presence."[24] Here, too, among the ripening vineyards and the hazelnut and almond trees, the *periodicos murals* blossomed, and Lardner, a corporal and squad leader by July, contributed verses to the Company Three wall board lamenting the fact that the other battalions of the Fifteenth had been shifted

by truck, while the Lincolns had to march a good part of the
distance from Mollerusa on the Lérida road, to Marsa. Using the
marching cadence of *"oop au ay arro"* (the soldiers' corruption
of the first four Spanish numerals, *uno, dos, tres, quatro*), and
setting his lyrics to the Gilbert and Sullivan "Tit Willow," he
composed a satirical complaint:[25]

> *In the hills by the Ebro the Fifteenth Brigade*
> > *Marched oop au and oop au ay arro*
> *And they kept right in step while their officers brayed*
> > *Loudly "Oop au and oop au ay arro."*
> *Oh, the MacPaps* and British and Spanish as well*
> *Get no practice in marching, it's easy to tell,*
> *And compared with the Lincolns they're lousy as hell,*
> > *Singing "Oop au and oop au ay arro."*
>
> *Yes, the Lincoln Battalion gets more than its share*
> > *Of oop au and oop au ay arro,*
> *But because our morale is high none of us care,*
> > *Singing "Oop au and oop au ay arro."*
> *Oh, we don't give a damn for a ride in a truck;*
> *If the others get carried it's just their hard luck;*
> *For as long as we're marching, we don't give a . . . .*
> > *Singing "Oop au and oop au ay arro."*

Early in the summer, Sheean, visiting the Lincolns both as
reporter and as bearer of a pair of replacement glasses for
Lardner (who received them as a drowning man might a life
preserver), found him indistinguishable from the others in his
column. He had a bristling beard, dirty khaki shirt, ragged
trousers, and sockless canvas *alpargatas*. To Sheean he admitted
that he had given away the new clothes with which he had arrived
—they were too fine.

A few days after the attack across the Ebro had begun,
Lardner was wounded by bomb fragments. In the hospital, he
was visited by Joseph North of the *Daily Worker*, who found him
lying on his stomach in a cot, completely absorbed in a compli-

---

* The Mackenzie-Papineau Battalion (Canadian).

cated mathematical puzzle he was pencilling out. "You know, Jim," he suggested, "it would be a good idea if arrangements could be made for a speaking tour for you in the States. You could get big crowds out—give them the lowdown on Spain. You know, Lardner's boy, wounded. Think of the crowds you could speak to."

Lardner shook his head. He had enlisted for service at the front, he said.[26] He left the hospital with his wounds still raw, insisting that he could finish healing back with his battalion. It took him until September 6 before he could get back to his own squad, although the front was now moving in his direction, the Fascists counterattacking with steadily increasing strength, the Loyalist, drained of outside support, steadily weakening.

It was just before the Internationals were to be pulled back and withdrawn from Spain, as the Republic had promised. On the night of the twenty-second, the Americans, knowing that a Spanish brigade would be relieving them by the twenty-sixth, were trying to hold their weakening lines against an enemy artillery barrage. A little after midnight, Lardner went out as leader of a three-man patrol to try to contact a platoon of twenty Americans and Spaniards which was supposed to have occupied a low hill forward to the right flank, but which had not been heard from for two hours. Two previous patrols had failed to locate them. Still they found no trace of the platoon, and continued on in the darkness for several hundred more feet. Then Lardner stopped his companions, telling them that he heard what seemed to be the sound of men digging: "You stay here while I go ahead to see who it is."

In Spanish, Lardner challenged the unknown group ahead. Behind him his patrol waited. A few moments later they heard shouts, then rifle fire, and grenades exploded around them. One of the pair—the Spaniard—was killed, and the American crawled to cover, returning to the battalion alone. The enemy had offered enough fire to repel a larger attack, and the next day captured the two hills from which the American probe had come. There was no chance to look for the bodies of the dead. The next evening the Lincoln Battalion was withdrawn from the lines for the last time. Perhaps the last American to volunteer, Lardner had been the last to be killed.

Weeks later, Hemingway, seeking confirmation of Lardner's death, found out through a correspondent on the Fascist side that press credentials had been found on a body on that battlefield from which the Lincolns had pulled back. Nothing more definite was ever known.

In Barcelona, on October 29, 1938, the surviving Internationals marched down the broad *Diagonal*, the highway which cut a slanting path across the city.* It was a farewell parade, and the Catalans who lined the streets, and hung from balconies and palm trees, wept. There was much to weep for. A cause had been lost.

Gradually, as the Nationalists pushed more deeply into Catalonia, the exiting Internationals managed, in small groups, to get across the frontier into France amid a chaos of Loyalist refugees. Repatriation was not easily accomplished, and often turned out to be unpleasant, while readjustment to civilian life was even more so. Alvah Bessie received his first hint that this would be the case when his friend Aaron Lopoff, not long before he was killed in the Sierra Pandols, said to him, "You really started something when you came over here, baby." Bessie thought that Lopoff was only referring to the slender chances they had for getting back alive; but a quarter-century later he understood that Lopoff might have meant something different: "You see, I had something of a reputation as a writer when I left. But that vanished. And ever since, everything that's happened to me personally has happened in one way or another because of Spain."[27] Like a dozen others (including Rolfe and Gates) he wrote a book about his experiences, Bessie's *Men in Battle* realistically complete to four-

---

* Ironically, this was the boulevard to be renamed after the war the *Avenida del Generalisimo Franco*.

letter barracks language rare in American books in 1939, but at the same time less than honest—as with his reference to Harry Pollitt as a "British working-class leader." It was a telling evasion, for most literate people (and even some others) knew in 1939 that Pollitt was the boss of the Communist Party in England.

Because of Spain, Bessie spent the war years in Hollywood as a film writer, after writing *Bread and a Stone*, a bitter novel which belonged more to the depression decade than to the year it was published (1941). As what some of the Lincolns later called, wryly, a "premature anti-fascist," he was *persona grata* as long as anti-fascism was in fashion, and the Soviet Union a wartime ally. But because of Spain, more than anything else, he was, five years later, in contempt of the House Un-American Activities Committee* (and then in jail) as one of the Hollywood Unfriendly Ten. The literary outcome was a novel for which he had trouble finding a publisher, *The Un-Americans* (1957), clearly based on the witch-hunting activities of the Un-American Activities Committee in the late forties, especially Bessie's own involvement. The fictional persecuted witness is Francis Xavier Lang, a playwright who, among other things, had written a play about the civil war in Spain called *Die on Your Feet*—the title taken from a speech by Pasionaria. (Lang had also written a best-selling journalistic book about the defense of Madrid.) Sarcastic in his responses to ignorant Congressmen who have just completed their persecution of the Hollywood Ten, he is, in turn, attacked by them as a Communist. As the weary cross-examination goes on, Lang's mind flashes back to his experiences in Spain in 1938, memories

* Another writer imprisoned for contempt was playwright John Howard Lawson, who in 1938 was engaged by Walter Wanger to revamp a Clifford Odets script on the Spanish Civil War. Lawson turned out a screen play which was only similar in characters and setting, *Blockade*. Although it was cited in 1949 by the House Committee as subversive, it was mainly an espionage melodrama set in Spain, and more pacifist than pro-Loyalist. Granville Hicks recalled waiting excitedly for *Blockade*, hearing that it "was going to strike a great blow for the Loyalist cause in Spain. But when the picture was released, it did not even indicate on which side the hero was fighting" (*Where We Came Out* [New York, 1954], p. 57).

which are interleaved with the progress of his testimony. There are a trinity of villains, for the Committee is abetted by the "Federal Bureau of Intimidation" and the "Department of Injustice."

Dedicated to two comrades killed in combat, Aaron Lopoff and Joseph Hecht[28] (there are characters based upon them as well), the novel often has moments when its purpose as a tract can be forgotten, for Bessie's film-writing skill rises intermittently in *The Un-Americans*' crisp dialogue and cinematic flashbacks to Spain. Nevertheless, with that novel, Bessie's career as a writer of fiction was, it seemed, over.* But it had already lasted longer than the careers which ended, some of them almost before they had begun, at the Ebro, at Jarama, at Belchite. Perhaps, though, Hemingway was right—that there was little significant literary potential among the Americans in the Brigades. Talent, after all, is relatively expendable; genius is irreplaceable, and it might be more consoling to think that—aside from the profound human loss—the waste of a Joseph Seligman or a James Lardner was not an expense of greatness. If so, the least which must be said for them was said by the father of another young American volunteer, the letter received by the son a day or two before his death in the last months of the war in Catalonia: ". . . I am glad you went over. A man may as well die young having died for a purpose than live a whole life without one."[29]

* There was a little-noticed autobiographical account roughly parallel to the novel, *Inquisition in Eden*, published early in 1965; while Bessie published early in 1967 what he called "the first and probably *only* successful book of a lifetime"—*The Symbol*. A *roman à clef* about a sexy, lonely Marilyn Monroe-like protagonist, it was a commercial success even before publication. For the publisher's jacket blurb about the author, Bessie filled out a long questionnaire in which he stressed the two things in his life about which he still stubbornly felt proud—his year in Spain and his year in prison. The jacket's copy-writer gingerly evaded the references.

9

THE AMERICAN VISITORS

We had writers and poets who came for in-
spiration and to find the truth; and writers
and poets who came because at one time it
was distinctly unfashionable in literary cir-
cles not to have visited Spain.
    Constancia de la Mora,
    IN PLACE OF SPLENDOR *(1939)*

I believed that all one did about a war was
go to it, as a gesture of solidarity, and get
killed, or survive if lucky until the war was
over. . . . I had no idea you could be what
I became, an unscathed tourist of wars.
    Martha Gellhorn,
    THE FACE OF WAR *(1959)*

AT A GATHERING of Helen Hokinson's club ladies in a 1937 *New
Yorker* cartoon, one matron introduced another with "Mrs. Purvis
is just back from Spain. She says they're wearing their skirts
quite short." Few travellers to Spain in the war years were that
obtuse, and perhaps the most unusual aspect of the drawing was
that it was a mention of Spain in the aloof *New Yorker*, where
Janet Flanner, the magazine's "Genêt," had written early in the
war that the "Spanish civil struggle isn't worth wasting ink on."
Editor Harold Ross felt no personal moral outrage about the war,

and—if anything—thought that the Americans in Spain were getting in the way. When the United States, two months after the start of the rebellion, dispatched "four battleships" to the area— to assist American nationals in leaving Spain, according to Secretary of State Hull—"The Talk of the Town" column was sure that the warships were being sent "so that any stray shell might have something solid to bring up against." The *New Yorker* found no citizen worth the risk of accidentally embroiling the U.S. "We don't know who our nationals are, exactly, but if they were the hundred handsomest folks in all Christendom, we don't believe they should be taken off in four battleships.* It is our opinion that nationals should be removed from warfaring countries in stone barges, hired for the occasion. . . . This is only fair to the stay-at-homes. . . ."[1] The Spanish Civil War "did not impinge" upon editor Ross, S. N. Behrman recalled. "Somewhere in his consciousness he felt that perhaps it should, but it didn't. He felt [eventually] that the *New Yorker* must reflect the moral sense it abraded in others. He therefore nurtured one of the most sensitive social consciences in this country, that of E. B. White, and gave him the run of the magazine in matters involving social conscience. In effect, he substituted E. B. White's conscience for his own. As long as the conscience of the *New Yorker* was all right, he rested easy."[2]

The *New Yorker* actually had a point about the American visitors. The tragedy going on in Spain was, in Claud Cockburn's

---

* Late in the war, Ernest Hemingway, who naïvely assumed that his literary fame gave him some political leverage, suggested that he could summon the U.S. Navy to rescue any Lincoln Brigade troops who might otherwise be trapped as they backtracked in Catalonia. "Look!" he told a group of American volunteers and correspondents in Barcelona. "Why the hell let our guys get trapped by the Fascists? If it has to be done, I'll get an American warship and we'll evacuate every single American." André Marty, then still war commissar of the Brigades, had either heard, or heard of, the conversation, and, when difficulties did crop up with exit permits, he proposed a solution and then added, "And by God, if that doesn't work we'll get Hemingway to get that battleship" (Arthur H. Landis, *The Abraham Lincoln Brigade* [New York, 1967], pp. 496–97).

term, " 'photogenic' in the widest sense of the word. Not just the press photographers turned up, everyone turned up who wanted to be in on the decisive thing of the century, the thing that was going to prove either that Democracy was going to stand up to the enemy there and then, or else that Democracy—it was the phrase people used at the time, and they believed in it—was going to take a terrible beating, and after that there would be a bigger and worse war. The massacres and the battles and the subsequent massacres took place, too, in lovely surroundings."[3] Some who went made the pilgrimage with a sense of despair and doom, as if they knew they were visiting not "the tomb of Fascism" (as Loyalist exhortations hopefully viewed Spain) but the tomb-to-be of European freedom. Inevitably, though, Republican Spain became what Arthur Koestler called, wryly, "the rendezvous of the international Leftist bohemia. Bloomsbury and Greenwich Village went on a revolutionary junket; poets, novelists, journalists and art students flocked across the Pyrenees to attend writers' congresses, to bolster morale on the front by reading from their works from mobile loudspeaker-vans to the militia-men, . . . and 'to be useful,' as the phrase went. . . ."[4]

To Constancia de la Mora, who handled foreign press relations for the Republic, fell the task of separating those visitors who could be useful from the "war tourists" and sensation seekers. It was "simply monstrous," she felt, "that some people could come to Spain only to watch us die." Aside from the stream of foreign politicians, she saw "writers and poets who came for inspiration and to find the truth; and writers and poets who came because at one time it was distinctly unfashionable in literary circles not to have visited Spain."[5] Most of the American visitors were intellectuals interested in seeing Spain's agony for themselves in order to make a cause for which they had worked hard at home, and for which, in some cases, it took courage to stand, less vacuous, less a matter of pamphlets and speeches. They came without publicity, and often with their own stock of food, in order not to deplete the dwindling Loyalist supplies. But sometimes they came not to see what they could do for the war effort, but what the war could do for them. To Constancia de la Mora, the classic example was neither politician nor writer—it was the swashbuckling Hollywood war tourist, Errol Flynn.

When Flynn arrived in Valencia, he presented himself imperiously at the Press Office at a time when events had made Government business chaotic, and demanded an automobile, permits, passes, gasoline slips, guides—whatever was needed to go to the Madrid front. Gasoline was so short that correspondents were deferring trips until new supplies arrived, but the actor had no time to spare. Too famous a personage to snub, he was dealt some of the precious gasoline slips and lent a car. And, two days later, the Paris papers reported that Errol Flynn had been wounded at the front in Madrid.

"We make a point of not allowing our front-line visitors to be killed," Stephen Spender had been told on his first visit to lines around Madrid; and even that was an understatement. As a result, the Government's Press Office wired frantically to Madrid to find out to what hospital Flynn had been taken, and how seriously he had been hurt. In Madrid, people from the Foreign Office combed the city looking for a dying or dead Hollywood star, and the Press Office furiously enjoined its guides in Madrid not to let any visitor close enough to the front to be in shooting range.* They wired back denials. No one had seen the movie star, and no one had conducted him to the line.

Just as the Press Office had decided that Flynn was probably lying unidentified in some morgue, one of the foreign news agency men drifted in and surveyed the panic. "What's all the excitement?" he asked casually. "Your Hollywood friend isn't really hurt. Just a scratch with a penknife on his arm, or something like that. Just to fix it so that we could plant a story in Paris about it."[6]

* Actually, so much of Madrid was within artillery range that to have followed the order literally would have meant sealing off Madrid to visitors.

Some of the American visitors had been in Spain at the beginning. Poetess Muriel Rukeyser—then twenty-two—had been in Barcelona, and, on the evening of July 25, 1936, five days after the war had broken out, was among the Americans at the Anti-Fascist Olympic Games evacuated at the order of the Catalonian Government. The "Workers' Olympiad" had been a reaction to the holding of the official Olympics in Hitler's Berlin, but had to be abbreviated, and some of the spectators and participants had even fought in the street battles in Barcelona. One was a woman, the first English volunteer to be killed—Felicia Browne, a Communist painter who went on from street fighting to the militia, and was killed in the Aragon on August 25, shot through the head. It was exactly a month after the evacuation in which Muriel Rukeyser left Spain in a small, overcrowded coastal steamer, the *Ciudad de Ibiza*. The local consulates reacted helplessly to the fighting in Barcelona, and the Belgian team had chartered the boat. Meant to hold two hundred, it was packed with five hundred, including the Belgian, Hungarian, and American teams, for the overnight voyage to Sète, the nearest port in France. The only ones who remained were men—and the one woman—who had volunteered for service with the Loyalist forces.

"Your job," a street meeting speaker had told a group of foreigners which included Miss Rukeyser, was to "go tell your countries what you saw in Spain." This she did, in a number of poems, several savagely partisan, their object, in her terse style:

> *The picture at our eyes, past memory, poem,*
> *to carry and spread and daily justify.*
> *The single issue, the live man standing tall,*
> *on the hill, the dock, the city, all the war.*
> *Exile and refugee, we land, we take*
> *nothing negotiable out of the new world;*
> *we believe, we remember, we saw. . . .*

For Muriel Rukeyser, having been an involuntary "war tourist" only confirmed the need for social concern on the part of the writers:

if we had stayed in our world
between the table and the desk
between the town and the suburb
slowly disintegration
male and female.
If we had lived in our city
sixty years might not prove
  the power this week
  the overthrown past
  tourist and refugee. . . .[7]

It was not the end of Miss Rukeyser's involvement with Barcelona. When the city fell, she wrote its elegy, "1/26/39."[8] She had seen the war there at its start, and celebrated both the beginning and the end.

Another unexpected "war tourist" was spade-bearded novelist Elliot Paul, who, since 1923, had lived a mostly expatriate life, first in Paris at a place in the Rue de la Huchette; then in the Balearics, on the island of Ibiza, where he was collecting material for a book on the life of an unspoiled Spanish town. The town Paul had chosen was Santa Eulalia del Rio, "very much like any American seaboard town except that the various races there had had six thousand years in which to be blended, and consequently the population was more homogeneous. Also the young men did not, as a rule, leave the island to seek their fortune elsewhere. . . . I loved them and their animals and the shadows of the trees that fell upon their houses. They divided their last *pesetas* and red wine and beans and gay spirit with me."[9]

Twice during his six-year idyll on Ibiza he made trips back to America. On the second trip, he became so homesick for Santa Eulalia that he decided to return there ahead of schedule, build a home, and settle down. With his wife and stepson he went back to Spain, and took the weekly steamer *Ciudad de Barcelona* from Alicante to Ibiza on July 14, 1936. It was the last regular passenger sailing, for five days later the Civil War began.

On Ibiza, the military garrison joined the rebellion and established a Fascist government. Before long, a transport, two destroyers, and four submarines loyal to the Republic had deposited four thousand mostly Anarchist volunteers on the island, overwhelming the rebels in a destructive battle. Nationalist sympathizers among the Ibicenos were plucked out of their homes and hiding places, and added to the military prisoners in the island's lone fortress. A few days later, the same amateur force joyously set out for the larger Balearic island of Majorca, made an ineffectual feint, and sailed back to Barcelona. Nothing had been accomplished except to announce by implication that Ibiza was being left to its fate. The Italians occupied Majorca and turned it into a supply and replacement depot for their "volunteers" in Spain, and an airfield and submarine base from which to harass shipping headed for Barcelona and Valencia. Then they turned to tiny Ibiza and showered the island with leaflets urging surrender, and bombs to reinforce the suggestion. Nothing of military importance was hit, but fifty-five Ibicenos were killed, forty-two of them women and children. "Our turn is coming now," one of the younger Fascist prisoners remarked to the Anarchist guards.

Outraged by the bombings and inflamed by the insolence of the young Fascist, the guards shot the prisoner and the men around him, marched other prisoners out of their cells and executed them, too, burying some of them in a common trench. Then the Anarchist members of the Ibiza militia hastily evacuated the island on two large boats, taking with them all the militiamen who insisted that they would be butchered by the Fascists if they were left behind. The Ibicenos did not know it yet, but they were completely defenseless. The dead from the Italian bombings and the dead from the Anarchist massacre littered the narrow streets of the harbor area and the halls of the old town fortress. Alone, "too numb to be saddened or horrified, faint from the unspeakable smell, . . . alone in blaming or not blaming . . . , alone in yesterday's riddled hopes and illusions," Paul wandered through the streets of Ibiza, wondering why the Civil War had to reach out its terror to the innocent island. Then he thought, "Of the two hundred and thirty-nine [dead] in the fortress, perhaps five were innocent, and of the fifty-five dead in the streets *all* were innocent, and the port was innocent, and the island and my town, and honest people everywhere."

Snapping out of his numbness, he found "the fascist boy survivor and the militia boy remainder," and quizzed them for information about events he "did not actually see but only heard and smelled the morning following." It was an act done "dutifully, as being the only man alive for miles around who tapped nightmares on typewriters." And there was little time, for soon there was a German gunboat in the shattered port, to take off foreign nationals before any suspicious Ibicenos left would be shot against the wall. The next day the Italian troops landed.

Elliot Paul's projected book on the *life* of a Spanish town became *The Life and Death of a Spanish Town*. By the time he came back to Loyalist Spain in June, 1937, the book had been written. From Valencia, it was only a few hours across a stretch of Mediterranean to the Ibicenos with whom he had spent four years. "I got away, and they did not," he had concluded his preface. "Their land is dying. Mine is not. This book is a debt I owe them." It was a relatively small skirmish on a small and isolated island, but Paul used the event to symbolize the impact of mechanized war on simple people maintaining their traditional culture. To a later generation, his sympathy smacked of windy rhetoric and "syrupy primitivism," for he was as much preoccupied with his own emotions as with the fate of his friends. The pity was as much for the life he could never live again, as for Santa Eulalia.[10] It was not that Elliot Paul was consciously using false tones, but that he had not, in the romantic haze with which he had quickly surrounded the scene, reached an end to innocence.

Although Paul returned regularly to visit Madrid, Valencia, and Barcelona while it was still possible, he settled in Paris again in the Rue de la Huchette, where most of his *Spanish Town* book was written. Most of the inhabitants of the St. Michel quarter, he discovered, wanted Franco to win in Spain, and Fascism to succeed as well in France: "The situation in France was so similar to that in [pre-war] Spain that my friends reacted to events there as if they were seeing themselves in a dream."[11] Before long, he was writing another book. He had become a specialist in nostalgic farewells to places so egocentric in outlook that their inhabitants could not see, even in a world where the terror was closing in, the connection between aloofness and complacency. In a few years German tanks were clattering across the Île de la Cité, over the Pont St. Michel, and even as far as the impenetrably narrow Rue de la Huchette. And Elliot Paul, once more an expatriate refugee, began writing *The Last Time I Saw Paris*.

Like most writer-visitors, John Dos Passos came to Spain by way of Barcelona, and, like the others, he was impressed at the start by the gutted churches, the "war posters signed by every imaginable committee and political party" and plastered everywhere there was a wall standing, and the papertaped windows, sometimes in unimaginative crisscrosses, more often "worked into all kinds of designs. The spiderweb with a spider in the middle of it was popular, as were fish, monograms of CNT and UGT, and linked squares and rays and interlacing triangles." Catalonia was still Anarchist-controlled, which to the outsider was represented by the banks with *"Taken Over by the Generalitat"* signs, stores with signs reading *"Employee Control"* or *"Taken Over By the C.N.T."* and trolleycars and buses repainted black and red with "C.N.T." in small letters on them.

Valencia to Dos Passos had a more international flavor than he remembered from past visits, and the bullfight posters had given way to martial ones. Indoors, the change in tone was more marked: the militiamen in the hotels were often newly arrived Internationals, a cross section of radical Europe, and the talk was of the mysteries of the Mediterranean just off Valencia's wharves—the unannounced blockades, the unreported sinkings, the anonymous freighters (names painted out) slipping by the watchful Italian warships by running at night without lights. From Valencia, he

drove west toward Madrid, as busy and noisy as he remembered
it, but more grim and more gray. He understood why when his
driver parked the car that evening in front of the Hotel Florida:
"The noise that went on when the motor stopped was machineguns.
We listen. Not very near but getting nearer; up the street from
the front night, shattered and dented with gunfire, pours into the
city."[12]

Much in the Madrid of sandbag trenches and paving-stone
barricades reminded Dos Passos of other Madrids he had known
over two decades—the same bustle, the same sallow faces, the
same streetcars—but the "Best People" were no longer visible:
"They are in Portugal or Seville or in their graves." Although
he had already inaugurated his own literature of anti-Communism
with the closing pages of his *U.S.A.* trilogy (in *The Big Money*),
he saw little reason then for anything but dedication to the Republic's cause, observing at an International Brigade barracks
"French faces, Belgian faces, North of Italy faces; German exiles,
bearded men blackened by the sun, young boys; a feeling of
energy and desperation comes from them; they have lost their
homes, their families, their hopes of a living or a career; they
are fighting back." It was April, 1937, the time of the Brihuega-
Guadalajara victory, and the fighting back had a temporary air of
success, even to a parade through the shell-pitted streets of captured Italian flags, guns, and trucks. But at night he would think
of the shells, and the bloodstained sidewalks and gutters, and,
while staring at the ceiling, or at the oasis of his clean electric-lit
room, "of the pleasantfaced middleaged chambermaid who'd
cleaned it that morning and made the bed and put everything in
order and who'd been coming regularly every day, doing the job
ever since the siege began just as she'd done it in the days of
Don Alfonso, and wondered where she slept and what about her
family and her kids and her man, and how perhaps tomorrow
morning coming to work there'd be that hasty loudening shriek
and the street full of dust and splintered stone and instead of
coming to work the woman would be just a mashedout mess of

blood and guts to be scooped into a new pine coffin and hurried away. And they'd slosh some water over the cobbles and the death of Madrid would go on."

Dos Passos had not come to Spain this time as novelist or vacationer, but to help Hemingway write the film script which became *The Spanish Earth*. The originator of the venture, Dos Passos was convinced that the only way to make Americans aware of the facts about Spain, when so many newspapers were isolationist, was through a film. Even in that medium, he knew, the message would be hard to get through. In Pennsylvania, for example, the Board of Censorship was refusing to pass newsreels of the Civil War unless all references to General Franco's troops as "Fascists" were removed, even when the troops were actually Mussolini's. But a few nights before Dos Passos had sailed, he had had dinner with Carlo Tresca, then editor of an Italian-language weekly in New York. Tresca, who had spent a lifetime in various libertarian causes, warned his friend about the Communists in Spain, "John, they goin' to make a monkey outa you . . . a beeg monkey."

"Impossible," said Dos Passos. He and Hemingway would have complete charge of the script.

The old ex-Anarchist laughed. "How can you? When your director [Joris Ivens] is a Communist Party member, when everywhere you go you will be supervised by Party members. Everybody you see will be chosen by the Party. Everything you do will be for the interests of the Communist Party. If the Communists don't like a man in Spain right away they shoot him."*[13]

Dos Passos' much delayed arrival, according to Hemingway, was an anticlimax. "He had been in Paris . . . , writing me notes heatedly in favor of our cause," Hemingway told A. E. Hotchner, "but now he announced that he was actually coming down to join us and we eagerly awaited his arrival because we were all starving and he had been instructed to bring food. He arrived with four

* Tresca was murdered in January, 1943—gunned down as he left his office. A Communist political assassination was suspected, but the murder was never solved.

chocolate bars and four oranges. We damn near killed him."[14] Beyond the grotesque *ex post facto* exaggeration lies the obvious fact that disenchantment with Dos Passos set in early, and that the feeling was reciprocal.

One night, several months later, Elliot Paul, back in Valencia from a visit to Madrid, began to talk about Dos Passos to his sixteen-year-old guide Coco (Francisco) Robles, and to Constancia de la Mora. "I don't know what's come over Dos Passos," he said. "I saw him in Paris and he won't take an interest in Spain any more—says he doesn't care. He is full of some story about a friend of his being shot as a spy, some college professor from Johns Hopkins."

Coco—so Constancia de la Mora reported—looked at Elliot Paul gravely. "I hope that will not make Dos Passos lose his interest in the fight against fascism in Spain," he said. "The man he spoke of was my father."

One of the mysteries of the war was the case of José Robles, Dos Passos' old friend and translator of one of his books, and Professor of Spanish Literature at Johns Hopkins University. When the Civil War began, he had been spending the summer in Spain with his family, and had immediately offered his services to the Republic. He had never belonged to any political party, and had never participated in Spanish politics. In the fall of 1936, during the siege of Madrid, he worked—with the rank of Lt. Col.—as English interpreter for a tall, gray-haired Russian general, Berzin (known there as "Goriev"). General "Goriev"— officially the military attaché to the Soviet ambassador—had his office a few doors away from General José Miaja, the Republican commander in Madrid, and how much of the defense of Madrid was planned in one office and how much in the other was always a matter of doubt. "Goriev" trusted Robles, who "had a fine open face and pleasant personality, and looked the disinterested idealist."[15]

In the winter of 1937, Robles disappeared from sight, and the story circulated in Valencia that he had been shot as a spy.

People who claimed special knowledge intimated that he had been smuggled out of Spain against his will and taken by boat to Russia. Some said it was because he had talked too much and revealed military secrets in Madrid cafés. In Madrid, Dos Passos said later, he learned from "the then chief of the republican counter-espionage service that Robles had been executed by a 'special section' (which I gathered was under the control of the Communist Party). He added that in his opinion the execution had been a mistake and that it was too bad." It had nothing to do with café indiscretions, Dos Passos was sure, and the Fascist spy theory seemed to him "the fabrication of American Communist sympathizers."[16]

The day that he had first walked into the Press Office in Valencia, in March, 1937, and Coco ran to greet him, was just about twenty-four hours after the Robles family had been informed of the execution. Dos Passos raced about Madrid and Valencia frantically trying to find out more information, but there was not much information to be had. It was general knowledge that Robles had a brother who was an officer on Franco's side, and that hardly improved the outlook. What might have been more to the point— although one Republican story had it that he might have been framed by the Anarchists—was that Soviet secret agents could have concluded that Robles had learned from "Goriev" and Miaja too much about the extent to which the Republican War Ministry was controlled from the Kremlin, and, as a non-Communist, was not sufficiently reliable to "forget" the information he had acquired.

Some of his associates in the documentary film project, Dos Passos recalled, "were disgusted with me for making all these inquiries. What's one man's life at a time like this? We mustn't let our personal feelings run away with us. . . ." It was impossible for him. He felt the Spanish Republic was being destroyed from within, although—paradoxically—the rest of the Robles family kept right on working for the Republic, wife and daughter first in Valencia and then in Barcelona, and son with the Press Office until he went off into the Republican militia in the last-ditch fighting in Catalonia, where he was captured in the final month of the war.

Dos Passos stayed with the film unit, reluctantly. There was some discussion as to what the main theme of the documentary was to be. An obvious subject was the beseiged capital and its stubborn citizenry. It was easy enough to photograph the city's wounds, and such battles as Dos Passos, Matthews, and Hemingway could watch from a battered apartment house on the Paseo de Rosales, a perch Hemingway wryly christened "the old Homestead." But there was little humor Dos Passos could see in the city's agony. To him, Madrid was "a great stony theater of tragedy." Part of the tragedy, he added to himself, was the invisible Communist terror, but "this was something you couldn't very well get into a documentary particularly when the communists had charge of it. Our Dutch director did agree with me that, instead of making the film purely a blood and guts picture we ought to find something being built for the future amid all the misery and massacre. . . . We settled on an irrigation scheme being put through by a village collective."[17] So Dos Passos helped provide the scenario for a film to do missionary work for a cause in which he had already lost faith.

To Hemingway, death was the price of war, and one had to expect the irrationality of lives wasted, or the wrong lives taken. As a result, he found the obsession of his old friend Dos Passos difficult to accept. "Dos," he said, "spent his whole time in Madrid looking for his translator. We all knew he had been shot but no one had the heart to tell Dos, who thought the translator was in prison and went all around checking lists. Finally, I told him. I had never met the translator, nor had I seen him shot, but that was the word on him; well, Dos turned on me like I had shot him myself." Then Hemingway insisted on a second reason for Dos Passos's withdrawal. "The very first time* his hotel was bombed, Dos packed up and hurried back to France. Of course, we were all damned scared during the war, but not over a chicken-shit

* This is clearly hyperbole.

thing like a few bombs on the hotel. Only a couple of rooms ever got hit anyway. . . ."[18]

Hemingway had not wanted to tell Dos Passos, but something had to be done, he told Josephine Herbst, to get him "to lay off making inquiries about Robles. It was going to throw suspicion on all of us and get us into trouble. This was a war." Hemingway might admit that someone had told him Robles was dead—but, Miss Herbst insisted, the information must be attributed to "someone from Valencia who was passing through but whose name . . . he must withhold." All three had had lunch at Russian headquarters, and, when Hemingway caught Dos Passos momentarily alone, he told him. From Dos Passos' abstracted air afterwards, Josephine Herbst knew he knew. Finally, a little coffee cup trembling in his hand, "Dos came up to me, and in an agitated voice asked why was it that he couldn't meet the man who had conveyed the news, why couldn't he speak to him too? The only thing I could think of was to tell him not to ask any more questions in Madrid. It would be better to wait until he got to Valencia and then see someone like [Álvarez] del Vayo and find out what he could."

The ride back into Madrid was silent, and Hemingway bolted from the car as soon as it halted at the Hotel Florida, leaving the others standing on the street. Forlornly, they walked toward the Place Mayor, where the setting sun illuminated the "flushed skeletons" of once beautiful houses. In the square was a still whole statue of a great horse, its flanks glinting coppery rose in the sunlight. On one side was painted in red the initials of the Anarchist syndicate: *C.N.T.* In the hand of the rider had been thrust a tiny Anarchist flag.[19]

From Madrid, Dos Passos went on to Valencia, and before he left Spain he visited the headquarters of the POUM in Barcelona. It was just before the suppression of the Party, and the confused, internecine warfare in the streets, in which Orwell had been involved and about which he would write with such anguish. At the POUM office Dos Passos asked some questions about party rivalries in Catalonia of a man at "a big battered fakegothic desk," and learned that "It's complicated. . . . You know Spain." It was only later that he discovered that the gaunt Englishman at his hotel with the sick, drawn look had been George Orwell. "We didn't talk very long, but I can still remember the sense of assuagement, of relief from strain I felt at last to be talking to an honest man." Orwell, he thought, already then must have been suffering not only from his wounds but from the tuberculosis which later killed him. "Men who are about to die regain a certain quiet primal dignity. Orwell spoke with the simple honesty of a man about to die."[20]

Dos Passos had been full of doubts before he went to Spain, but the old loyalties to the country had temporarily magnetized him. The Spanish episode—in particular the Robles case, which became a lens through which Dos Passos afterwards viewed the struggle—became (in Malcolm Cowley's words) "a final and definite turning point in his career. Hemingway had tried to explain it to him privately (I imagine) and in an article published in *Esquire* but obviously written for Dos Passos alone. There are always traitors in a civil war, Hemingway said. Some of them are likeable people in ordinary life, but a revolutionary government has to protect itself against them if it is going to survive. Malraux also answered him; at least it is likely that some passages of *Man's Hope* were written with Dos Passos in mind. But Dos Passos had crossed a gulf so wide and deep that his friends were lost in it."[21] Having no faith in the justice of such trials as Robles must have had, and sure that his friend had been guilty only of not being a Communist (and even this often proved no safeguard), he had a different point of view which went beyond the individual case. "Of course," he insisted, "this is only one story among thousands in the vast butchery that was the Spanish Civil War, but it gives us a glimpse into the bloody tangle of ruined lives that underlay the hurray-for-our-side aspects. Understanding the personal histories of a few of the men, women and children really involved would, I think, free our minds somewhat from the black-is-black and white-is-white obsessions of partisanship."[22]

Returning from Spain, Dos Passos wrote a piece for a magazine, *Common Sense*, titled "Farewell to Europe!" He meant it literally. Feeling let down by events, he was proclaiming his personal declaration of isolationism. "The Atlantic," he concluded, "is a good wide ocean."[23] The Communist *New Masses* attacked the manifesto as the statement of "a tired radical," and Dos Passos responded that activism in the interests of another country had to have its limits: "*After all*, we must remember where our enthusiasm for brave little Belgium led us." He was all for offering the Loyalists ambulances, and even machine guns, he insisted, but he was not for intervening on a broad scale. "Our business," he wrote, "is now to learn the lessons. . . . We have the enormous luck, shared by few of the inhabitants of Europe, of not having yet to take sides for life or death in any of these quarrels. The place to fight the Fascists is in your own home town. Fascism thrives on the war spirit."[24]

Several months after Dos Passos had left Spain—it was the summer of 1937—he was the chief subject of a conversation *Esquire* publisher Arnold Gingrich had with Hemingway. They were fishing out of Key West, where Gingrich had flown to battle with the author of *To Have and Have Not* and Moe, Hemingway's lawyer, over the questionable taste of the finished manuscript. "I felt," the publisher remembered, "based only on my hard-earned knowledge of what is and isn't libelous, that large gobs of this were libel *per se*. Three people were libeled right up to their eyebrows. . . ." One was Hemingway's erstwhile friend.

The parts about Dos Passos were rough, Hemingway admitted, but he had thought of a neat stratagem: "You know, all I have to do to get Dos to okay everything in here that you object to about him? All I have to do is tell him *you* don't like it! . . . Moe, you draw up the tightest-ass release you can dream up, and I'll get it signed."

The lawyer was baffled. "But Ernest, I thought your defense of that part was that it *isn't* about Dos Passos. I frankly don't see how I can draw up a release for a man to sign that isn't *about* him—"

The logic of the law had escaped Hemingway, as had the shift in the literary climate. Cockily, he assumed that Dos Passos would, for old times' sake, freely consent to be fictionally libeled by the writer-pal who had not only broken to him reluctantly the withheld news about Robles but had rationalized it away. But Hemingway's stratagem was never put to the test; his thoughts were still across the Atlantic, and he solved the immediate literary dilemma by killing large portions of the novel, leaving it malformed because neither were the objectionable episodes replaced nor the remaining sections re-integrated.[25]

Whatever the guilt or innocence of José Robles, it was a point of no return for Dos Passos, and the total disillusion with Communism of his next fictional hero was symbolically parallel to his own. Glenn Spotswood, in *The Adventures of a Young Man* (1939), joins the Communist Party because it seems to be fighting for a better life for the average man. He works as a union organizer among Kentucky miners, suffers beatings at the hands of mine owners, but persists in serving the cause of the miners until his refusal to hew to all the twists in the Party line makes him a renegade. The vindictiveness of Party leaders follows him all the way to Spain after he joins the International Brigade. In Spain, he sees the Party rivalries beneath the surface of the Republican cause. Perez, one of his old Spanish acquaintances from the States (now an empty-sleeved Catalan ex-soldier) warns him, "Here [are] several different kinds of war. We fight Franco but we also fight Moscow. . . if you go to the Brigada you must not let them fight us. They want to destroy our collectives. . . . We have to fight both sides to protect our revolution."[26] But merely talking to Perez is too much, and Spotswood is arrested as a "Trotskyist-Bukharinist wrecker" after the suppression of the POUMists in

Barcelona. The fact that he keeps a diary is the clinching "evidence" that he is a spy, and he is released only when a sudden enemy attack overruns the area and someone is needed to go out to die on an utterly futile mission. Rather than release for him, it is the carrying-out of his death sentence. A bullet brings him down when he is halfway up the hill, and he goes "spinning into blackness."

The grim saga of the Spotswood family was continued by Dos Passos in two other novels. *Number One* (1943) concerned a Huey Long figure whose success was further evidence of the author's disillusionment with the ability of the people to choose their own government. In *The Grand Design* (1956) the message is Communist duplicity beneath Communist appearances of co-operation in combatting depression and in fighting the Second World War. The complete disillusionment with social and political reform reflected by the Spotswood books, John Aldridge has observed, left its mark on their quality as novels: "He can no longer protest with the great power and conviction of *U.S.A.*, for his protest depended on the existence of those hopes. The best he can do is expose with a kind of listless irritation the evils he is now able to see but helpless to attack." The three novels—more fictional tract than fiction—are pervaded with the futility Dos Passos brought home with him from Spain, his career afterwards "a long process of running through and destroying the ideals which seemed to him worthy of belief." After Spain he had "run through them all and been left with nothing. In *U.S.A.* he [had] achieved a perfect blend of protest and negation which gave the book and its characters their power and value."[27] When he had left what remained of his idealism in Madrid, Valencia, and Barcelona, he had lost the formula with which he had turned into art some of the great social issues of his time. There are good reasons for considering Dos Passos, who neither bore arms nor absorbed any bullets in Spain, the major American literary casualty of the Civil War.

Dos Passos had found the tragedy of Spain not restricted to the trenches. It was a fact most sensitively recorded by the women "war-tourists" among the Americans. Novelist Josephine Herbst survived an encounter with a Spanish *soldado* who greeted her warmly with a four-letter English word which was the only one the Americans had taught him up to then. Two American officers in the Lincoln Battalion quickly took her in tow and gave her a tour of front-line positions. Later, she toured the ruined towns, and saw what happened to communities in the wake of a retreat. Her next novel recorded the memory.[28] But afterwards, verbalizing her experience came hard, although she had been irresistibly drawn to Spain early in the war. "Later you may dress it up with reasons; some of them may very well apply. But *because* is the soundest answer you can give to an imperative. I didn't even want to go to Spain. I had to. Because." When she returned, Spain was already becoming "locked up inside of me. There was one thing you couldn't do when you came back from Spain. You couldn't begin to talk in terms of contradictions. . . . What was wanted was black or white."

More than twenty years later, Miss Herbst finally unlocked her impressions in *The Starched Blue Sky of Spain*.[29] If the pen had ever seemed mightier than the sword, the typewriter nonetheless seemed to have little chance against the new weapons, she had thought even while packing her typewriter for the journey. But she had hoped for a miracle—"and there were intimations of possible miracles in Spain." She had acquired an assignment to write feature pieces—what the news in the daily dispatches usually failed to cover—but she was primarily fulfilling her imperative. Dutifully, she forwarded her human interest pieces, while the intimations of possible miracles faded on closer view. "Doubtless many of the soldiers in the International line were under the old spell of 'workers of the world, unite' in the full belief that the true causes back of the war in Spain were revolutionary, and that, *this time*, a great new world might once more have a chance. But the mirage of the future did not blind them to the present; it induced the opposite to an easy optimism. To be stupidly optimistic does not give courage." Only at the Hotel Florida, among the correspondents, did she find that easy optimism, generated by the popping of corks and the camaraderie of writers who could sometimes write dispatches which convinced even their authors. Madrid, even with the bombardment, often "seemed utterly remote from the more meaningful scenes you might witness in the villages," and her room at the Florida "was hardly bearable" after a day or two with the people of the Guadarrama.

The Florida's worst was the regular occasion when the German artillery found the range. Miss Herbst recorded one shelling just before daybreak when a hit burst pipes and sent water into her room. She pulled on a dressing gown and ran out into the corridor toward the rooms at the back, where Hemingway, fully dressed and calm, greeted her with "How are you?" Ashamed of her cowardice, she headed back toward her room to dress. Then, seeing Claud Cockburn in the hall, coffee pot in hand, pale but impeccable, she rushed up to him and took the pot.

> We went to a room toward the front where the banging was heaviest. Thousands of rats seemed to be scrambling for their lives in the plaster of the walls. We got the coffeepot plugged in, but there was no coffee. Someone else brought coffee and someone else some stale bread. A toaster came from somewhere. Dos Passos, fully dressed and composed, even to a necktie, came in. A French correspondent in a vibrant blue satin robe emerged carrying an armful of grapefruit, which he passed out to each of us, bowing to us in turn. Who would give away a precious grapefruit if this was not to be our last hour? No one ate the fruit, but each one, when the shelling was finally over, stole off with the loot. Hemingway blew breezily in and out. . . . When the shelling was over some people ran at once to the street. Hemingway came back with the report that the Paramount Theatre had got it, including the big sign advertising Charlie Chaplin's "Modern Times." . . .

Early in May, 1937, Josephine Herbst decided that it was about time to move on. She was eating food others needed, and, even so, she had already lost twenty pounds. Like Dos Passos, she prepared to leave Spain just as the suppression of the POUM in Barcelona had begun, and, cornering Claud Cockburn in Madrid, asked him what the truth was. "They are putting out the usual line of accusations," he shrugged; "they claim they've got documents to prove collaboration with Franco." She put only one more entry in her journal—the record of a stop at a filling station en route to Valencia, where she had unexpectedly renewed acquaintance with a young Spanish officer she had first met at a mountain outpost near Guadalajara. He was happy and proud, and that was the way she had hoped to remember Spain.

In the summer of 1936, Martha Gellhorn, a young American novelist, was researching background material for a novel in the Stuttgart *Weltkriegsbibliothek* when the Nazi newspapers published their first news about the fighting in Spain. There was no talk of revolution or rebellion: According to the controlled German press, bloodthirsty rabble were attacking the forces of decency and order. But the Spanish rabble, she discovered by careful reading, was the legal government of the Republic, referred to only as "Red Swine-Dogs." She was convinced: "The Nazi newspapers had one solid value: Whatever they were against, you could be for. . . . But there I was, working with miserable determination on a novel about young pacifists in France. I stayed some months in Germany discussing, with anyone who still dared to discuss, the freedom of mind, the rights of the individual, and the Red Swine-Dogs of Spain. Then I went back to America, finished my novel, shoved it forever into a desk drawer, and started to get myself to Spain. I had stopped being a pacifist and had become an anti-fascist."[30]

In the winter of 1937, Martha Gellhorn was back in France, applying to the authorities in Paris for permission to cross into Spain. When the permission was not forthcoming—the typical French petty official, she was sure, was "a certified brute"—she acquired a map and took a train to the Andorran border. In tiny, landlocked Andorra, no one was very concerned about non-intervention. It was easy there to walk from one country to another, then take a Spanish train—of "ancient cold little carriages" full of soldiers—to Barcelona. Since she spoke no Spanish, and assumed that questions might be asked about a young American blonde—who claimed to be a writer—in Spain, she prudently had come equipped with a letter from a friendly editor at *Collier's*, which told whom it might concern that the bearer was a special correspondent for the magazine in Spain. It was only to smooth things with authorities in France and Spain, and it worked as effectively in Spain as it had failed in France. In her soon lost innocence, she had come believing "that all one did about a war was go to it, as a gesture of solidarity. . . . I had no idea you could be what I became, an unscathed tourist of wars."

In the first days of spring, 1937, there was renewed hope that the Loyalists would contain the rebellion and eventually win out, and the atmosphere she saw in Barcelona was bright with March sun, optimism, and red banners. The taxi driver even refused money. On trucks and in jammed cars she made her way across Spain, "handed about like a package, with jollity and kindness." It was on the dark, cold evening of March 30 that she arrived in Madrid, equipped with a knapsack, good looks, and what was left of the fifty dollars with which she had crossed the frontier. Tagging along behind the war correspondents who had transportation and gasoline, she had learned a little Spanish and a little military science, and visited the wounded. On her first visit to the front she arrived just in time to be marooned there by an enemy attack, and was forced to spend the day at a brigade first aid station, helplessly watching the bodies of the dead and the wounded being brought in. It was a poor effort for the *Causa*, and one journalist-friend—very likely Hemingway*—suggested a few weeks after she had arrived that she could serve the Cause better by writing than by touristing. She knew nothing about war, but she had seen life in Madrid. (It was not everybody's daily

---

* She had met Hemingway in Key West before the war, when she came, chaperoned by her mother, to interview him.

life, he pointed out. It was what was new in war. The civilians of the Republic had the war brought literally home to them.) She also put the April 5 attack she had seen at closer range than expected into a magazine piece, and, when copies of it reached Spain later, it was carefully read by the American volunteers who remembered the fair-haired girl in slacks.

She had mailed her Madrid piece to *Collier's* and became a war correspondent as well as a novelist when the article was accepted. Hemingway took her to the *Telefónica* and saw to it that the Spanish press relations and censorship personnel took good care of her: "That's Marty—be nice to her—she writes for *Collier's*—you know, a million circulation."[31] There were to be more pieces from Spain, and, for eight years, Martha Gellhorn found more war to write about. The first war was the most curious, when, to fill the days, one might—with green chiffon scarf wound around one's head, and slacks from Saks Fifth Avenue hitched up firmly—take a walk from the hotel to the trenches. "So we strolled to University City and Usera, to the Parque del Oeste, to those trenches that are a part of the city and that we knew so well. No matter how often you do it, it is surprising just to walk to war, easily, from your bedroom where you have been reading a detective story or a life of Byron, or listening to the phonograph, or chatting with your friends." To *Story* magazine, she observed that "it is really too strange. I walked from my hotel to the front as easily as you would walk from the Metropolitan Museum to the Empire State Building."[32] It may have been a useful image to Americans who only thought of war as an impalpable something that happened a long way from home.

Back from Spain after her first visit, Martha Gellhorn sat on the platform at the July Writers' Congress with a journalist-friend she had acquired in Spain named Hemingway, and among the speeches following his offered a brief talk of her own on writers fighting in Spain, identifying some of the Germans, French, Spanish, English, and American authors she had observed there. Like herself, she said, they had all gone "because it is immensely important to them to do something beyond them, to do something about which they believe. They have gone to Spain to do whatever work they can do. . . ."[33] For the committed writers, she declared,

> There is no reward of special recognition, credit, praise, money or consideration. They have the immense privilege of being there. They have the immense privilege, not only as writers but as human beings, of being a part of a living thing in which they believe.
>
> One morning in Madrid, during a bombardment, we went to the theater. An amateur performance was being put on for the benefit of the hospitals. The boy who was acting the part of the hero scarcely knew his lines. At the end he came out and said he was sorry about it, and he apologized for having forgotten his lines. He said he had tried to learn the lines while in the trenches and that learning them had been hard because an attack had been going on. On the other hand, he said, he had time during the attack to write a poem, which he proceeded to read. It was very fine. He had written the poem for the men serving in the trenches with him. It meant something to them for him to do it and to him to have done it. He is an example of another kind of writer fighting in Spain.

Except for a broader social commitment, it was a Hemingwayish performance, concluding with the peroration, "We have the obligation of seeing and understanding what happens, of telling the truth. . . . A writer must also be a man of action now. Action takes time, and time is what we all need most. But a man who has given a year of his life, without heroics or boastfulness, to the war in Spain, or who, in the same way, has given a year of his life to steel strikes, or to the unemployed, or to problems of racial prejudice, has not lost or wasted time. He is a man who has known where he belonged. If you should survive such action, what you have to say about it afterwards is the truth, is necessary and real, and it will last."

In the fall of 1937 she was back in Madrid, describing its trenches and its streets, "those calm young men who were once . . . bank clerks or law students," and the children who made clay houses and cardboard dolls and "missed school only when the shelling was too bad." She was even back again in the fall of

1938 for the third winter of the war, reporting what home life had been reduced to in Barcelona—the skimpy rations and the food queues, the elderly at home unemployed because factories had run out of raw materials, the mature away fighting somewhere, the young no longer going to school because of the daily air raids. She was there to report the first and last parade of the withdrawing Internationals, down the Diagonal, the soldiers who "looked very dirty and weary and young," and many of whom had no country to go back to. She was at a Catalan munitions factory now resorting to re-boring the prehistoric guns whose grooved rifling had been worn smooth from the many thousands of rounds they had fired, and for which there would be no replacements from outside. She was there at a home in Barcelona where, bidding the worn, brave people goodbye, she said, impulsively, after shaking hands all around, "The third winter is the hardest."

"We are all right, señora," said the lady of the house. "We are Spaniards and we have faith in our Republic."

All that Martha Gellhorn wrote about the war afterwards, even in the guise of fiction, was towards the ends she had talked of that evening on the speaker's dais with Hemingway, from the visit to the peaceful oasis of the Madrid Zoo to the hints about her attraction to Hemingway in the early days of their reporting out of besieged Madrid. (" 'I hope this war lasts long enough for him to say something,' I thought.")[34] He had read what she wrote, given her literary advice, and fallen in love (in Malcolm Cowley's description) "like a big hemlock tree crashing down through the underbrush."[35] According to a story he told A. E. Hotchner, he even offered to fight a duel over her in Spain. "General Modesto was in love with Miss Martha, made three passes at her in my presence, so I invited him to step into the men's can. 'All right, General,' I said, 'let's have it out. We hold handkerchiefs in our mouths and keep firing till one of us drops.' We got out our handkerchiefs and our guns, but a pal of mine came in and talked me out of it because money was scarce and our side could not afford a monument, which all Spanish generals get automatically."*[36]

When Hemingway came back from the war for the last time and began work on *For Whom the Bell Tolls*, divorce from his second wife Pauline was in the air, and, by January, 1941, he was answering (as "Hemingstein") former Lincolns Major Milton Wolff, who had objected to the alleged vilification of André Marty in the novel, "You have your Marty and I've married my Marty. . . ."[37]

For both Martha Gellhorn and Hemingway the Cause would have more permanence than their marriage. Twenty years later, she could write that she had upheld the *Causa* for twenty years, and was weary of explaining

> that the men who fought and those who died for the Republic, whatever their nationality and whether they were Communists, anarchists, Socialists, poets, plumbers, middle-class professional men, or the one Abyssinian prince, were brave and distinterested, as there were no rewards in Spain. They were fighting for us all, against the combined force of European fascism. They deserved our thanks and our respect and got neither. . . .
>
> All of us who believed in the *Causa* of the Republic will mourn the Republic's defeat and the death of its defenders, forever, and will continue to love the land of Spain and the beautiful people, who are among the noblest and unluckiest on earth.

The defeat of the Republic, Martha Gellhorn had declared for herself and others like her who were in Spain, "was ours; we

---

* Martha Gellhorn's short story "A Sense of Direction" (in *The Heart of Another* [New York, 1941]) may deal with the origins of the episode. In it, the female correspondent-narrator is taken on a tour of the front by an International Brigade "Commandante" who uses his opportunities to be alone with the attractive young American by attempting to paw her. Returning to her Madrid hotel much later than expected, she stops by the room of fellow writer "Fred Lawrence," who is in bed, reading. Knowing the amorous commandante's reputation, "Lawrence" admits, "I was worried about you," and adds, "Did he try anything?"

"Of course not," the narrator lies (while thinking about the query, "I was delighted.").

Hemingway more than repaid the gesture, his idealized Maria in *For Whom the Bell Tolls* resembling the new heroine in his life. The novel was dedicated to Martha.

carried it with us in our minds, in our hearts, where it mattered. I daresay we all became more competent press tourists because of it, since we never again cared so much. You can only love one war; afterward, I suppose, you do your duty. . . ."[38]

A most unusual place for an American woman "war tourist" in Spain to be published was the *Volunteer for Liberty*. A piece by Dorothy Parker appeared there in November, 1937. "I want to say first," she began, "that I came to Spain without any axe to grind. . . . I am not [even] a member of any political party. The only group I have ever been affiliated with* is that not especially brave little band that hid its nakedness of heart and mind under the out of date garment of a sense of humour."[40] With her husband Alan Campbell, the small, dark-haired writer had visited Barcelona and Valencia, sitting out four German air attacks upon the refugee capital, impressed by the unreasonable beauty of night bombings and the terror of day raids. Afterwards, they went on to Madrid as part of an American delegation, and created a sensation in the hotel dining room when Miss Parker wore a fashionable (in Manhattan) and unwarlike pale yellow hat shaped like a sugar loaf. A waiter whispered to writer-propagandist Arturo Barea, "What d'you think's the matter with her so that she can't take the thing off? Perhaps her head is shaped like a cucumber. . . ."[39]

Shell-bespattered Madrid was far more a war sector, but Dorothy Parker had clearly been most impressed by an incident in Valencia, and described it later for the *New Yorker*. "Soldiers of the Republic" was a vignette of six Loyalist soldiers in a Valencia café, in the closing hours of a forty-eight hour leave

* From the late nineteen-twenties, when she was fined $5 for "sauntering" in a Boston demonstration against the execution of Nicola Sacco and Bartolomeo Vanzetti, Miss Parker had been active in liberal causes. During and after the Spanish Civil War she was national chairman of the Joint Anti-Fascist Refugee Committee, a post which caused her trouble long after the fact, for in 1951 she was cited by the House Un-American Activities Committee (along with three hundred other writers, artists, actors and educators) for affiliation with what the Committee designated as "Communist-front" organizations.

from the line. "There were many soldiers in the room," she wrote, "in what appeared to be uniforms of twenty different armies until you saw that the variety lay in the differing ways the cloth had worn or faded." The worst thing they had to face, they tell the narrator's companion, is the lack of communication with their families. Some had been without news for a year. Six months before, one comments, he had heard through a brother-in-law that his wife and children were all right and had a bowl of beans a day; but what troubled her, he had been told, was that she had no more thread to mend the children's ragged clothes. "She has no thread," he keeps repeating.

After the soldiers leave, the two women left at the table get up to go, too, and summon the waiter; but he only shakes his head and moves away. The soldiers had paid for their drinks.[41]

It was a more effective protest than the bitter picture of bombed children she had sent to *New Masses*. The understated eloquence of the plea for six soldiers of the Republic could stir readers already sated with atrocity stories, yet destined to endure more years of them. It was difficult, though, to avoid the compulsion to cry out against the wanton brutality that had become so much a part of war that, as Martha Gellhorn once noted, "another shelling of Madrid" was not even newsworthy.

Writing to Freda Kirchwey in May, 1938, Thomas Wolfe (sympathizing with the Republic at a distance) in caustically commenting on Franco's offer to reopen Spain's tourist trade in the Nationalist sector, suggested a sample letter of inquiry to the Franco tourist bureau: "I should like, if opportunity presents itself, to visit the various craters and ruined masonries throughout the town of Barcelona, paying particular attention to the subway entrance where a bomb exploded, and where one hundred and twenty-six men, women and children were killed in one economical gesture." Also, he offered, "I should like . . . to pay a visit of devotion and respect to the Chapel . . . where General Franco's wife and daughter go to offer prayers for the success of the Defender of the Faith."[42] What had infuriated Wolfe had been a Francoist travel advertisement he had seen in April. "Visit the sunny South of Spain this Spring," it had invited. "Seville will welcome you to its wonderful Holy Week processions."

Not waiting for Franco to open his tourist bureau in Barcelona, Lillian Hellman took a leave from polemical playwriting and went to Loyalist Spain late in 1937. It was educational, she thought. In Madrid, for example, she discovered that in the hour-and-a-half of the first shelling she had endured there were many different sounds in the darkness: "Some of those sounds have no name in English." In the kitchen of her hotel a blind woman had been holding the bowl of soup she came to get each night.

> . . . She was killed eating the bowl of soup. Afterwards an Englishman said to me, "Not much sense to this kind of killing. They don't even try for military objectives any more, or for men. When I was on the Franco side, a few months ago, I heard the German technicians call this 'the little war.' They're practising. They're testing, testing their guns. They're finding out the accuracy of the guns, they're finding the range." Finding the range on a blind woman eating a bowl of soup is a fine job for a man.[43]

When the *New Republic* published the Hellman piece, it was with a two-sentence preface: "The article was written at the request of Walter Winchell, to be published in Mr. Winchell's widely syndicated column. After it was prepared, however, the King Features Syndicate, owned by W. R. Hearst, refused to permit it to be distributed to the newspapers taking Mr. Winchell's column."

There were not only American visitors in Spain, but Spanish veteran visitors in America, appearing at rallies and mass meetings, and at fund-raising events as small as apartment cocktail parties, where one paid fifty cents a drink, and met a celebrity or a Loyalist veteran. A *New Yorker* cartoon cynically pictured a typical grouping at a benefit cocktail party for the Cause, with one dispassionate drinker commenting to another, "This is the round that starts them weeping for the Spanish Loyalists." There were pro-Loyalist benefits in Hollywood, too, throughout the war. At one, in Frederic March's home, Errol Flynn—a war tourist himself—, Dashiell Hammett, Robert Montgomery, and a dozen others saw a private showing of *The Spanish Earth*. When the Monterey *Herald* telephoned John Steinbeck to inform him that Congress—or, rather, its Dies Committee—had denounced him for contributions to the Loyalist cause, the novelist (then working on *The Grapes of Wrath*) noted that other California celebrities had also contributed to the Loyalist cause. "What's good enough for Shirley Temple," he explained, "is good enough for me." Other cinema stars besides the famous moppet supported the Republic—Paul Muni, Orson Welles, Edward G. Robinson—and *Life* even went to a Hollywood party where Mr. Oscar Hammerstein II raised money for Spanish children's welfare.[44]

Star of the war tourist-in-reverse circuit was André Malraux, whose journalistic Spanish War novel *Man's Hope* was in press in an English-language edition as he spent the spring and summer of 1938 raising American dollars for Spain with tales of his air adventures over Madrid. "To big audiences," *Time* reported, "he talked with almost untranslatable rapidity and eloquence; to small groups of writers from Princeton to Hollywood he preached his favorite literary message: the value to literature of active political careers by its creators. . . . In Hollywood he made three money-raising speeches. . . . When esthetes asked him how he could write in Spain with the War going on, he replied, 'It gets dark at night.' The ivory tower, he told them forcibly, was no place for writers who had in democracy a cause they could fight for. If they lived, he insisted, their writing would be better for the experience gained in the fight; if they died, their deaths would make more living documents than anything they could write if they remained in ivory towers."[45]

It was a grim invitation, but Malraux rallies and meetings

were seldom inspirational in the expected manner, whether they were a send-off dinner for the "First American Writers-Artists Ambulance Corps" at the Hotel Pennsylvania (sponsored, among others, by Edna Ferber, George S. Kaufman and Stuart Davis) or a rally at the Mecca Temple sponsored by the North American Committee to Aid Spanish Democracy. At one of his first meetings (it was long after the suppression of the POUM in Barcelona), Communists were carefully planted in the audience to ask him leading questions about the allegedly dark doings of the POUMists. Wasn't it true, Malraux was asked, that the POUM was sabotaging the Republic? His reply was cold, and to the point: "I will not say anything critical of any human being who fought and died in the defense of Madrid." As Koestler, too, had dis-covered, those in the audience dismayed by the non-Party Line response remained uncomfortably silent while they worried over another possible victim of the infection of heresy. But Malraux's intensity and eloquence disarmed the most narrow partisans, as he turned to an anecdote about the distribution of toys to the bombed and shelled children of Madrid:

> When it was all over, there remained in the immense empty space one little heap, untouched. . . . It was a pile of toy airplanes. It lay there in the deserted bull ring, where any child could have helped himself. The little boys had preferred anything, even dolls, and had kept away from that pile of toy airplanes . . . with a sort of mysterious horror.[46]

One listener at the Mecca Temple in March, 1937, had been a very young literary critic, Alfred Kazin, who recalled Malraux's "stabbing phrases" as driving "the agony of Spain like nails into our flesh." That night, not only did Malraux tell the story of the Madrid children and the toys, but also the tale, to appear in *L'Espoir* as well as in the film made of the novel, about one of the planes of his International Air Squadron which had been brought down high among the mountain villages. Only mule paths led down the mountain, and single file, the wounded aviators were brought down by stretcher-bearers, while the entire population of each village through which they passed stood reverently, the men in silence, the women and children in tears. And, said Malraux, *"when I raised my eyes, the file of peasants extended now from the heights of the mountain to its base; it was the grandest image of fraternity I have ever encountered."* Although he had to pause every few sentences for his interpreter to catch up, "and would draw in his breath like a swimmer, he spoke with such fire that his body itself seemed to be speaking the most glorious French. He was magnificently the writer as speaker, the writer as the conscience of intellectual and fraternal humanity, the writer as master of men's souls." His very rhythms, Kazin thought, "were so compelling that audiences swayed to them. *'We destroyed the airdrome of Seville, we did not bombard Seville. We destroyed the airdrome of Salamanca. I destroyed the airdrome of Ávila at Olmedo, but I did not bombard Ávila. For many months now the Fascists have been bombarding the streets of Madrid.'* "[47]

Like Malraux, Ralph Bates had metamorphosed from fighter for the *Causa* to its ambassador to the intellectual world. Blond, florid, and energetic, with a revival meeting style and fluency, the British novelist was the center of attention in chic Manhattan or Hollywood "parties for Spain" as well as on the platform at mass meetings. Already the author of the Spain-set—and highly regarded—*Lean Men* and *The Olive Field*, as well as the more experimental (but unsuccessful) *Rainbow Fish*, he knew Spain from long residence, and the war from his months as a political commissar. *The Olive Field* had to be sent to him in galley proof in Spain, where he was already so politically active during the months which preceded the civil war that he was unable to read it—and the galleys had been set by Cape from a typescript he had never seen, one made in England from the handwritten manuscript he had left behind. Turbulent Spain, which had inspired the book, had made it impossible for him to correct, clarify, tighten or elaborate the inevitable passages which, to an author, look agonizingly different in print.[48] Nevertheless, *The Olive Field* described the attachment of people to their soil with the passion and vividness of a D. H. Lawrence, and the chapters of his novel about the aborted revolution of 1934, one London critic wrote, succeeded each other "like ringing blows on an anvil."

Some of his war memories were even more passionate and vivid, particularly one "chilling experience" he recalled which had "so completely transcended anything I had ever known that I seemed to have walked into a vast and deliberately fashioned drama or religious rite." He had come down from the hills into Villanueva one windy night during the Brunete battle. The town, raked by shellfire, was burning.

> At one moment a blazing roof beam would be flung into the sky, describing a yellow scroll, or a huge inverted cone of sparks would soar up and illuminate the billowing smoke, or a column of flame would rush out and burst above the stubbled fields, sending wave after wave of sparks running down the valley. . . . For safety I entered the church. It was an evacuation station and its floor was covered with wounded men, groaning and screaming. . . . Doctors were going among the men; the church was lit by a few acetylene flares placed in the ground. The long shadows writhed on the walls, like figures in a mobile El Greco. All the church was full of the echoing litany of death. I went up to the dismantled high altar to write my report. Suddenly my imagination, my mind, and my heart were frozen. Bowed over the center of the altar, his head upon his hands, was a wounded man, blood streaming from his head. He was standing as a priest stands when he murmurs: "Hoc est corpus meum." The man was dying, I thought. He seemed to be pleading the sacrifice of Spain. I stood frozen in imagination, hearing that echoed wailing. Far off, the machine guns rattled.
>
> Afterwards I went outside and was sick. I was not sick at the spectacle of pain, but because of the unaccepted sacrifice.[49]

Committed as he was, by the time Bates left Spain he was in political trouble which made his absence imperative. He had been there too long. In Latin (and, afterwards, Asian) fashion, he was sent on missions which made use of his reputation while keeping him out of the country.[50] Still, his Party loyalties while a Republican missionary to America appeared impeccable. Unlike

Malraux, he had come to preach the Stalin line against the Anarchists, Syndicalists, Trotskyites, and other splinter groups who were fighting against Franco but not for the Communists. But he offered his message subtly through his passionately told tales of Communist-led troops of the Fifth (and truly Red) Regiment spearheading the Madrid defense, and (according to him) Communist-inspired citizens defending the Madrid barricades. Kazin heard him one warm spring evening at Muriel Draper's house on lower Lexington Avenue, when he spoke "with so much conviction, so many ready facts, so much pleasure in his own oral gifts," that John Chamberlain, who had introduced him humbly, and the crowd, mostly from the staff of *Time*, was "shaken by the torrent of Bates's words" and impressed by its proximity to a novelist-adventurer in the tradition of Malraux and Hemingway. Bates, Kazin recalled, "stood in the center of the artful Victorian parlor and spoke to a fascinated circle gathered at his feet as if it were an orchestra out of which he was drawing beautiful sounds with a few slight gestures of his hands."[51] By then, Bates had already written some of the short pieces about Spain he published in 1939 as *Sirocco*, an uneven collection of short and novella length documentary fictions about Mediterranean fishermen, mountain farmers, peasant feuds—and the war. The title story, of the conversion of a revolutionary from revenge to love within the same cause, and "43rd Division," which told of a guerrilla individualist and his solo war in the mountains, had much of the mood, and some of the style and power, of the Spanish War novel Hemingway was still composing. "Everything," Clifton Fadiman hazarded about Bates in a *New Yorker* review, "is in favor of his writing a great book, perhaps the classic novel of the Spanish civil war." But, although he never stopped writing,[52] Bates had left the wellsprings of his fiction to live on the American side of the Atlantic, settling down eventually to journalism and teaching in New York. The great novel of the civil war would be written by somebody else.

As a missionary for the Cause, Bates had won, through his platform manner and his zeal, an audience which went far beyond the committed Stalinists, who never numbered significantly among the writers on the American Left, and who made—as Granville Hicks later put it—"scarcely a dent on any of the media that reached the masses of the American people—the popular magazines, the movies, the radio."[53] Even later, when in the last desperate year of the Spanish Republic's life, Kazin and other American intellectuals had become revolted by the Moscow trials and disgusted by Soviet duplicity in Spain,* they could not help but consider—as Czechoslovakia and Austria disappeared into the Nazi maw—Fascism as the major threat to peace. It seemed to those whose mood Kazin echoed that it was essential that the Spanish Republic somehow survive: "I did not want to dwell on what the Stalinists were doing in Spain. I wanted only to see Fascism destroyed, to see the stone roll away from the tomb." When a City College classmate of his just back from the front told Kazin of the persecution in Barcelona of the anti-Stalinist Left, he was reluctant to believe the tales he inwardly knew were true. After years of reading Malcolm Cowley's literary essays and reviews in the *New Republic*, where Cowley was the immensely influential Literary Editor, and several years of review writing for him, Kazin was prepared to go along with the Popular Front leanings of that sophisticated veteran of the Left Bank and the Village. Kazin personally disliked the Hemingwayish-looking, pipe-smoking, military mustached Cowley in the way, perhaps, that one instinctively dislikes the samaritan upon whom one has been dependent for a livelihood. Still, Cowley had not only been at Harvard with Dos Passos, in an ambulance unit in France with E. E. Cummings, in the Village with Hart Crane, and in Paris with Hemingway, he had *also* been a visitor to Spain, and had

---

* Some intellectuals waited until the even more revolting Stalin non-aggression pact with Hitler in August, 1939, made Communist cynicism impossible to rationalize further.

come back convinced that any division of the Left would weaken resistance to the common enemy, Fascism.

Cowley had gone to Spain in July, 1937, to attend the Writers' Congress, and had not come back enthusiastic over Stalinist influence in Spain, but kept his inferences guarded. It was important to retain at least the facade of an uncorrupted cause, and that meant—at the least—an air of scepticism toward the Anarchists. For the *New Republic* he noted that in Barcelona, when he passed the former headquarters of the POUM, "the Left Communist organization more or less allied with the Trotskyists," he saw "half a dozen blue-capped Assault Guards standing watch at the door. Inside was a great heap of broken plaster and anti-government pamphlets." He quoted a conversation with European journalists whose protective armor of cynicism, he felt, was "mixed with an almost sinister type of revolutionary dilettantism." One of them had remarked that he did not plan to go to Madrid: "Madrid is too orderly; it is entirely devoted to winning the war. But here in Barcelona you can always be sure of trouble. It is *formidable, épatant.*" Another correspondent advised Cowley to be sure to see the Aragonese villages then under Catalonian Anarchist control. "They try all sorts of experiments," he said. "I was in one village where they had abolished money. In another, they had divided their possessions equally and spoke of returning to the Golden Age. It is all quite crazy and I love it." But then Cowley observed, the newsman offered to change the American's French money into pesetas. Later, Cowley discovered he had been cheated on the transaction.[54]

In a later report, Cowley fell into a cliché of the Popular Front (for which an Orwell could not have forgiven him), sarcastically contrasting the Americans of the International Brigade to the "brave stay-at-homes of the FAI and the POUM." But, for the most part, what Cowley saw of the war while in Spain for the Congress he reported as reasonably as his conclusions. What would happen, he asked, if the Nationalists should win out? The people, he thought, would sink back into apathy, their land exploited by the Germans and the Italians. There would be reforestation and irrigation projects, but nothing which would interfere with the big landed proprietors. The schools would be returned to the Church. And the country "would sleep and decay, as it slept and decayed in the eighteenth century." It was a fair assessment, and, but for pressures generated by American military expenditures and commitments in Spain after the Second World War, might have been entirely accurate a generation later. And if the Republic survived? "There will be a period of incompetence and disorder, there are certain to be quarrels and trials and scandals, but all these will be signs that the people are fighting their own battles. . . . There will be new irrigation projects, new dams, power plants, mines, smelters, factories, universities; the printing presses will be busy and the schools crowded. . . . Under a people's government, the dead land will spring to life."[55] Significantly, he did not capitalize *people's* or *government*. Whatever his "protective benevolence" (in Kazin's terms) toward proletarian literature—nearly the only dynamic literary mood in the thirties—Cowley had come back from Spain without ideological blinders, but no less convinced that a politically fragmented Spain might satisfy idealism, but could not win.

The war-tourist writers were numerous and articulate, and ranged the gamut of American writing, from poet Langston Hughes, who came to observe the Negro soldiers among the Internationals, and stayed to write poetry, to Erskine Caldwell, tale-spinner of the Southern poor whites, who saw a different kind of grimness in Catalonia. They ranged from young novelist Meyer Levin, who visited the Madrid trenches, and then went on to Palestine, later admitting guiltily, "It seems to me that I am still apologizing a little for not having remained to fight in Spain,"[56] to the anti-Semitic, anti-Catholic had-been novelist Theodore Dreiser, who arrived in nearly isolated Catalonia close to the end, and came back, self-inflated, to the States.

In hopes, dreams, and failings, Dreiser was the embodied caricature of the war-tourist. Sour, selfish, and floundering at the ragged edge of genteel penury, whatever had made him a writer was, by this time, gone, and he was ready for almost any kind of literary prostitution. But almost no one was asking him. He was for the Republic, he thought, and was particularly against bombing defenseless cities; but in the words of an "exasperated organizer" of anti-embargo protests, "the old dope" was for enforcing the arms embargo rather than lifting it.[57] Still, he was a great name out of the past, and, recognizing this, the League of American Writers—of which he was not a member—invited him to junket over to Paris for meetings of the International Association of Writers and the less left-winging *Rassemblement Universel pour la Paix*. It was a free adventure, easily worth the two lectures he would have to cancel, and, as for *The Living Thoughts of Thoreau* he was "editing" for Longmans—his secretary Harriet Bissell was going to be doing that anyway.

Dreiser sailed on the *Normandie*, and, immediately on arriving in Paris, sent out for some American gin for his "morning depressions." "When I get enough whiskey in me I'm all right for a while," he wrote his secretary, "but then come the blues again. . . ." He battled his "blue devils" with gin and at least one bedroom involvement with a French female, gave a platitudinous speech at the Peace Conference in which he endorsed "fair play" and "sharing peacefully what had been given us by nature," and accepted an invitation from Loyalists at the Conference to visit Spain. On July 29, 1938, he took the train to Perpignan and was driven in an old Republican car to Barcelona, later writing for NANA a piece (published September 11, in the *New York Times*) describing his ordeal. The recurrent air raids, the food shortages, the lack of replacement clothing, the totality of the tension under which Catalans lived, appalled him. There was no sugar, butter, or milk, and almost no bread or meat, but the people endured their privations stoically, and Dreiser was impressed. "The courage of them," he wrote Harriet Bissell. "The pride. They won't beg!"

As a Very Important Person he was given audiences with President Manuel Azaña, Premier Juan Negrín, and Foreign Minister Álvarez del Vayo, and out of the talks came a suggestion that Dreiser intercede somehow with President Roosevelt to get American food shipments to Republican Spain. As a visiting dignitary, Dreiser even permitted himself to be interviewed, and twenty correspondents, he boasted to his secretary, showed up at the Ritz for the privilege. After a three days' sampling of the Catalan atmsophere, including a visit to a military hospital, an army camp, and an underground Barcelona air raid shelter, he raced off for London,[58] but not before a farewell party was thrown in his honor at the Hotel Majestic. It was in the days of the last battles across the Ebro, and correspondents had just returned to the comparative safety of Barcelona, to be regaled by Dreiser's theories that Franco was secretly a Mason, and Hitler and Stalin secret Catholics, and that all the troubles of Europe were the result of a strange Masonic-Catholic conspiracy. Dreiser, newspaperman Robert Payne later wrote, could hardly have enjoyed a more distinguished—and, on the surface at least, respectful—audience. "André Malraux was there, his face convulsed in dreadful tics, his handshake limp, his hair damp and matted over his forehead. Ernst Toller was smiling his sad refugee smile. . . . There was Boleslavskaya of *Pravda* and Herbert Matthews of the *New York Times* and Louis Fischer, dark and saturnine, and sometime during the conversation James Lardner drifted in, looking pale and ghostly from his wounds." Nothing could budge Dreiser from his obsession. He was going back to America, he declared, to tell people about the accomplishments and struggles of the Loyalists, but the whole mess had been the fault of the Masons and the Catholics, and now it would lead to a terrible war no one could prevent.

"Dreiser's voice quavered with passion," and, Payne thought, "he evidently believed all this nonsense. He was a little drunk, for the Majestic had plentiful supplies of wine and almost no food. We lived on pale soup, bread cobs, squid and corn husks which pretended to be coffee."

His dewlaps shaking and his face suddenly radiant, the old war-tourist prophesied "a war more terrible than any war that has been visited on man," and the handful of farewell-wishers sat politely, waiting for the diatribe to end. "I think Malraux was the one most perplexed. . . ," Payne recalled. "It was not that he did not believe Dreiser: it was simply that he saw deeper, and more perturbing, causes for the war which was coming. Toller, too, was uneasy. . . . Matthews listened with appalled politeness, and only Boleslavskaya was gently amused by the sight of the doddering old man weaving his spell of doom, while the chandeliers twinkled overhead and the lights went out and the white-gloved waiters set candles in wine bottles round the table."[59]

In London, Dreiser set about trying to see Government officials in the Republican cause, but finally had to write Harriet Bissell that "seeing the people the poor Loyalists wanted me to see is difficult. England is an autocracy. The masses are underpaid; stupid, silent. The gang at the top wants not only to rule England but the world. They want beggars & stupid slogan-fed workers and they have them—while they loaf and entertain and shoot deer in great preserves!" He had more success in the United States, but it was nearly meaningless. He first wrote to President Roosevelt to ask for an appointment, but the letter was answered by Assistant Secretary of State Berle. Dreiser wrote a second time, pointing out that, although he was willing to discuss his unstated message from Spain with any official the President saw fit, he had promised Azaña and del Vayo he would talk with the President himself, if he could. This time Dreiser was invited to meet with Roosevelt at Hyde Park the next Wednesday, and fifteen minutes was set aside in the Presidential calendar. Meanwhile, Dreiser moved in briefly with a female sleeping partner in New York and spoke of his experiences in Paris and Catalonia (the public side of them, at least) to several public meetings, one of them the League of American Writers at the City Club. "It was a terrible shame," he told them of the Fascist bombings of Barcelona, "that they made a hash of that beautiful city." Suddenly there were big moments for a writer now sixty-seven and passé. The *New York Times* even interviewed him on his birthday. (And through his agent he sold three articles on Spain for nine hundred dollars.)

On September 7, Roosevelt lunched with him on the Presidential yacht *Potomac*, on the Hudson off Hyde Park, and offered sympathy, but pointed out that his administration could not legally initiate even non-partisan food shipments to Spain. Instead, he suggested that Dreiser organize a committee of several eminent citizens to devise means of raising funds, food, and clothing for both sides from the United States and other American countries. Since it was the only way to achieve any kind of help for Republican Spain, Dreiser agreed to try; but the committee idea failed. Still, the project bore some fruit, for Roosevelt afterwards formed a civilian committee himself, and, through the International Red Cross, attempted to get shipments of such foodstuffs as flour to Spain. "That you should have applied the mechanism of the plan you suggested so accurately and effectively," Dreiser wrote Roosevelt on January 7, 1939, "and particularly in the face of the stalemate that any ordinary citizen was certain to encounter, makes still more clear to me the enormous value of a great executive in the Presidential chair at all times but most particularly in periods of stress and change." Dreiser was gratified. He had, briefly, involved himself with the world's movers and shakers. It had been thirty years since he had met a President—the other Roosevelt. And, suddenly, in the space of three months, he had dined with the Presidents of Spain and the United States, and had been a luminary at an international conference in Paris. Nevertheless, it was too late for Loyalist Spain: Barcelona would fall in three weeks. Dreiser had been perhaps the last, and certainly one of the least attractive, but also—however belatedly—one of the most effective of the American visitors.

EPILOGUE
The Persistence of Rudinism

When a man hath no freedom to fight for at
home,
Let him combat for that of his neighbors;
Let him think of the glories of Greece and of
Rome,
And get knocked on his head for his labors.
George Gordon, Lord Byron,
November 5, 1820

IN PARIS ON THE TWENTY-SIXTH of July, 1848, a cause was being lost on the barricades. That sultry afternoon, the Revolution of '48 was nearing its final collapse, and Ivan Turgenev, who had been in Paris for several months, stood by watching it fall. "He watched, he noted, he deplored," V. S. Pritchett has commented;[1] "but when it was all over he did not, for all his love of liberty, share that sense of personal tragedy which overcame the Herzen circle."

Now that it was too late, Alexander Herzen confessed to Turgenev that he was sorry that he had not taken a rifle a workman had offered him that afternoon, and at least attempted to do something useful. The worst that could have happened, he explained, is that he might have taken with him to the grave "one or two beliefs." Turgenev shrugged his shoulders. Political activism —its dogmas and its violence—had no attraction then for him.

301

Yet, seven years later, when he began working on a political novel, he turned to that afternoon in Paris, and the last twitch of the dying cause, when, in the narrow alleys of the Faubourg St. Antoine, a battalion of the line was breaking through one of the last barricades, and its surviving defenders, thinking desperately of their own safety, were taking flight.

As the last defender fled, at the close of Turgenev's novel, a solitary figure suddenly appeared on the very top of the barricade, "a tall man in an old overcoat, with a red sash, and a straw hat on his grey, disheveled hair. In one hand he held a red flag, in the other a blunt curved sabre, and as he scrambled up, he shouted something in a shrill, strained voice, waving his flag and sabre." A Viennese soldier took aim at him and fired; and the slender young Russian drooped like his flag, and toppled over, face downwards, a bullet in his heart.

"*Tiens!*" sneered one of the escaping revolutionaries, "*one vient de tuer le Polonais.*" Alone, with an insult for his epitaph, Dmitri Rudin, writer, had died on a foreign barricade for a lost cause.[2]

"There was a touch of Rudin, it used to be said, in every Russian," Pritchett observed in 1937, "and now, when some English intellectual goes out to the trenches of Castile and the Spanish militiaman calls out, 'God, they've shot the German,' one wonders if Rudin is not a universal figure. . . . Now, has Rudinism once more returned?"

It had never really disappeared. The persistence of Rudinism is the persistence of causes which jolt the intellectual into activism. Byron—however sophisticated and cynical—was a Rudin before Rudin. Even before Spain, the apparently non-political Hemingway had observed that a writer might hone his pen on a cause.* Rudinism propels the intellectual back into touch with his society, sometimes even at the cost of his life. It is, Pritchett wrote, "that bug for good and ill [which] gets into most thoughtful men in times of social frustration. And if Turgenev's non-com-

---

* "Writers are forged in injustice as a sword is forged" (*Green Hills of Africa*).

batant instinct put the hint of futility into Rudin's end . . . one can argue that Rudin was not futile on the barricade in the Faubourg St. Antoine, that '48 *was* his cause, and that he had the sense to see it." As Turgenev had said of Rudin, "He has enthusiasm; and believe me, who am a phlegmatic person enough, that is the most precious quality of our times. We have all become insufferably reasonable, indifferent, and slothful; we are asleep and cold, and thanks to anyone who will wake us up and warm us. . . . Who has the right to say that he has not been of use?"

The persistence of Rudinism, with its twentieth-century apogee in the rugged hills and valleys between Madrid and Barcelona, and in the twisted concrete-and-steel of cities blasted by the first modern war, has given a mythic distance to the experience of Spain. Writers now dead lived out that myth in their lives and work; while writers who survived exorcised only with great difficulty the impact of the Spanish Civil War upon their literary careers. In some cases, Rudinism touched their works with the only brilliance they were to achieve; in others, the excitement of the Cause, or the despair of disillusion, effected profound changes. And, in a plethora of works by writers whom Spain touched only through the newspapers—or, afterwards, the history books—the Last Great Cause continues to provide frame, plot, background, theme, atmosphere. Strangely, though, the after-image of Spain has appeared in little post-war poetry. It had been a poets' war but the war had drained—or claimed—its poets.

In mythic distance behind Tom Wingfield, Tennessee William's narrator in *The Glass Menagerie,* are memories of Guernica. In Edward Albee's play *The Death of Bessie Smith* "there is dying going on in Spain." In Robert Penn Warren's novel *Flood* the hero is a caricature of the thirties writer, which calls for one good book (and later failures), marriage, Spanish Civil War, disillusion, retreat to the South, sex, Hollywood. In Ellick Moll's novel *Image of Tallie* the central character is a dashing, cynical novelist and Hollywood script writer, great lover, and eventual casualty in Spain. Even Iris Murdoch's novel of Easter Monday in Dublin in 1916, *The Red and the Green,* concludes with an epilogue in 1938 in which the eldest son of a veteran of the Irish Civil War tells his parents that he wants to fight for the Loyalists in Spain. James Baldwin has recalled that his first publication (he was twelve) was a short story about the Spanish War; while in John Barth's first novel, *The Floating Opera,* a father's testamentary injunction that his son must have "kept clear of communist sympathy since 1932" disinherits the son five years later when it is proven in court that he had been donating money to the Spanish Republican cause. "Aren't you aware," the Red-baiting judge snarls, reversing the bequest, "that the Loyalist movement is run by the Communist Party? Directed from the Kremlin?"

The war in Spain appears in Irwin Shaw's "Main Currents of American Thought" and "The City was in Total Darkness," as well as through the opening sections of his novel *The Young Lions.* In William Faulkner's *The Mansion,* Linda Snopes and her husband both go off to Spain, Linda to drive an ambulance, her husband to be killed in action within a few months. (And afterwards her Communist affiliations cause her investigation by the F.B.I.) In Budd Schulberg's *The Disenchanted,* Spain is pervasive ("One minute to six. Just time to meet his girl, grab a bite and go on to the rally for the Lincoln Brigade.") Shep, Schulberg's writer-hero, who later tries unsuccessfully to sell a screenplay on the Loyalists, muses over a drink at the beginning of the novel, ". . . . won't it be awful when my grandchildren ask me what I was doing the day Barcelona fell and I have to say I was synopsizing Faith Baldwin!" Similarly conscience-plagued is Gus Leroy in Mary McCarthy's *The Group,* a publisher's editor awash in psychoanalysis and guilt over not joining the volunteers in Spain; while in Muriel Spark's *The Prime of Miss Jean Brodie,* in spite of Miss Brodie's militant pro-Fascism, her pupils remain somewhat confusedly Loyalist. Later, a man asks one of them, Sandy, about the climate in her school then, for they had both been students in Edinburgh in the thirties. "We boys," he recalls, "were very keen on Auden and that group of course. We wanted to go and fight in the Spanish Civil War. On the Republican side, of course. Did you take sides . . . at your school?" Some did.

One of Joyce Emily's boasts was that her brother at Oxford had gone to fight in the Spanish Civil War. This dark, rather mad girl wanted to go too, and to wear a white blouse and black skirt and march with a gun. Nobody had taken this seriously. The Spanish Civil War was something going on outside in the newspapers and only once a month in the school debating society. Everyone, including Joyce Emily, was anti-Franco if they were anything at all.

One day it was realised that Joyce Emily had not been at school for some days, and soon someone else was occupying her desk. No one knew why she had left until, six weeks later, it was reported that she had run away to Spain and had been killed in an accident when the train she was travelling in had been attacked. The school held an abbreviated form of remembrance service for her.*

After hope had given way to hopelessness, despair became the keynote of the best fiction begotten by observers and participants. (Only early in the conflict could Malraux have written a novel titled *L'Espoir.*) Hemingway's novel concerned those for whom the bell already tolled; and Humphrey Slater,* once a commissar in the XVth Brigade, during the frigid and futile battles around Teruel, renounced the Party afterward and wrote his bitter *The Heretics* (1947), about the fate of those who in any age are far-seeing enough to dissent, even from Communism. Less political, but desolate, realistic, and powerful (yet afterwards forgotten amid the prolificacy of his publications) was Robert Payne's *The Song of the Peasant* (1939), which did for the war itself what Ralph Bates's *The Olive Field* had done for its seed-years. Payne's Pere Campo, an Anarchist leader of a fishermen's cooperative, and Tomas Mora, a Communist stonemason, join in fighting Fascists in the exhilarating early days of the war; and then, two years later, reappear in the hopeless battles along the

* Ironically, Miss Brodie afterwards confided that she sometimes regretted urging Joyce Emily "to go to Spain to fight for Franco, she would have done admirably for him, a girl of instinct. . . ."
* He used the name Hugh Slater while in the British Communist Party, because it sounded more proletarian.

Ebro, from where Payne had reported the war. At the end of the novel, one is dead and the other wounded, the village destroyed in a belated and pointless air raid, and the cause lost. To the victors belongs the rubble.

Even among the writers who remained relatively aloof during the war, the event took on symbolic value, Edmund Wilson using a money-raising cocktail party for Loyalist Spain as a vehicle for exposing some of his characters to satire in *Memoirs of Hecate County*. Among the few writers who supported the winning side, there was little of the after-image of Spain in their work (Evelyn Waugh's *Officers and Gentlemen* is one of the rare novels in which the Francoist point of view crops up). The rebels owned the country; it was the side of the dispossessed, and of the writers upon whom its impact continued, who clung to the receding legend.

The Spanish War is the setting for the gun-running in Leonard Woolf's play *The Hotel*, and Graham Greene's "entertainment" *Confidential Agent*; and the hero of *Casablanca* loses his idealism while running guns for the Loyalists. The war in Spain turns up more significantly in Maxwell Anderson's verse drama *Key Largo*, where King McCloud, in the play's Prologue, tries to pull his men back off a hill before they are destroyed, for the Loyalist cause is lost and further resistance is hopelessly suicidal:

> *Why should we die here for a dead cause, for a symbol,*
> *on these empty ramparts, where there's nothing to win,*
> *even if you should win it?*

The men refuse to leave with McCloud, and die; and the rest of *Key Largo* is McCloud's drama of expiation and redemption, his arrival at an understanding of why volunteers die for causes:

> *... In the last analysis one dies*
> *because it's part of the bargain he takes on*
> *when he agrees to live. A man must die*
> *for what he believes—if he's unfortunate*
> *enough to have to face it in his time—*

*and if he won't then he'll end up believing
in nothing at all—and that's death, too.*

Sean O'Casey, who had been passionately Loyalist, put the war into three of his plays: in *Purple Dust,* for example, the high-spirited O'Killigain has fought in Spain. Michael Blankfort's *The Brave and the Blind* dramatized the siege of the Alcazar, and Irwin Shaw's *Siege* dramatized the plight of a group of Loyalists surrounded in a mountain fort. John Osborne's Jimmy Porter (*Look Back in Anger*) not only mourns the fact that there are no more "good, brave causes left" after Spain, but remembers bitterly, "For twelve months, I watched my father dying—when I was ten years old. He'd come back from the war in Spain, you see. And certain god-fearing gentlemen there had made such a mess of him, he didn't have long to live. . . . Every time I sat on the edge of his bed, to listen to him talking or reading to me, I had to fight back my tears. At the end . . . I was a veteran."

Arnold Wesker—of the same "angry" generation of English playwrights as Osborne—was only four years old when the war in Spain began; but in the trilogy of plays which made his reputation in the late fifties[3] the struggle for a better world gravitated about such events as the Spanish Civil War. It was "every man's war," but to most of Wesker's characters the aftermath was disillusion. Twenty years after his International Brigade service, Dave Simmonds, reminded of Spain, asks angrily, "Am I expected to live in the glory of the nineteen thirties all my life?" Yet, when he had volunteered for Spain he had thrown off his pacifism with "I'm not even sure that I want to go, only I know if I don't, then—well, what sense can a man make of his life?" For Dave, it becomes the last ideal worth fighting for. Disillusioned by the senseless fratricide which fragments the Left,* he comes home to withdraw into himself.

* "Remember Spain? Remember how we were proud of Dave and the other boys who answer the call? But did Dave ever tell you the way some of the Party members refused to fight alongside Trotskyists? And one or two of those Trotskyists didn't come back and they weren't killed in the fighting either?" (Monty to Sarah in Wesker's *Chicken Soup with Barley*)

Dozens of heroes of novels run a gamut of incident which includes a stint as volunteer in Spain: Lionel Trilling's *The Middle of the Journey*, Frederick Prokosch's *The Skies of Europe*, David Karp's *The Last Believers*, Norman Mailer's *Barbary Shore*, among them. Malcolm Lowry's great novel *Under the Volcano* takes place during a November day in 1938, when the war in Spain is grinding to a close; and one of its leading characters, Hugh, is an anti-Fascist journalist haunted by his experiences of the Spanish war, a foil to his half-brother Geoff—a sodden ex-consul—who has abdicated from any kind of political action. (Guiltily, Hugh feels that he belongs back in Spain, rather than in Mexico wet-nursing an alcoholic from whose life meaning seemed to have disappeared.)

On the satiric side, Anthony Powell's "Music of Time" novel, *Casanova's Chinese Restaurant,* includes Erridge, a left-wing peer who, picturesquely for his social set, goes off to fight against Franco, and is dismissed as a "typical aristocrat idealist." Frustrated by dysentery, he returns. His time in Spain, Norah remarks, "seems to have been a total flop. He didn't get up to the front and he never met Hemingway." Even worse, Erridge's behavior in Barcelona had brought him close to losing his life for some cause or other, a Member of Parliament points out, for he "seems to have shown a good deal of political obtuseness—perhaps I should say childlike innocence. He appears to have treated POUM, FAI, CNT, and UGT,[4] as if they were all the same left-wing extension of the Labour Party. I was not surprised to hear that he was going to be arrested at the time he decided to leave Spain. If you can't tell the difference between a Trotskyite-Communist, an Anarcho-Syndicalist, and a properly paid-up Party member, you had better keep away from the barricades."

Since Spain there have been more barricades than Rudins. Perhaps Spain took more than its share of the emotional and physical toll Rudinism regularly exacts—the last overwhelming appeal to the writer-activist. "How curious the society which uproots its intellectuals and sends them abroad to discover their wills!" Pritchett had written. "Do they discover them? And if they are right—and we admire their passionate sincerity—and Rudin was right when he stood up on the overturned omnibus in the Faubourg St. Antoine, whose war shall we be fighting in? In their war—our war for something we need—or, as happened before, in somebody else's? . . . How seductive is the foreign barricade, how exotic the international, as distinct from the national situation!" Yet, it is not that every foreign barricade exerts the same epic appeal, for it has never been enough that the cause be exotic or international. To hone one's pen on an epical cause— or discard the pen for a sword—requires the magnetic force of the grand, foredoomed tragedy. This is the dilemma—and the glory—of Rudinism.

After the defeat—"and it has often seemed to me," Claud Cockburn wrote twenty years after, "that intellectuals somewhat tend to exaggerate both defeats and victories, as though taking it for granted that either of them might be final—a lot of European intellectuals left their souls dead on the soil of Spain and never again were able to face the continuing realities of life." But, Cockburn confessed, "There were also some intellectuals who faced the Spanish realities with such sturdiness that they left their bodies on that soil too." They were "the first proof to the nineteen-thirties that when some people talk about dying for a cause they mean it."[5] "The writers and artists," Daniel Aaron observed, "who spoke for the Spanish Loyalists, who raised money for medical aid, or who smuggled themselves into Spain as volunteers were not consciously furthering party interests, nor was there anything ulterior or sinister in their devotion to the Spanish peasantry. The issues appeared clear-cut, the cause of Spain was the cause of democracy and morality. Sectarian bickerings seemed contemptible in the light of such awesome events, and for more than a few, the nobility of the Spaniards engendered a comparable nobility in themselves."[6] But among those seized by the Marxist religion, there was an even further inspiration, for the Communist blessing upon the Republic had doubly ennobled the cause. It also doubled the impact of the disillusionment and despair. Among these writers, John M. Muste has written, "the true disillusionment came because many of them thought they had found in Marxism a means to contain and control the element of violence which is so clearly the center of twentieth-century life and of twentieth-century fiction. . . . This explains the desperation with which so many embraced Marxism in the thirties; it was the last chance, and for awhile it seemed the best chance. When the hurricane passed, those whom it had shaken [often] came to believe that it had been no chance at all."[7] For the less rigidly political Edgar Z. Friedenberg looked back on the still irresistible myth:

> And yet . . . when all is said and done, one's heart somehow stopped beating with the defeat of the Loyalists. For history lost meaning in Spain. We—the liberals of our generation—conceived of Spain as the Armageddon where the forces of evil would be smashed and the world would finally turn to light and love. We thought history was on our side, the good side, and that the very gods themselves would rise up in righteous fury and smite down the foe. And, since the defeat of the Loyalists, nothing has ever seemed quite the same. For many a tired liberal, in his heart of hearts, would have longed to have been shot down fighting for Absolute Right on the Jarama River, near Madrid, to die content in the supreme Kamakazi of the intellect. We have turned to the arts, to sensuality, to the accumulation of possessions; but we are no longer what we were. We have lost our innocence and the sword no longer flames to the east of the garden of Eden.[8]

To Louis Fischer too, it was "probably the zenith of political idealism in the first half of the twentieth century."[9] Still, nobility and idealism remain unstable commodities in the shifting world market: passionate commitment to the *right* cause is ever honored, but *right* and *wrong* depend upon current political realities. Looking back on the persistent symbolic overtones of the Spanish Republic's struggle for survival, an English historian has reflected that "distortion" is the price of "symbolic significance and international resonance." Spain, he minimized, was primarily an internal affair, internationalized as much by "visiting intellectuals and professional propagandists" as anything else.[10] Yet—thanks to Mussolini and Hitler—the war had already outgrown its domestic origins before the Republic acquired any help from outside, even the quickly offered support of the intellectual activists, or of the opportunistic Party *apparat*.

So the controversies about Spain—and the role of the engaged intellectual—continue. Pronounced dead almost from the beginning, the *Causa* refuses to lie still in its grave, and "keeps haunting memories, arguments, books and loyalty files."[11] It had been prophetic of ambulanceman James Neugass in 1938 to write of the persistent ghosts which haunt the aftermath of idealism,

> *When in the evening secret service men*
> *lock vaults of cross-indexed finger prints*
> *and the morgues of passport photographs*
> *Where the faces of the Brigades*
> *fade and bleach but do not die*
> *longer than the memory of police chiefs*
> *Grow the shadows of footstone olive trees*
> *deep in battlefield orchards at sunset. . . .*

The impact upon literature has often been to render suspect much of the writing inspired by the lost, and afterwards unfashionable, cause, although writers of real worth—whatever history's eventual verdict on the Republic—were no less mistaken or misled than the politicians or the journalists, nor did they take refuge in dogma or fall back less on slogans. For those who remained true to themselves and their convictions, John Lehmann has observed, the war in Spain "also demonstrated that there are occasions when poetry concerned entirely with a political creed and the action resulting from it can have an enduring poetic power: warmly applauded in the political surge of the moment, rejected when disillusionment sets in," such writings are often found found later "to have some uranium content that still makes them impressive and valid as poetry."[12] The tarnish, in other words, often rubs off, while little else written in the thirties has collectively survived as well; for Spain came at the conclusion of a myopic, discreditable decade. For all its traces of shabbiness when examined close up, and its persistent mythos when seen at a distance, much of the moral grandeur of the Last Great Cause was solid coin, negotiable in the next generation. "It is the fate of my own generation," one of its representatives, Dan Wakefield, observed, "to find ourselves respectful visitors at the shrines of our fathers' departed passions.[13] *Homage to Catalonia* in hand, we search Barcelona for the spots where the bricks were torn out of the streets and built into barricades; the buildings that once bore posters proclaiming the revolution are now plastered with announcements of the coming of Britain's Tommy Steele, 'El Rey de Rock and Roll.' "[14] But the legend dies hard. There are already too many shrines to it in literature which show inescapable signs of permanence. "Those of us who were there," author Robert Payne has written, "sometimes feel that the Civil War in Spain has already entered into legend. We see the olive groves and the parched plains and the faces of those proud and dark-eyed people, and an incandescent light seems to fall on them. They are larger than life, and very bright against the skyline, and there is something about them which reminds us of the Homeric heroes as they strode across the plains of Troy."[15]

"Countries do not live only by victories," Premier Juan Negrín told the last meeting of the Cortes of the Republic, after the fall of Barcelona, "but by the examples which their people have known how to give in tragic times." For those who were not there, even in spirit, the tragic Cause of the Republic, nearly blotted out by the catastrophe of the Second World War and the Orwellian reversals of the Cold War, has receded in memory or receded into the library. There remains that written legacy—the fading Legend of Spain, now and then still reshaped into a form which communicates some remnant of the great burst of hope that momentarily fired a generation which had discovered in Madrid and Guernica, in Teruel and Barcelona, an antidote to a world sunk in cowardice, hypocrisy and cynicism. In 1702, a London critic, looking for a reason for the degeneracy of the English drama at the time, declared that the writers' preoccupation with politics had led to a deadening of the "imaginative faculty of the soul." If there were any vestiges of soul in the discreditable thirties, it may have been in the sometimes naively fought, and not entirely innocently lost, Last Great Cause.

Notes and Sources

In 1958, the late Charles Fenton (*The Apprenticeship of Ernest Hemingway*) was beginning to assemble notes for a book on what he called the "American literary backgrounds" of the Spanish Civil War. Writing to Mark Schorer about the project, he spoke of the war as the last great cause for intellectuals of that generation; and Professor Schorer, in answering, noted that Fenton had the title of his projected book right there—"the last great cause."

Fenton's death occurred before he had gone beyond collecting a mass of preliminary notes from the published record, material I did not get to see until just before this book—coincidentally long scheduled to be called *The Last Great Cause*—was completed. His files of notes at Yale remain, nevertheless, a substantial contribution to the research on the American response to the war in Spain.

Other research on the response of writers to the war in Spain has resulted in two valuable studies—Allen Guttmann's *The Wound in the Heart: America and the Spanish Civil War* (New York, 1962); and Hugh Ford's *A Poet's War: British Poets and the Spanish Civil War* (Philadelphia, 1965). There have been, and continue to be published, studies of a more specialized nature; and rather than list the usual three or four thousand titles, I call the reader's attention to the sources cited in the following end-notes.

INTRODUCTION

1. Cedric Salter, *Try-Out in Spain* (New York, 1943), pp. 6–7.
2. Dante A. Puzzo, *Spain and the Great Powers 1936–1941* (New York, 1962), p. v.
3. Quoted as epigraph to Allen Guttmann, *The Wound in the Heart* (New York, 1962).

4. Quoted by Hugh Thomas, *The Spanish Civil War* (New York, 1961), p. 143.

5. Jerrold tells his story of his involvement in the plot in *Georgian Adventure* (New York, 1938), pp. 370–77. Bolin's parallel account appears in his *Spain: The Vital Years* (Phila., 1967), pp. 11–48.

6. Salter, pp. 13–15. The reader will have to evaluate how apocryphal the tale is for himself, as no further identification of the writers is made.

7. Neal Wood, *Communism and British Intellectuals* (London, 1959), p. 57.

8. Jerrold, Introduction to René Quinton's *A Soldier's Testament* (London, 1930), quoted by Herbert Read in *Poetry and Anarchism* (London, 1939), p. 67.

9. Claud Cockburn, *In Time of Trouble* (London, 1956), p. 253.

10. W. H. Auden, "Spain" (based upon the London, 1940 text, slightly revised from the original Faber text of 1937).

11. "Night Before Battle," *Esquire*, XI (February, 1939), 97.

CHAPTER ONE

1. *Authors Takes Sides on the Spanish War* (London, 1937).

2. *Ibid.*

3. Quoted in Peter Stansky and William Abrahams, *Journey to the Frontier: Two Roads to the Spanish Civil War* (Boston, 1966), p. 316. (This volume appeared in England in the same year under the title *Julian Bell and John Cornford: Their Lives and the 1930's.*)

4. Stansky and Abrahams, p. 318.

5. John Cornford, "On the Catalonian Front," *New Republic*, December 2, 1936, pp. 136–38.

6. "Diary Letter from Aragon" to Margot Heinemann, quoted in Stansky and Abrahams, p. 331.

7. "Diary Letter," p. 335.

8. *Poems for Spain* (London, 1938), pp. 26–29.

9. The other three vignettes describe panic among the women during the shelling of a village, a view from "the clean hospital bed," and his "leave-taking from Spain."

10. John Sommerfield, *Volunteer in Spain* (New York, 1937), pp. 97–98. (Ellipses are the author's own.)

11. Sommerfield, pp. 101–02.

12. Sommerfield, pp. 137–38.

13. From an obituary in *Left Review*, III (February, 1937), 67.

14. *Poems for Spain,* pp. 26–29. Originally in *New Writing,* IV (Autumn, 1937), 37, titled "Poem."

15. *John Cornford,* ed. Pat Sloan (London, 1938), pp. 193 and 238.

16. *The Whispering Gallery* (New York, 1955), p. 282.

17. There was at least one more memorable work Spain inspired in Sommerfield, a short story, "The Escape," published shortly after his book in the fifth quarterly volume of *New Writing,* pp. 59–67. It was the story of wounded Asturian militiamen attempting to escape by sea to France, hoping to get to a safe frontier point, cross over, and fight again. As they make their trek they encounter the scattered bodies of the dead, described with striking imagery. Later, the story was included in a short story collection, *The Survivors* (1947), where it was the only reminder of the Spanish experience. Sommerfield's subsequent novels were not successful.

18. Extracts from Ralph Fox's letters are from *Ralph Fox: A Writer in Arms,* ed. John Lehmann, T. A. Jackson, and C. Day Lewis (New York, 1937).

19. "A Conversation with Claud Cockburn," *The Review* [Oxford], No. 11–12 (1965), pp. 51–52.

20. Philip Toynbee, *Friends Apart* (London, 1954), p. 105.

21. Esmond Romilly, *Boadilla* (London, 1937), p. 129. Unless otherwise noted, quotations from Romilly are from this edition.

22. She was Jessica Mitford, later a well-known writer (*The American Way of Death* and other books).

23. *Poems for Spain* (London, 1938), pp. 33–34.

24. From the anonymous introduction to Caudwell's posthumous *Poems* (London, 1939).

25. From a letter quoted by George Thomson in his introduction to a reprint edition of *Illusion and Reality* (New York, 1948 and 1963), p. 4.

26. Stanley Edgar Hyman, *The Armed Vision: A Study in the Methods of Modern Literary Criticism* (New York, 1952), pp. 173, 207–08.

27. *Poems* (London, 1939), pp. 49–50.

28. *English Captain* (London, 1939), pp. 204–05.

29. Quoted in Lehmann, *New Writing in Europe* (London, 1940), p. 119.

30. "British Medical Unit—Granien," dated Barcelona, November, 1936, first published in *Volunteer for Liberty,* Nov. 17, 1937, p. 3. The poem is generally abbreviated in title to "Granien."

31. Vincent Brome, *The International Brigades* (London, 1965), p. 216 (quoting verbal evidence, Mrs. Wintringham to Brome).

32. Hugh Thomas, *The Spanish Civil War,* p. 348n. (Spender in the

1960's could not recall the Byron reference.) See Chapter Two, below, for more on Spender.

33. *New Writing in Europe,* pp. 120–21.

34. *Poems for Spain,* p. 40.

35. Dominic Behan, *My Brother Brendan* (London, 1965), p. 18.

36. Brendan Behan, *Confessions of an Irish Rebel* (New York, 1966), p. 133.

37. Dominic Behan, p. 18.

38. Brendan Behan, p. 134.

39. *Left Review,* July, 1937, pp. 318–19.

40. Quoted in Hugh D. Ford, *A Poet's War* (Philadelphia, 1965), p. 124.

41. *Poems for Spain,* pp. 50–51.

42. "Critic," "A London Diary," *New Statesman and Nation,* July 24, 1937, p. 139.

43. Letter to John Lehmann, in Stansky and Abrahams, pp. 120, 416.

44. Letter to "B," in Stansky and Abrahams, p. 121.

45. Letter to Vanessa Bell, December 12, 1936, in Stansky and Abrahams, p. 297.

46. Virginia Woolf, entry for June 23, 1937, in *A Writer's Diary* (New York, 1954), p. 274.

47. Extracts from Bell's letters are from Quentin Bell, ed., *Julian Bell, Essays, Poems, and Letters* (London, 1938), and from Stansky and Abrahams.

48. Stansky and Abrahams, pp. 412, 421. The authors note that they base their account on contemporary accounts as well as conversations with Cochrane and Rees.

49. Stansky and Abrahams, p. 413, quoting a letter to them from Sir Richard Rees.

50. Julian Symons, *The Thirties* (London, 1960), p. 136.

CHAPTER TWO

1. Christopher Isherwood, *Exhumations* (New York, 1966), p. 59.

2. Stephen Spender, *The God that Failed* (New York, 1963), p. 245.

3. Stephen Spender, *World Within World* (London, 1951), p. 198. Quotations from Spender are from this work unless otherwise noted.

4. Nathan of the gold-tipped talisman was a former Guards officer of almost incredible courage. On July 14, he was killed near the old battlefield of Boadilla, cut down by a bomb fragment.

5. See footnote in Chapter Seven about the origin of the term "fifth column."

6. Donald Hall, "The Experience of Forms" [Part II of a profile of Henry Moore], the *New Yorker*, December 18, 1965, p. 70.

7. *The God that Failed*, pp. 247–48.

8. The incident and some of the lines are found in *World Within World*, p. 207; the poetry appears in full in *The Still Centre* (London, 1939), pp. 55–56. *Centre* contains all of his Spanish War poetry Spender cared to print in 1939.

9. *The Creative Element* (London, 1953), p. 153.

10. "Ultima Ratio Regum," *Centre*, p. 58.

11. *World Within World*, p. 221. For obvious reasons, Spender does not identify him by name.

12. Symons, *The Thirties*, p. 128.

13. Harold Nicolson, *Diaries and Letters 1930–1939*, ed. Nigel Nicolson (London, 1966), p. 321 (entry for 26 January, 1938).

14. "Impressions of Valencia," *New Statesman and Nation*, January 30, 1937, p. 159.

15. Arthur Koestler, *The Invisible Writing* (New York, 1954), 336–37.

16. "Impressions of Valencia," *New Statesman*, Jan. 30, 1937, p. 159.

17. "A Conversation with Claud Cockburn," *The Review* [Oxford], No. 11–12 (1965), p. 50.

18. Introduction to *The Poet's Tongue*, quoted in Monroe Spears, *W. H. Auden* (New York, 1963), p. 189.

19. W. H. Auden, "In Memoriam: Ernst Toller," *The New Yorker*, June 17, 1939, p. 80.

20. T. E. Lawrence to C. Day Lewis, November 1934, in *The Letters of T. E. Lawrence*, ed. David Garnett (London, 1938), p. 825.

21. *Ibid.*, 20 December, 1934, p. 839.

22. Quotations otherwise unidentified are from C. Day Lewis, *The Buried Day* (London, 1960), pp. 219–22.

23. Lines from *The Nabara* are quoted from C. Day Lewis, *Overtures to Death and Other Poems* (London, 1938), p. 41.

24. Peter Lowbridge, "The Spanish Civil War," *The Review*, No. 11–12 (1965), p. 49.

25. *Buried Day*, p. 223.

26. *Collected Poems* (London, 1954), p. 228.

27. *Anarchy and Order: Essays in Politics* (London, 1940), p. 58.

28. *Ibid.*, p. 48.

29. *Ibid.*, p. 58.

30. "A Song for the Spanish Anarchists," *Thirty-Five Poems* (London, 1940), p. 41.

31. "The Heart Conscripted," in *Poems for Spain*, pp. 39–40.

32. *Poems for Spain*, pp. 74–77.
33. "A Conversation with Edgell Rickword," *The Review*, No. 11–12 (1965), p. 19.
34. *Left Review*, April, 1937, p. 139.
35. Jack Lindsay, *Fanfrolico and After* (London, 1962), p. 264.
36. *Loc. cit.*
37. From *Lament and Triumph* (London, 1940), pp. 71, 76.
38. Constantine FitzGibbon, *The Life of Dylan Thomas* (Boston, 1965), pp. 136–38, 199.
39. Letter to Glyn Jones, March 1934, in FitzGibbon, p. 80.
40. FitzGibbon, p. 236.
41. George Barker, in *Coming to London*, ed. John Lehmann (London, 1957), p. 55.
42. John Lehmann, *The Whispering Gallery*, pp. 283–85.
43. "The Tourist Looks at Spain," *New Writing*, No. 4, p. 231.
44. Rex Warner, a.l.s. to S.W., October 25, 1965.
45. *Autumn Journal* (London, 1939), pp. 27–29.
46. "Postscript to Iceland, for W. H. Auden," *Collected Poems, 1925–1948*, (London, 1949), p. 93.
47. Auden and MacNeice, *Letters from Iceland* (New York, 1937), pp. 240, 258.
48. *I Crossed the Minch* (London, 1938), pp. 125–29.
49. "Today in Barcelona," *The Spectator*, January 20, 1939, p. 84.
50. *Autumn Journal*, Part XXIII in *Collected Poems*, p. 170.
51. *Ibid.*, p. 173.
52. "The Poet in England Today," *New Republic*, March 25, 1940, pp. 412–13.

CHAPTER THREE

1. All quotations from Orwell in this chapter, unless otherwise identified are from *Homage to Catalonia* (New York, 1952, originally published in London, 1938).
2. FitzGibbon, pp. 138–39.
3. *Tribune* (London), September 15, 1944, quoted in George Woodcock, *The Crystal Spirit: A Study of George Orwell* (Boston, 1966), p. 166.
4. "Inside the Whale," quoted in Woodcock, p. 178.
5. Cyril Connolly, "Barcelona," *New Statesman and Nation*, December 19, 1936, p. 1020.
6. Orwell, unlike the stereotype Englishman, regularly found experiences "moving"—and confessed as much.

7. From the essay, "Looking Back on the Spanish War," in *A Collection of Essays by George Orwell* (New York, 1954), pp. 214–15.
8. Josephine Herbst, "The Starched Blue Sky of Spain," *The Noble Savage* I (March, 1960), 109.
9. *Illusion and Reality*, p. 112.
10. "Looking Back on the Spanish War," (1943), in *Essays*, p. 199.
11. "Castilian Drama," *New Republic*, October 20, 1937, p. 287. Later Bates, in effect, retracted this. See Chapter Nine, Note 50.
12. "Looking Back," p. 211 ("A resolution, fight to the end. . . .").
13. Quoted in Woodcock, p. 170.
14. *George Orwell* (London, 1954), p. 140.
15. Quoted by Heppenstall in *Four Absentees* (London, 1960), p. 140.
16. Edward Hyams, *The New Statesman, 1913–1963* (London, 1964), p. 199.
17. Heppenstall, p. 141.
18. Koestler, in an obituary notice in the *Observer*, January 29, 1950, reprinted in *The Trail of the Dinosaur* (New York, 1955), p. 104.
19. Woodcock, pp. 259, 260.
20. "Why I Write" (1947), in *The Orwell Reader*, ed. Richard Rovere (New York, 1956), p. 394.

CHAPTER FOUR

1. Koestler, *The Invisible Writing* (New York, 1954), pp. 314 ff. Unless otherwise credited, quotations in this chapter are from *The Invisible Writing*.
2. A.l.s., Koestler to S.W., June 7, 1965.
3. Claud Cockburn, *Crossing the Line* (London, 1958), as quoted in *The Thirties*, pp. 132–33.
4. *The God That Failed*, p. 66.
5. *Spanish Testament*.
6. *Enemies of Promise* (London, 1938); the quotation is from the Anchor reprint edition (New York, 1960), p. 113.
7. Koestler, Preface to the *Danube Edition* of *Dialogue with Death* (London, 1966), p. 6.
8. "Looking Back on the Spanish War," in *Essays* (New York, 1954), p. 202.
9. *Dialogue with Death* (New York, 1942), p. 203.
10. *The God That Failed*, p. 67.
11. *Ibid.*, p. 68.
12. Koestler to S.W., June 7, 1965.

13. John Atkins, *Arthur Koestler* (London, 1956), p. 118.
14. "The Fraternity of Pessimists," quoted in Atkins, *Arthur Koestler*, p. 36.
15. Koestler to S.W., June 7, 1965.
16. Pritchett, "The Art of Koestler," p. 171.
17. *Dialogue with Death*, pp. 113–14.
18. *The Invisible Writing*, pp. 359–60.
19. George Orwell, "Arthur Koestler," *Collected Essays* (London, 1961; originally pub. 1944), pp. 222, 225.

CHAPTER FIVE

1. *The Invisible Writing*, p. 374. Koestler's reference was to Thomas Mann.
2. *Authors Take Sides*.
3. William Rothenstein, *Since Fifty* (London, 1940), pp. 282–83.
4. *Authors Take Sides*, inside front cover.
5. "This Danger of War," broadcast from London, November 2, 1937. Printed in *The Listener*, 10 November, 1937, and in *Platform and Pulpit*, ed. Dan H. Laurence (New York and London, 1961), pp. 282–86.
6. Leeds, March 12, 1937.
7. Quotations from *Geneva* are from the first American edition, in *Geneva, Cymbeline Refinished and Good King Charles* (New York, 1947).
8. A Fabian lecture delivered November 25, 1932; reprinted in *Platform and Pulpit*, p. 235.
9. *Authors Take Sides*.
10. Nicolson, diary entry for 6 October 1936, *Diaries*, p. 274.
11. Richard Ellmann, *James Joyce* (New York, 1959), pp. 716–17, quoting a letter to him from Nancy Cunard, 1957.
12. *Ibid.*, p. 722.
13. Behan, *Confessions of an Irish Rebel*, p. 133. The often ludicrous tale of the O'Duffy battalion is told (not always seriously) by the General himself in *Crusade in Spain* (Dublin, 1938), and (disenchantedly) by Seumas McKee in *I Was a Franco Soldier* (London, 1938). When the six months were up, 654 survivors elected to go home, while nine stayed to continue the crusade.
14. Quoted in Richard Ellmann, *Yeats: The Man and the Masks* (New York, 1958), p. 277.
15. Adapted from Yeats's "Three Songs to the Same Tune."

16. Quoted by Hugh D. Ford in *A Poet's War* (Philadelphia, 1965), pp. 149–50, from *Salud!* (London, 1937). Macalastair's actual name is Desmond Fitzgerald.
17. Ellmann, *Yeats*, p. 278.
18. Yeats to Ethel Mannin, Feb. 11 [1937], in Allan Wade, ed., *Letters of W. B. Yeats* (London, 1954), p. 881.
19. "Those Images" (1938).
20. Posthumously published in *Last Poems* (London, 1939).
21. *Authors Take Sides.*
22. William Van O'Connor and Edward Stone, *A Casebook on Ezra Pound* (New York, 1959), p. 15.
23. Charles Norman, *The Magic-Maker* (New York, 1960), p. 321.
24. See Eliot's "Commentary" in *Criterion*, April, 1931, as well as other issues of this period.
25. *Authors Take Sides.*
26. *Right Review*, July, 1938, pp. 2–3 (in an editorial).
27. Eliot to C. L. Sulzberger, quoted in Sulzberger's column, "Foreign Affairs," *New York Times*, January 9, 1965, p. 24.
28. C. Day Lewis, "The Volunteer," in V. de Sola Pinto, ed., *Crisis in English Poetry, 1880–1940* (London, 1951), p. 196.

CHAPTER SIX

1. The story of his beating and conversion is from Campbell's *Light on a Dark Horse* (Chicago, 1952), pp. 306–12, and his poem "In Memoriam of 'Mosquito,'" in *Collected Poems*, II, (London, 1957), 23.
2. J. Artega de Leon, "Roy Campbell Through Spanish Eyes," *Spain*, No. 85 (May 18, 1939), 140.
3. From a review of *Flowering Rifle*, quoting a letter from Campbell, *Spain*, No. 72 (Feb. 16, 1939), 139.
4. Robert Graves, "A Life Bang-Full of Kicks and Shocks," *New York Times Book Review*, January 5, 1958, p. 6.
5. "Letter from San Mateo Front," in *Collected Poems*, II, 48 and 42, footnotes and text.
6. *Rifle, Collected Poems*, II, 195n.
7. "The Singer," *Right Review*, April, 1939, unpaged. A *jota* is a Spanish folk dance.
8. *Rifle*, pp. 236–38.
9. *Ibid.*, p. 224n.
10. *Collected Poems*, II, 72.

11. *Rifle*, pp. 245–46.
12. "Letter from the San Mateo Front," p. 41n.
13. *Rifle*, p. 226.
14. "Talking Bronco," *Collected Poems*, II, 91–92.
15. *Right Review*. A less ambiguous supporter was Lawrence Durrell, who wrote a carefully phrased but enthusiastic letter to the *Review* which included such lines as "Power to your right arm! . . . And every man who feels the same will be more interested in your writing than in the prodigious squeaking and chirping that goes up from the Leftist barnyards (January, 1939).
16. Graves, "A Life Bang-Full," p. 6.
17. Hugh Thomas, pp. 602–03.
18. Robert Speaight, *The Life of Hilaire Belloc* (New York, 1957), pp. 464–65.
19. *European Jungle* (Philadelphia, 1939), p. 281.
20. Jerrold's remarks come from "Spain: Impressions and Reflections," *Nineteenth Century*, CXXI (April, 1937), 470–92; and *Georgian Adventure* (New York, 1938), pp. 386–87.
21. Arnold Lunn, *Spanish Rehearsal* (London, [1937]), pp. 7–9.
22. *Ibid.*, p. 139.
23. Farmborough, *Life . . .* (London, 1938), p. 200.
24. *Ibid.*, p. 2.
25. *Ibid.*, p. 122.
26. Evelyn Waugh, "Fascist" [letter to the editor], *New Statesman*, March 5, 1938, pp. 365–66. The magazine had labelled several Mayfair jewel robbers as having a "typical Fascist mentality," and Waugh declared that intellectuals were creating a "bogy" of English Fascism.
27. Evelyn Waugh, *Robbery Under Law: the Mexican Object Lesson* (London, 1939), p. 44.
28. "Evelyn Waugh's Impressions of Spain," *Venture*, I (February, 1965), 61.
29. Lewis to Campbell, October 25, 1936, in W. K. Rose, ed., *The Letters of Wyndham Lewis* (London, 1963), pp. 239–40. The excerpt from Campbell's letter is from Rose, p. 240.
30. *The Revenge for Love* (first American edition; Chicago, 1952), pp. 132–33.
31. Geoffrey Wagner, *Wyndham Lewis* (New Haven, 1957), pp. 84–85.
32. Wyndham Lewis, "A Derelict Author in Search of a Public," in *The Writer and the Absolute* (London, 1952).

CHAPTER SEVEN

1. The description is from a Hemingway dispatch from Madrid, September 30, 1937, about a shell hitting the Florida.
2. Claud Cockburn ("Frank Pitcairn"), *In Time of Trouble* (London, 1956), pp. 257–58.
3. Alvah Bessie, *Men in Battle* (New York, 1939), p. 136. The entire incident is recounted in Bessie, pp. 136–38.
4. Ernest Hemingway, Preface to Gustav Regler's *The Great Crusade* (New York, 1940), p. vii.
5. Richard Freedman, "Hemingway's Civil War Dispatches," *Texas Studies in Literature and Language*, I (Summer, 1959), 171–72.
6. *Ibid.*, pp. 172–73, quoting an Ira Wolfert dispatch, February 28, 1937.
7. *Ibid.*, p. 173, quoting a cable to NANA, March 12, 1937.
8. Sidney Franklin, *Bullfighter from Brooklyn* (New York, 1952), p. 231.
9. Freedman, p. 174, quoting Wolfert dispatch.
10. Herbst, p. 93.
11. Quoted in Hemingway, Preface to *All the Brave* (New York, 1939), p. 7.
12. Hemingway's dispatches are quoted throughout from their reprinted appearance in *The Spanish War*, No. 16 in a sixpenny booklet series called *Fact*, edited by Raymond Postgate, who made some abridgements. No. 16 was the issue for July, 1938.
13. Regler, *The Owl of Minerva* (New York, 1960), p. 290.
14. Preface to Regler's *The Great Crusade*, p. viii.
15. *Owl*, p. 298. Cf. a similar Dos Passos experience in "The Fiesta at the Fifteenth Brigade," in *The Theme is Freedom* (New York, 1956), pp. 131–36.
16. Preface to *The Great Crusade*, pp. viii–ix.
17. "The Heat and the Cold," reprinted from *Verve* (Spring, 1938) as "Afternote to *The Spanish Earth*" (Cleveland, 1938), p. 57.
18. *The Spanish Earth*, commentary from reel six, p. 51.
19. *Owl*, p. 293.
20. *Ibid.*, pp. 293, 296.
21. Sinclair Lewis never went to Spain, and there is no record of a Hemingway-Dos Passos visit to Raven afterwards.
22. Malcolm Cowley, "Mister Papa," *Life*, January 10, 1949, pp. 87–101.

23. Freedman, p. 178, quoting the original NANA cabelese, Madrid, May 10, 1938.
24. Whit Burnett, "Writers Smell Gunpowder," *Story*, XI (August, 1937), 8.
25. "The Writer and War," as published in Henry Hart, ed. *The Writer in a Changing World* (New York, 1937), pp. 69–73.
26. *Owl*, p. 311.
27. Preface to *The Great Crusade*, p. ix.
28. Sinclair Lewis, "Glorious Dirt," *Newsweek*, October 18, 1937, p. 34.
29. *New York Times*, November 15, 1937, p. 2.
30. Quoted from Nazi documents captured after World War II in Carroll Quigley, *Tragedy and Hope* (New York, 1966), p. 602.
31. After many delays, it opened in New York, in a Theatre Guild production, in the winter of 1940.
32. Vincent Sheean, *Not Peace But a Sword* (New York, 1939), pp. 236–38.
33. "The Time Now, the Place Spain," *Ken*, April 7, 1938, pp. 36–37. *Ken*, it must be noted, was both anti-Fascist and anti-Communist.
34. John Gates, *The Story of an American Communist* (New York, 1958), pp. 59–60.
35. Hemingway, "The Old Man at the Bridge," in *The Fifth Column and the First Forty-Nine Stories* (New York, 1938); and in *The Short Stories of Ernest Hemingway* (New York, 1953), pp. 78–80.
36. *I Wonder as I Wander* (New York, 1956), p. 365.
37. In August, 1958, Hemingway employed a lawyer to attempt to prevent reprinting of any of his *Esquire* stories about the Spanish War in *The Armchair Esquire*, insisting that the stories "were not as good as I wanted them. . . ." Eventually the case was settled by the reprinting of only one of them, "The Butterfly and the Tank." When the affair caused some conjecture that he had changed his mind about the Cause of the Republic, he told the *New York Times:* "In these stories I did not try to be pro-Loyalist or anti-Loyalist. But if anyone wants to know how I feel today let me say that I have not changed my attitude about the Spanish Civil War. I was for the Loyalists and I still feel that way about the Loyalists. The only change is that I know more about the war" (August 7, 1958, p. 27). Perhaps literary reasons were also behind his refusal to permit NANA to reprint several of his dispatches in a release, "The 20th Anniversary of the Battle of Madrid."
38. *World Within World*, p. 209.

39. Sheean, *Not Peace, But a Sword*, pp. 328–34.
40. *Ibid.*, pp. 336–37.
41. *Enemies of Promise* (London, 1938); the quotation is from the Anchor reprint edition (New York, 1960), p. 73.
42. Hemingway to Malcolm Cowley, in "Mister Papa."
43. Carlos Baker, *Hemingway: The Writer as Artist* (Princeton, 1956), pp. 238–39.
44. *Ibid.*, p. 242.
45. *For Whom the Bell Tolls* (New York, 1940), p. 235.
46. *Ibid.*, p. 305.
47. *New Masses*, XXXVII (November 5, 1940), 25–29.
48. Letter dated January, 1941, quoted in "The Last Commander and the Unpublished Letters," *American Dialog*, I (October–November, 1964), 11.
49. "The 1930's Were an Age of Faith," *New York Times Book Review*, December 13, 1964, pp. 15–17.
50. *For Whom the Bell Tolls*, p. 248.

CHAPTER EIGHT

1. James Caldwell, *Defense in University City* (Cincinnati, 1939). This pamphlet—part 3 of a series of 8—was actually written and published by Robert J. C. Lowry, in a series he called *The Little Man*. Reprinted in Lowry's short story collection, *Happy New Year, Kamerades!* (New York, 1954), pp. 15–39.
2. A.l.s., Robert Lowry to S.W., October 18, 1965.
3. Alvah Bessie, *Men in Battle* (New York, 1939), p. 182.
4. Quoted from a letter from Mendelson to his sister Jeannette, July 15, 1938; in Joseph Leeds, *Let My People Know: The Story of Wilfred Mendelson* (New York, 1942), p. 75.
5. Gertrude Stein, *The Autobiography of Alice B. Toklas* (New York, 1933), p. 269.
6. Introduction to *Men at War* (New York, 1942), pp. xxv–xxvi.
7. For much of my information about Shipman I am indebted to Malcolm Cowley.
8. Quotations from Fischer unless otherwise noted are from Louis Fischer, *Men and Politics* (New York, 1941).
9. Louis Fischer, in *The God That Failed*, p. 218–20.
10. Bessie, *Men in Battle*, p. 302. Further references to Bessie, unless otherwise identified, are from his memoir.
11. *Volunteer for Liberty*, October 6, 1938, p. 10; Bessie, *Men in Battle*,

pp. 280–81, 318; Rolfe, *The Lincoln Battalion* (New York, 1939), p. 284.

12. Sandor Voros, *American Commissar* (Phila., 1961), pp. 409–10.

13. From an introduction by Gold to a pamphlet of proletarian poems (including Rolfe's), *We Gather Strength* (New York, 1933), p. 8.

14. *The Civil War in Spain* (New York, 1962), p. 278. (Rolfe died in 1954.)

15. "City of Anguish," in *First Love* (Los Angeles, 1951).

16. Daniel Hutner (posthumously) in *Volunteer for Liberty*, September 20, 1937, p. 6.

17. *The Lincoln Battalion*, p. 73.

18. Murray Kempton, *Part of Our Time* (New York, 1955), p. 316.

19. Printed in Ted Allan's *This Time a Better Earth* (New York, 1939), p. 188. Allan, however, puts Seligman's death as 1938.

20. Pre-Spain biographical data from material Neugass submitted to Harper's in 1948.

21. Quotations are from *Story*, XIII (November–December, 1938), pp. 83–93. "Give Us This Day," in the lines quoted here, may echo Hemingway's "A Clean Well-Lighted Place" ("Give us this nada our daily nada . . .").

22. The image is from Neugass's "On the Road" vignette, "Transsubstantiation," in *Salud!*, p. 12.

23. Sheean, p. 244.

24. Ring Lardner, Jr., "Somebody Had to Do Something," a pamphlet published by the James Lardner Memorial Fund, Los Angeles, California, 1939.

25. Printed in Rolfe, *The Lincoln Battalion*, pp. 243–44.

26. Joseph North, *Men in the Ranks* (New York, 1939), pp. 46–47.

27. Brock Brower, "The Abraham Lincoln Brigade Revisited," *Esquire* (March, 1962), p. 66.

28. Hecht fought in Spain but was killed in World War II.

29. From the father of John Cookson to his son, dated from Green Bay, Wisconsin, August 20, 1938. Cookson was adjutant of the Fifteenth Brigade's Transmission Company, and before Spain a promising young scientist who had done research in crystallography. *Volunteer for Liberty*, October 6, 1938, p. 5.

CHAPTER NINE

1. The *New Yorker*, September 19, 1936, p. 73 (Genêt's "Letter from Paris") and September 26, 1936, p. 8 ("The Talk of the Town").

328 THE LAST GREAT CAUSE

2. S. N. Behrman, "Harold Ross: A Recollection," in *The Suspended Drawing Room* (New York, 1965), p. 15.
3. *In Time of Trouble*, p. 252.
4. *The Invisible Writing*, pp. 326–27.
5. *In Place of Splendor* (New York, 1939), p. 294.
6. *Ibid.*, pp. 297–98.
7. "Mediterranean," from *U. S. 1* (New York, 1938).
8. Published in *A Turning Wind*.
9. Elliot Paul, *The Life and Death of a Spanish Town* (New York, 1937), p. 3. Further quotations are from this edition.
10. John M. Muste, *Say That We Saw Spain Die* (Seattle, 1966), pp. 47–52.
11. Elliot Paul, *The Last Time I Saw Paris* (New York, 1942), p. 321.
12. Entries dated Madrid, April, 1937, in *Journeys Between Wars* (New York, 1938), p. 363. Further references to Dos Passos in Spain, unless otherwise noted, are from this edition.
13. John Dos Passos, *The Theme is Freedom* (New York, 1956), p. 116.
14. *Papa Hemingway* (New York, 1966), p. 132.
15. Louis Fischer, *Men and Politics*, p. 429.
16. Dos Passos, "The Death of José Robles," *New Republic*, July 19, 1939, p. 309.
17. *The Theme is Freedom*, p. 137.
18. *Papa Hemingway*, p. 133.
19. Herbst, pp. 96–100.
20. *Theme*, pp. 143, 145–46.
21. Malcolm Cowley, "Disillusionment," *New Republic*, 99 (June 14, 1939), 163.
22. Dos Passos, "The Death of José Robles," p. 309.
23. "Farewell to Europe!", *Common Sense*, VI (July, 1937), 10–11.
24. "The Communist Party and the War Spirit, *Common Sense* (Dec., 1937), 11–14.
25. Arnold Gingrich, "Scott, Ernest and Whoever," *Esquire*, 66 (December, 1966), 189, 322.
26. *The Adventures of a Young Man* (New York, 1939), p. 305. Further quotations from the novel are from this edition.
27. John W. Aldridge, *After the Lost Generation* (New York, 1951), pp. 79, 80, 81.
28. For the episode of the *soldado* see *The Lincoln Battalion*, p. 70. The Herbst novel was *Rope of Gold* (New York, 1939), the concluding section dated "Tortosa, Barcelona Road, 1938."
29. Herbst, *Starched Blue Sky*, pp. 76–117.

30. Martha Gellhorn, *The Face of War* (New York, 1959), p. 10. All quotations from Miss Gellhorn's work, including her Spanish dispatches, come from this edition unless otherwise identified.
31. Arturo Barea, *The Forging of a Rebel* (New York, 1946), p. 643.
32. "Visit to the Wounded," *Story*, XI (October, 1937), 59.
33. Martha Gellhorn, "Writers Fighting in Spain," in Hart, ed., *Writers in a Changing World* (Philadelphia, 1938), pp. 63–68.
34. See "Zoo in Madrid," and "A Sense of Direction," in *The Heart of Another* (New York, 1941). Hemingway is not referred to by name but is thinly disguised.
35. "Mister Papa."
36. *Papa Hemingway*, p. 133.
37. "The Last Commander and the Unpublished Letters."
38. Martha Gellhorn, *The Honeyed Peace* (New York, 1953), p. 126.
39. *The Forging of a Rebel*, p. 686.
40. "No Axe to Grind," *Volunteer for Liberty*, November 15, 1937, p. 4.
41. "Soldiers of the Republic," *New Yorker*, XIII (February 5, 1938), 13–14. Dorothy Parker also wrote two pieces for *New Masses* about her visit, published November 23, 1937 and March 14, 1939.
42. Wolfe, *Letters*, ed. Elizabeth Nowell (New York, 1956), pp. 353–54.
43. "A Day in Spain," *New Republic*, XCIV (April 13, 1938), 298.
44. Guttmann, p. 131.
45. "News from Spain" (cover story on Malraux and *Man's Hope*), *Time*, November 7, 1938, p. 62.
46. Malraux, "Forging Man's Fate in Spain," *Nation*, 144 (March 20, 1937), 316. It was also part of his speeches in the U.S.
47. Alfred Kazin, *Starting Out in the Thirties* (New York, 1965), pp. 106–08.
48. The first edition of the novel Bates actually saw through the press was the 1966 first American edition, which differs in some particulars from the English text published thirty years before.
49. Ralph Bates, "Of Legendary Time," *Virginia Quarterly Review*, Winter, 1939, quoted in Payne, *The Spanish Civil War*, p. 331.
50. Private information. Bates's public break with Stalinism came with the Russian invasion of Finland, after which he wrote (*New Republic*, Dec. 13, 1939, pp. 221–25) "A specter is haunting the world, the specter of a revolution that is dead." He referred to the "Russian crime against Finland," and the "shame" and "bad faith" of the Communists, but added, "Lest I be thought to be unfairly critical of the Spanish Communist Party, let me say that that party throughout the civil war exercised marvelous patience, showed great wisdom,

demonstrated its magnificent courage and worked with an exhausting intensity in the service of the Spanish cause. The Communists of the world, in their degrees, did the same. The tragedy in Spain was that the effective fighting forces were more or less limited to the Communist regiments. The theological bitterness of the Communist Party, however, could be seen in its attitude toward the POUM party. That party's policies would have been disastrous had they been put into effect. That indisputable truth was made the basis for the utterly unscrupulous charge that the POUM was in actual contact with Franco, and was working exclusively and consciously in the interests of the fascists." It was a charge he had earlier (see Chapter Three, above) made himself.

51. *Starting Out in the Thirties*, p. 109.
52. Bates published some stories in the forties, and a semi-autobiographical novel of adolescence, *The Dolphin in the Wood*, in 1950, but he was unable to find publishers for several novels he completed during the next decade. Although he had broken with the Communist Party, the fifties were the years of the notorious blacklists, when the entire communications media were often short in political courage.
53. *Where We Came Out* (New York, 1954), p. 56.
54. Malcolm Cowley, "To Madrid: I," *New Republic*, August 25, 1937, p. 65.
55. "To Madrid: III," *New Republic*, October 6, 1937, p. 238.
56. Quoted from Levin's autobiography in Walter Rideout, *The Radical Novel in America* (Cambridge, 1954), pp. 252–53.
57. Guttmann, p. 163; Daniel Aaron, *Writers on the Left* (New York, 1961), p. 361.
58. The accounts of Dreiser in France and Catalonia, unless otherwise noted, come from *The Letters of Theodore Dreiser*, III, ed. Robert Elias (Philadelphia, 1959), 801–15; and W. A. Swanberg, *Dreiser* (New York, 1965), pp. 450–55.
59. Robert Payne, *The Civil War in Spain*, pp. 288–89.

EPILOGUE

1. I am indebted to Pritchett's essay, "A Hero of Our Time," *London Mercury*, 36 (August, 1937), 359–64, for his observations on Turgenev and Rudin. Later, Stephen Spender thought, too, that Spain "offered the twentieth century an 1848."
2. Quotations from Turgenev's *Rudin* are from the Constance Garnett translation (London, 1920).

3. *Chicken Soup with Barley* (London, 1958), *Roots* (London, 1959), *I'm Talking about Jerusalem* (London, 1960).

4. POUM (Marxist Labor Party, with Anarchist-Trotskyist leanings); FAI (Spanish Anarchist Party); CNT (Anarchist Trade Union); UGT (General Union of Workers, a Socialist group eventually under Communist domination).

5. *In Time of Trouble,* pp. 252–53.

6. *Writers on the Left,* p. 157

7. Muste, p. 191.

8. Edgar Z. Friedenberg, "The Paradoxes of the Spanish Civil War," *New Republic,* June 28, 1954, p. 19.

9. *The God That Failed,* p. 218.

10. Raymond Carr, "The Spanish Tragedy," *New York Review of Books,* November 25, 1965, p. 23.

11. "The Old Melodrama," *Time,* June 21, 1954, pp. 114–15.

12. *The Whispering Gallery,* p. 281.

13. Some of the best second-generation writing inspired by the Spanish Civil War has been historical, as with Cecil Eby's *The Siege of the Alcázar* (New York and London, 1966).

14. Dan Wakefield, *Between the Lines: A Reporter's Personal Journey Through Public Events* (New York, 1966), pp. 120–21.

15. *The Civil War in Spain,* p. 14.

INDEX

References under individual authors include citations which appear elsewhere in this index under titles of works by these authors.